Folklore from Contemporary Jamaicans

Folklore from Contemporary
JAMAICANS

by Daryl C. Dance

Drawings by Murry N. DePillars

The University of Tennessee Press / Knoxville

15 T   4/88

The paper in this book meets the guidelines for permanence and durability of
the Committee on Production Guidelines for Book Longevity of the Council
on Library Resources. Binding materials have been chosen for durability.

Tales Nos. 10, 48B, 49, and 105A were originally published in Daryl C. Dance,
"Aunt Sue's Stories" (*Afro-American Perspectives in the Humanities,* ed. Chester M.
Hedgepeth, Jr. [San Diego: Collegiate Publishing, Inc., 1980]).

Library of Congress Cataloging in Publication Data

Dance, Daryl Cumber.
     Folklore from contemporary Jamaicans.

     Bibliography: p.
     Includes index.
     1. Folklore—Jamaica. 2. Jamaica—Social life and
customs. I. Title.
GR121.J2D36 1985   398′.097292   84-5061
ISBN 0-87049-436-8 (alk. paper)

Frontispiece photograph. Boys in the Jamaican countryside pose with their donkey
for the photographer. Jamaica Tourist Board photo.

For my daughter, Daryl Lynn Dance
The greatest little five-year-old trooper who
ever took to the folklore trail

Acknowledgments

A Fulbright-Hays Research Grant in 1978 from the Council for International Exchange of Scholars enabled me to undertake the fieldwork for this book. Most of the tales were transcribed and annotated during the 1979–80 school year with the support of a grant from the Robert R. Moton Memorial Institute. I am grateful for the support of both of these agencies.

During the six months that I spent in Jamaica from June through November 1978, innumerable friends and colleagues assisted me in various ways. They secured an apartment for me, provided me with draperies and kitchen utensils, stocked my refrigerator, furnished my bar, saw that I was supplied with difficult-to-obtain items, lent me typewriters, books, and various other supplies and equipment, introduced me to informants, aided me in arranging interviews, chauffeured me, entertained me, babysat, and in every conceivable manner facilitated my work on this project and made my stay in Jamaica one of the most pleasant and productive periods of my life. For such assistance I wish to thank Dr. and Mrs. Everett Allen, Mrs. Bailey, Dr. Eddie Baugh, Dr. Malcolm Biddlestone, Mr. Eladio Bottier, Miss Erna Brodber, Dr. Vivinne Bryant, Mr. and Mrs. Dean Brown, Mr. Eddie Chang, Dr. Arthur Drayton, Dr. and Mrs. John Engledew, Dr. and Mrs. Carl Gibbs, Ambassador and Mrs. Fredrick Irving, Mr. Donald Jackson, Ms. Cynthia James, Dr. and Mrs. Ronald Lampart, Mr. and Mrs. Alston Lewis, Miss Rowena Lewis, Mrs. Ivy Marrett, Mr. and Mrs. Mervyn Morris, Mr. Harold Pierson, Mr. and Mrs. Cecil Phillips, Mrs. Velma Pollard, Mr. and Mrs. Asquith Reid, Dr. and Mrs. Ashok Sahney, Mrs. Beryl Thomas, Mrs. Jackie Turpin, Mr. and Mrs. John Thompson, and Miss Rose Walcott.

I am indebted to the University of the West Indies for extending me library privileges, furnishing me an office, and granting me membership privileges at the Senior Common Room. I am likewise beholden to the Institute of Jamaica and the Kingston and St. Andrew Parish Library for allowing me the use of their facilities. I also wish to express my appreciation to the officials at the Gun Court Rehabilitation Center for providing me a conference room to interview inmates and for allowing me to visit that institution numerous times, both to collect materials for this work and to attend programs sponsored by the Gun Court Culture Movement, a group to which most of my informants belonged. I am grateful as well to the faculty of St. Joseph's College who allowed me to tape in their classes, who arranged sessions for me with several groups of students, and who sent me additional materials in writing.

For such favors I particularly wish to thank Ms. Cherry Robinson, Ms. Joan Irvin, and Mr. Bryan Heap.

Grateful acknowledgment is made to the Jamaica Tourist Board, the Jamaican Embassy in the United States, and to Aldric Crawley for permission to use photographs which appear in this book.

Among the friends in the United States who kindly assisted me in preparing for the trip to Jamaica in numerous ways, including giving me letters of introduction to friends and relatives, I wish to thank Miss Ruth Richardson, Mrs. Frankie Hutton O'Meally, Mrs. Jennifer Royal, and Dr. and Mrs. Dennis Warner.

I am also very grateful to Mrs. Elsa Ettrick for her help in transcribing my tapes; to my son Allen Dance for his assistance in preparing the index; to Mr. Carlos Nelson for his critical reading of this manuscript; and again to Mrs. Jennifer Royal, whom I consulted throughout the preparation of this manuscript with a plethora of questions regarding spelling, transcription, and interpretation.

My greatest debt is, of course, to the many informants who graciously received me and generously shared their folk materials with me. Unfortunately, I do not have the names of all of them, but I am delighted to be able to gratefully acknowledge the contributions of Henry Baillie,[1] Alvin Beckford, Faith Beckford, Kirk Beckford, Richard Beckford, Mrs. Louise Bennett, Rohan Biley, Mr. Constantine Blackwood, Mr. Thomas Blair, Emelyn Brown, Mr. Edward Brown, Headley Brown, Mr. Herbert Brown, Janet Bryson, Rev. Eddie Burke, Mr. Vernon Campbell, Stepheney Carter, Herman Clarke, Maureen Clarke, Michael Clarke, Paul Clarke, Paulette Clarke, A. Clough, Winsom Cornwall, Karolene Dauley, Dawn Davis, Mr. Paul Dixon, Mr. Clive Duncan, Elaine Elliot, Avis Gayle, Mr. Michael Gibbs, Mr. Roger Gordon, Jennifer Gray, Durrington Guthrie, June Hamilton, Louise Harris, Sharon Harris, Jackie Haughton, Karen Haughton, Judith Haughton, Michael Haughton, Mrs. Theresa Henry, Clive Heslop, Rosemary Higgins. Camille Hinds, Mr. Shirley Hines, Elaine Hunter, Myrna James, Marva Jennings, Andrea Johnson, Mrs. Mary Johnson, Miss Thelmira Jones, Carman Kennedy, Mrs. Maureen Warner Lewis, Delroy Logan, Carlton McDermott, Daryl McFarland, Frank McKellop, Sonia McNeill, Lorna Marsh, H. Martin, Gervaise Mattocks, Ena Morgan, Eulette Murray, Mr. Clinton Palmer, Lorna Parkes, Mr. Franklin Parks, Millicent Ramsay, Lorna Reid, Blossom Richettes, Mr. J. P. Riley, Mr. Frank Rhoden, Mr. Granville Roach, Mr. Alfred Rose, Dawn Smith, Pauline Stephens, Veronica Sterling, Panchita Sybron, Mr. Vivian Talbot, Mr. Junior Thomas, Michael Thomlinson, Mr. Clive Thompson, Pamela Walcott, Sandra Walcott, Winnifred Walkers, Andrew Whittaker, Mr. Basil Williams, Mr. Phillip Williams, Yvonne Williams, and Inez Wright.

My indebtedness cannot be fully acknowledged without recognizing the contributions of my then five-year-old daughter, Daryl Lynn Dance, my constant companion and assistant, my occasional consultant, and my greatest asset for approaching informants and gaining entree into homes, yards, and especially children's groups.

---

1. My informants ranged in age from six to ninety. Those untitled here were under eighteen at the time of our sessions.

Contents

XI. Children's Games

Illustrations

Photographs

Boys on donkey, *frontispiece*
Fruit and vegetable peddler, *following page xxv*
Fruit stand
Roadside market
Fishermen
Classroom
Children rehearsing dance
Festival dancers
Festival dancers
Jonkonnu dancers
Jonkonnu dancers
Dancers at Port Royal
St. Joseph's Catholic Church
Linstead Market
Holy Cross Church
Country home
Street in Spanish Town
Shanty town lovers
Boys with gig
Rastafarian

Maps

Introduction

There is not now available, nor has there ever been, a general and comprehensive introductory collection of the rich folklore of Jamaica. This is a somewhat paradoxical situation in that it appears almost everyone who has ever had an opportunity to be introduced to aspects of the Jamaican folk tradition has been fascinated by it. American folklorists from Martha Beckwith through Zora Neale Hurston to Roger Abrahams have written ebulliently about what they have observed and recorded; historians have marveled at the many African survivals to be observed among the Maroons; music lovers from around the world have intoned the lyrics of the popular mento or calypso, and rocked to the beat of the ska or the rock steady or the reggae; race men and faddists alike have ardently embraced and adopted the Rastafarian philosophy, rituals, and speech patterns as well as the dreadlocks. Tourists to the island work at mimicking the Jamaican patois and copying the dance steps, and they would never dream of returning home without at least one piece of folk art or some of the handmade items to be purchased from higglers throughout the country. Those travelers who have ventured beyond the regular tourists paths have been fascinated by the drama of a Pocomania service or the witchcraft of the Obeah man. Yet, despite this widespread enthrallment with these better-known aspects of Jamaican folk life and culture, the fact remains that no extensive general collection of the vast range of Jamaican folklore has been assembled.

The closest approaches remain Walter Jekyll's collection of stories (almost all Anancy stories) and songs, *Jamaican Song and Story,* originally published in 1907; the early volume of stories (mainly animal stories), riddles, and songs collected by Martha Beckwith between 1919 and 1921, *Jamaica Anansi Stories;* and her collection of games, rituals and proverbs gathered between 1919 and 1924, *Jamaica Folk-Lore* (New York: G. E. Strecherd, published for the American Folk-Lore Society, 1925; rpt. New York: Kraus Reprint, 1969). Also deserving mention here are George E. Lawrence's unpublished "West Indian Folklore: Proverbs, Riddles, Stories and Songs," collected between 1929 and 1946 and available in the Special Collections of the University of the West Indies, Mona, Kingston; two boxes of unpublished Anancy, duppy, and Big Boy stories, dream and psychic experiences, beliefs and legends, games, rhymes, riddles, and songs from a folklore research project in Jamaica, directed by Jeanette Grant during 1967–69, which are reposited in the Institute of Jamaica in Kingston; Ivy Baxter's treatment of the songs, dances, and religious and social customs of Jamaica in *The Arts of an Island* (Metuchen, N.J.: Scarecrow Press, 1970); and Leonard E. Barrett's fine study *The Sun and the Drum:*

African Roots in Jamaican Folk Tradition (Kingston: Sangster's Book Stores, 1976).

There are of course numerous collections of specific areas of Jamaican folklore, particularly the songs and the stories. In addition to those volumes of songs to be found in the "Works Cited" section, other notable songbooks include "The Music and Song-Words of Jamaica: A Programme from Ormsby's Memorial Hall" (Kingston, March 4, 1931), an unpublished manuscript available in the Special Collections of the University of the West Indies in Mona; Thomas Murray's *Folk Songs of Jamaica* (London: Oxford Univ. Press, n.d. [the introduction is dated 1951]); Thomas Murray and John Gavall's *Twelve Folk Songs from Jamaica* (London: Oxford Univ. Press, 1960), which draws from Murray's earlier collection; and Olive Lewin's *Brown Gal in de Ring* (London: Oxford Univ. Press, 1974). In addition to the numerous collections of stories listed in "Works Cited," other important anthologies of Jamaican folktales include Philip Sherlock's *West Indian Folk-Tales* (London: Oxford Univ. Press, 1966); Louise Bennett's *Anancy Stories and Dialect Verse* (Kingston: Pioneer Press, 1957); Clinton Black's *Tales of Old Jamaica* (London: St. James's Place, 1966); and Philip M. Sherlock's *Anansi the Spider Man* (London: Macmillan, 1966). Other interesting studies of Jamaican folklore are Izett Anderson and Frank Cundall's *Jamaica Proverbs and Sayings* (1910, 1927; rpt. Shannon, Ireland: Irish Univ. Press, 1972); and Zora Neale Hurston's *Tell My Horse* (Philadelphia: Lippincott, 1938), which treats Haitian as well as Jamaican lore. Various collections of materials from the West Indies include Jamaican items as well.

Although all of the earlier folklore collections noted above and in the "Works Cited" section of this book represent significant contributions to the collection, interpretation, and preservation of Jamaican folk materials, even a cursory review of the list indicates some of the glaring omissions and problems that *Folklore from Contemporary Jamaicans* seeks to address and rectify. Aside from the apparent need for a more general and comprehensive collection of folklore, a glance at the list will also indicate that much of the work was done many years ago. Although a few important collections have been reissued, most of them are no longer in print; indeed, some of them were never published and have been accessible only to the most persistent of scholars who tracked them down in dusty boxes on remote shelves of various Jamaican libraries. Many of the collections have imposed certain limitations upon themselves. Some of them are very brief, such as Lewin's *Brown Gal in de Ring,* which contains only twelve songs; Burke's *Water in the Gourd,* which contains only seven selections; Black's *Tales of Old Jamaica,* which contains only ten tales; and Murray and Gavall's *Twelve Folk Songs from Jamaica.* In some instances the books are obviously limited because they were prepared for use in elementary schools, and at other times they were apparently kept brief in order to facilitate inexpensive publication as pamphlets. Furthermore, many of the available collections of tales and songs

Map 1. Jamaica.

often tend to reproduce the same or similar items and ignore other materials. Almost all of the folktale collections include the Anancy tales. A few collections include some of the more traditional legendary tales in Jamaica and the duppy tales. Many other tales that I found to be popular in Jamaica, such as the Big Boy tales, some of the etiological "myths," the Fader Forsythe cycle, and most of the obscene materials, have never been published, as far as I have been able to determine. Aside from this omission of complete cycles of stories, another shortcoming has resulted from the fact that most of the folklorists have tended to do their fieldwork only in remote, rural areas of Jamaica. While there is indeed an abundance of materials available from isolated groups in Jamaica, there is also a wealth of folklore to be found in the yards and prisons and living rooms of Kingston and other urban areas.

Though I was familiar with prior collections of Jamaican folk materials when I started my fieldwork for this volume, I attempted to begin with no preconceptions. Thus I did not aggressively solicit specific types of materials or particular tales that I already knew and had been led to expect to find. Rather I endeavored to create an environment in which Jamaicans of all ages (preschool children through octogenarians) and socioeconomic-educational backgrounds (peasant farmers to university professors) and areas (remote mountain villages to downtown Kingston streets)[1] would share with me the kinds of materials that they regularly enjoy and exchange. The contents of this volume may thus be viewed as representative of popular contemporary Jamaican folklore — the tales that present-day Jamaicans enjoy telling; the songs they sing; the rhymes they recite; the riddles they pose; the games they play, etc.

Brief biographies of many of my major informants are included in the back matter of this volume. In some instances, however, my methods of collecting made it impossible to gather biographical data. There were times, for

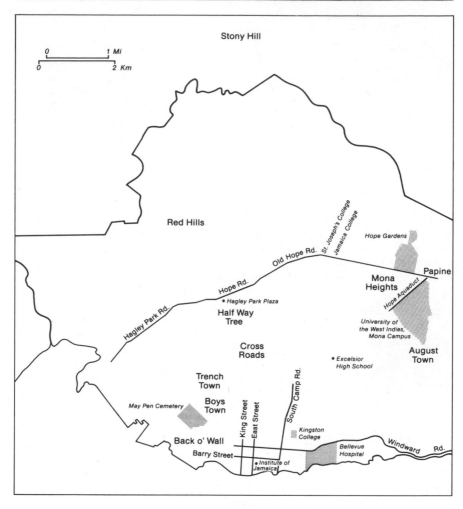

Map 2. Kingston.

example, when I stopped on a street corner and talked with and collected from a group gathered there. There were numerous instances when I set up in a Kingston yard and groups of ten, twenty, thirty, forty or more children and adults intermittently wandered in and out of the group. In almost every instance, I managed to get the name of the tale-teller and often the names of those playing games or singing group songs, but frequently when I attempted to secure additional information at the end of such a session, a particular informant had been called home by a parent or for some other reason was not still there. When I went back, it was often impossible to find those individuals because I never knew where many of them lived—only that they shared this common yard. On the other hand, some individuals were interviewed several times over a period of weeks, and for such informants I have extensive biographical information. The entries in the "Biographies of Major Contributors" section are, therefore, disproportionate. It is also important to note that several of my informants were in prison; to avoid any possible embarrassment to them, I have chosen not to call attention to that fact in their biographies.

Some Jamaicans will undoubtedly be disturbed by the presentation of certain of the "rude" materials in this volume because Jamaicans have characteristically practiced the stratagems that Zora Neale Hurston observed among Black Americans:

> The theory behind our tactics: "The white man is always trying to know into somebody else's business. All right, I'll set something outside the door of my mind for him to play with and handle. He can read my writing but he sho' can't read my mind. I'll put this play toy in his hand, and he will seize it and go away. Then I'll say my say and sing my song."[2]

Inevitably, when Jamaicans recognized that I was looking for folklore, they tended to offer me as a "play toy" the well-known Anancy tales and traditional folk songs that could "properly" be shared with outsiders, since the materials were appropriate (or at least the obscene allusions were not immediately apparent). As my informants got to know me better or as sessions livened up causing my presence to be less obtrusive, the performers/participants/tellers became more open and unrestrained and shared with me many items that are characteristically reserved for intimate groups. Interestingly enough, however, even the beggar woman who, to earn the daily dole that she required of me, became my guide and self-appointed bodyguard during my sallies into the rougher areas of Kingston, was appalled and vociferously protested whenever informants began to relate ribald materials—despite the fact that she herself obviously enjoyed them.

In selecting the contents of this volume, I have observed Jan Harold Brunvand's definition of folklore as *"those materials in culture that circulate traditionally among members of any group in different versions."*[3] While the materials were collected in Jamaica and while they are often uniquely Jamaican in dialect, subject matter, characterization, concerns, and the like, they are also often traditional and universal in motif and type. Any reader from any part of the world will recognize many familiar items. Obviously several of these tales have traveled to Jamaica from all corners of the globe. The most obvious source, of course, is Africa, but many items can also be traced to Europe, Asia, and other parts of America. Annotations for each item indicate in abbreviated form other printed sources, which are listed in "Works Cited." Additional geographic areas in which the item has been collected are noted as well. I have keyed references to Ernest W. Baughman's *Type and Motif-Index of the Folktales of England and North America* and Helen L. Flowers' *A Classification of the Folktales of the West Indies by Types and Motifs*. Because contemporary Jamaican materials have not been extensively collected and because they have not been fully indexed, there are numerous unannotated tales in this volume.

Following each item is an indication of where the tale was collected. If the informant was a child, his age is indicated. Initially I had considered identifying the contributor of every piece, but for varied reasons I decided against that: in a few instances the tellers themselves requested that they not be identified with specific tales; in other instances it occurred to me that it might be better not to identify a young child who gave me an obscene tale; finally, there would rarely be any significance to providing the names in an extensive collection such as this, where there are hundreds of contributors.

Each of the eleven chapters in *Folklore from Contemporary Jamaicans* is preceded by a brief introduction in which I attempt to provide a succinct exploration of the nature of the materials and occasionally to comment upon other relevant matters, such as what motivated them, how they developed, and how they relate to other similar folk items. These introductions are not intended as definitive statements about the materials presented, nor even as intensive interpretations of them. My goal has been to collect, present, and preserve the primary materials that will provide the groundwork for scholars in a variety of fields (folklore, anthropology, literature, sociology, history, etc.) to pursue more extensive analytical and interpretive studies.

One of the greatest thrills in observing or hearing the performance of a Jamaican folk tale, song, or rhyme is the distinctive Jamaican speech, which is most often rhythmic and musical; it is also marked by a variety of fascinating tonal variations, as well as characterized by unique language patterns from both Jamaican Creole and Rastafarian, or dread, talk. Though the reader of this volume who is not familiar with Jamaican patois may experience some initial difficulties in attempting to read the transcriptions of some of the tales because of these variations in speech, I have refused to make any efforts to standardize the dialect or to replace Jamaican expressions with more familiar ones, since to do so would be to seriously bastardize and destroy one unique character of the materials. To assist the foreign reader, I have explained any nonstandard word or expression upon its first appearance. The glossary at the end of this book includes a list of such words that appear several times throughout the volume, including variant spellings of words to suggest the dialectical pronunciations. I have attempted to reproduce each piece exactly as the informant delivered it. Just as I have avoided standardizing any slang or dialect, I have also avoided *imposing* any dialect. Thus, inconsistencies in pronunciations and speech patterns will be obvious throughout the tales. The same teller may sometimes, for example, form the plural of a word by adding an *s*; again he may use the word without an *s* as a plural; on another occasion he may form the plural by adding *them* or *dem*. Thus, in Tale 12A the plural of *egg* is at one time "egg," at another "eggs," and finally "the egg them."

Traditionally the Jamaican folktale has closed with the line, "Jack Mandora, me nuh chose none," which has been interpreted as "Jack, man of the door [or 'Jack, heaven's doorkeeper,' or 'Jack, Dora's man'], I am not responsible for this story, it is not of my choosing."[4] When Chaucer prepared his collection of folktales, he had to issue a lengthy apologia:

> But, first, I beg you in your kindness not to consider me vulgar because I speak plainly in this account and give you the statements and the actions of these pilgrims, or if I repeat their exact words. For you know just as well as I that whosoever repeats a tale must include every word as nearly as he possibly can, if it is in the story, no matter how crude and low; otherwise, he tells an untrue tale, or makes up things, or finds new words.[5]

Though Chaucer expressed my sentiments exactly, how much simpler it is for me to utter the same disclaimer to all of those who may be shocked or disturbed or ashamed or embarrassed or offended by the tales here! For all of you who turn this page and proceed further in this book, let me here and now declare, JACK MANDORA, *ME* NUH CHOSE NONE!

---

1. The map of Jamaica will provide the reader who is unfamiliar with that island a guide to those cities and towns in which I collected materials, where my informants lived, or to which they referred in their tales.

2. Hurston, *Mules and Men* (1935; rpt. New York: Harper and Row, 1970), pp. 18–19.

3. Brunvand, *The Study of American Folklore: An Introduction* (New York: Norton, 1968), p. 5.

4. Louise Bennett, *Anancy and Miss Lou*, p. xi; see also Barrett, *The Sun and the Drum*, p. 35. The meaning of this closing line was also discussed in my interviews with Louise Bennett (Gordon Town, Jamaica, November 4, 1978) and Eddie Burke (Santa Cruz, Jamaica, November 4, 1978).

5. *The Canterbury Tales of Geoffrey Chaucer*, trans. R.M. Lumiansky (New York: Washington Square Press, 1960), pp. 14–15.

Jamaican fruit and vegetable peddler in the marketplace in Ocho Rios sings, "Ackee, rice, salt-fish are nice," as she holds out the popular ackee to shopper. Embassy of Jamaica photo.

Left, above: Higglers and shoppers gather at a fruit stand in a shopping center. Even the most modern shopping centers usually have fruit and vegetable stands such as this one. The old and the new commonly exist side by side in Jamaica. Jamaica Tourist Board photo by Roy (Johnny) O'Brien.

Left, below: Roadside markets such as the one here are to be found in villages and along roadsides throughout Jamaica. Jamaica Tourist Board photo by Roy (Johnny) O'Brien.

Jamaica calls itself an angler's paradise. On the north coast big fighting fish may be caught close to land, and numerous varieties of fresh water fish are prevalent in streams and rivers throughout the island. Jamaica Tourist Board photo.

Left, above: Jamaican children are subjected to a severely disciplined, highly structured formal educational system, but when they escape the rigorous demands of the classroom, they enjoy a variety of free activities. Many of them proved to be for me a rich source of folk games, riddles, songs, rhymes, and tales. Embassy of Jamaica photo.

Left, below: Children from the Port Antonio Infant School rehearse a dance for the National Festival of the Arts. Embassy of Jamaica photo.

These dancers are among many who participate in the National Festival of the Arts, an annual competition in all the arts which culminates during Independence celebrations in August with spectacular shows at the National Stadium in Kingston. Embassy of Jamaica photo.

Many of the dances in the National Festival of the Arts are derived from popular folk dances that the performers learned as children. Embassy of Jamaica photo.

Right, above: The Jonkonnu festival is an important part of Jamaica's Christmas celebration, in which costumed dancers wearing masks parade through the streets. Sylvia Wynter suggests that these festivals are related to the Yam festivals of Africa, and like them are designed to increase the fertility of the earth. See Wynter, "Jonkonnu in Jamaica: Towards the Interpretation of Folk Dance as a Cultural Process," *Jamaica Journal,* IV (June, 1970), 34–48. Jamaica Tourist Board photo by Roy (Johnny) O'Brien.

Right, below: This group of Jonkonnu dancers includes participants with unusual names such as Horse Head, Devil, Belly Woman, Pitchy Patchy, and Actor Boy. The festival is variously spelled Jon Connu, John Canoe, Jankanoo, and Jonkunnu. Jamaica Tourist Board photo by Roy (Johnny) O'Brien.

These dancers are performing at an old fort in Port Royal. Forts such as this one were set up to guard the coasts and the mountain passes in Port Royal, which was reputed to be the wickedest city on earth and was a base for buccaneers in the 17th century. One of them, Henry Morgan (see Tale 100), was knighted and made Governor of Jamaica. The city was destroyed by an earthquake in 1692. Jamaica Tourist Board photo.

St. Joseph's Catholic Church at Tom's River was built in 1895. Catholicism, which was introduced into Jamaica by the Spanish settlers who arrived in 1509, remains popular in Jamaica, despite the fact that it was prohibited from 1655 (when English Protestants captured the island) until 1792. Jamaica Tourist Board photo.

The Holy Cross Roman Catholic Church is located near Half Way Tree in Kingston. Nearly all Christian denominations have churches in Jamaica, with the Anglicans, Methodists, Presbyterians, Roman Catholics, and Baptists being the most prevalent. There are also numerous nondenominational churches, such as Pentecostal and Evangelical. There are a Jewish Synagogue and a Baha'i Assembly in Kingston, and an Islam Mosque at Spanish Town. Jamaica Tourist Board photo.

Left: The market-house is an important part of Jamaican culture, having begun as a weekend carnival of trade and recreation. The market-houses commonly have gabled roofs and wrought iron decor. The market in Linstead was popularized by the folksong, "Carry me ackee go da Linstead Market." Jamaica Tourist Board photo.

Left, above: Comfortable country homes such as this one in the mountains in Cedar Valley offer a beautiful and cool retreat. Photo courtesy of Aldric Crawley.

Left, below: The Spanish settled Spanish Town (originally Sevilla la Nueva) early in the 16th century. This former capital of Jamaica is noted for its central square with its unmatched collection of 18th century buildings, including King's House, which was constructed in 1762, and the Court House. Photo courtesy of Aldric Crawley.

Lovers stroll near a yard of one of the many shanty towns scattered throughout Kingston, this one located near the University of the West Indies. Photo courtesy of Aldric Crawley.

Spinning gigs is a popular pastime with Jamaican youths (see Tale 148). The children chant "Gig lent, gig bite, gig dash away!" meaning that if one child's gig strikes that of another, the boy whose gig was hit may throw the offender's gig away. Photo courtesy of Charlotte Blum.

Some Rastafarians refuse to cut their hair for religious reasons, and allow it to grow into dreadlocks, suggestive of the lion's mane (they worship Rastafari, the Conquering Lion of the tribe of Judah). Dreadlocks have become popular throughout the Caribbean and in the United States, and one can no longer assume that everyone who sports dreadlocks is a Rastafarian. Jamaica Tourist Board photo by Roy (Johnny) O'Brien.

Folklore from Contemporary Jamaicans

I

Etiological Tales

Introduction

This first chapter is the shortest chapter in the collection, possibly because, as Helen L. Flowers has noted, "Aetiological stories of gods, animals and natural forces have declined sharply in distribution and popularity in the New World."[1] The kinds of "etiological" tales that I found in Jamaica are quite similar to those I found current in the United States a few years earlier.[2] Most of them focused upon the role of God in explaining why Blacks are black and poor. As in the American tales, generally the causes of the handicaps under which the Black Jamaican labors seem to be his own defects—tardiness, greed, ignorance, or aggressiveness—or God's carelessness. These tales, like their parallels in America, might at first appear to reveal an acceptance of Black inferiority. Though the body of materials available for consideration from Jamaica is too small to reach any definite conclusion about the function of these tales in Jamaican society, their similarity to the American tales and the fact that they grew out of a comparable historical situation suggest the possibility that one may argue, as I have done elsewhere regarding Black American tales, that these Jamaican tales are not self-denigrating tales, but rather veiled protests against a racist system in which the Black is destined to lose, fail, and suffer, no matter what he does.[3]

It is interesting to note that this group of tales, like the ribald materials that I collected, has not been previously published in studies of Jamaican folklore. The only version that I found in print was one in Madeline Kerr's sociological study.[4] That this absence represents something other than a paucity of such material among the folk in Jamaica was soon apparent to me in my study. The major reason seems rather to be the widespread insistence among Jamaicans upon denying the presence of racism and racial sensitivity. It was shocking to me to find in current situations, historical events, and literary accounts the most poignant evidences of the suffering of Black Jamaicans as a result of interracial and intraracial prejudice and then to hear numerous Jamaicans insist that their first acquaintance with racism came when they arrived in Miami or London. It must be conceded, of course, that the impact of white racism in countries such as the United States and Britain, where Blacks are a minority and where racism is considerably more direct and blatant and legalized, is much more acute. It is also very true that numerous West Indians, like novelist Michael Thelwell, recognized the racism that existed in their societies only after they experienced the American variety; in an interview in 1979 he told me:

> Going to Mississippi [during the Civil Rights movement] and looking at the plantation society, which had not evolved beyond that, and seeing a plantation society in which the racial attitudes which were prevalent during slavery had simply been taken and established in the code of law which governs the society was, first of all, an *enormous* kind of shock; and second of all, it enabled me to see certain things about Jamaican society, which at that time . . . were not quite so obvious; and in point of fact, regardless of whether there are overt signs of discrimination in a society, it is a victim of its history, a history very similar to the American South. . . . And what Caribbean people tend to term simply a *class* problem is basically a race problem which derives from patterns of relationships which evolved between the races during slavery and which still impose a kind of inertia on the class structure of the society and still . . . give form and content to social relationships. . . . The experiences in the South led me to a much clearer view and perception of the realities of the society which produced me.[5]

This kind of recognition and acceptance is not, however, common in Jamaica and accounts, I think, for the fact that such tales as those that follow are, despite their currency, suppressed and denied. When I asked the famed folklorist Louise Bennett if she were familiar with Jamaican tales such as the American ones about the hair, color, and economic status of Blacks, she exclaimed, "No, sir! . . . We don't have a great deal of that in the folklore. . . . I really never came up against any racial thing until the first time I traveled."[6] Another striking example of the denial of this kind of material occurred when I was invited to speak at a college in Kingston. I sent a copy of my Black American etiological tales to be duplicated and circulated among the audience, whereupon a teacher and the student who was in charge of the program rushed to my apartment and insisted that certain tales had to be deleted because in Jamaica they did not like materials that focused on differences between races or that touched upon racial characteristics in a derogatory way. After a long conversation during which I talked about the prevalence, the functions, and the interpretations of those tales, my two visitors, who still vociferously insisted upon the banning of such materials, went on to enthusiastically relate two tales explaining why the Black man is black, both of which appear in this chapter.

Three of the remaining tales in this section deal with the origins of words. Some tales explaining the origins of animals and animal behavior appear in Chapter 2.

1. Flowers, *A Classification of the Folktales of the West Indies by Types and Motifs*, p. 5, cited hereafter as *West Indian Types and Motifs*.

2. See my *Shuckin' and Jivin'*.

3. See my "In the Beginning: A New Look at Black American Etiological Tales," *Southern Folklore Quarterly*, 41 (1977), 53–64.

4. Kerr, *Personality and Conflict in Jamaica* (London: Collins, 1963), p. 152.

5. Interview with Michael Thelwell, Amherst, Massachusetts, December 9, 1979.

6. Interview with Louise Bennett, Gordon Town, Jamaica, September 15, 1978.

1A Jet Black

This is another one about why the Black man is black and the white man is white. Everybody was in front of God—the white man was in front of God, right? And God was giving him his color. So the Black man now came rushing in and say, "I want my color now; I want my color!" You know he can't wait any longer. He want his color. So God told him, "Stand back. Stand back!" And he thought that God said, "Jet black:" So that's the reason he's jet black.

Collected in Kingston on October 11, 1978.

See Motif A1614, "Origin of white and colored races," in Baughman, *Type and Motif-Index*. Versions of this tale appear in Dance, *Shuckin' and Jivin'*, No. 1; Hurston, *Mules and Men*, pp. 48–49; Hurston, *Dust Tracks*, pp. 74–77 (reprinted in Botkin, *Treasury of Southern Folklore*, pp. 482–83); Hughes and Bontemps, *Book of Negro Folklore*, pp. 125–27; and Brewer, *American Negro Folklore*, pp. 20–21.

1B Jet Black

Well, you have dis man now, you have dis yout' now. 'Im *jet black*. And a man ah mout' 'im now, say, "'Ow God mek 'im?" So 'im say is God and 'im apprentice now ah do some work—no, God and Satan ah do some work now—so Satan a mek di mold an ting, so Satan mek a bad move and God say, "Dress back!"[1]

So Satan tink God say "*Jet black.*" Say, "See it," and jus' trow a jet black pon di mold. It come, come *coal* black.

Collected in Kingston on October 6, 1978.
1. Move away.

2 How We Get Black

This is about the Indian. They call them Coolie. So the white man (they were giving colors), so the white man first go and he get the white color. So the Indian go and the Indian get color. So it wasn't time for the Negroes to get color. So they were throwing away—God was throwing away black paint, and the Negro just grab it and say, "Me will tek this; me will tek this," and that is how we get Black people.

Collected in Woodside on September 6, 1978.

3A Dat's Pe-e-r-fick

Well, the Chineyman philosophy about how people, 'ow the races, came about, why is Black and Chiney, because Black man dark, white man white, and Chineyman in between—a yellowish color. So the Chineyman say when God meking di mold now, 'im make di dough, put in di oven; so 'im never have di right timing. So 'im take out di dough too quick; so 'im look now di white man come, because di dough never get to bake good. So 'im say, "Cho!" Put dat one side and come again mek a nex' dough. Put it een dis time, say, all right, 'im goin' mek it stay longer, but dis time 'im mek it stay *too* long, and it get *burn* up now, and say is di Black man dat come. 'Im say, "A-hhh, shit, man!" Put it one side.

Say, "Awright." Him get di timing now, him mek a nex' dough and put in een now: "Ah-hhh!" Yellow man come, say: "Ah-h-h, dat's *pe-e-r-fick!*"

Dat is, di yellow man now is the Chineyman; 'im think his race is di perfick race, so that's why God mek him perfick.

Collected in Kingston on October 6, 1978.

In an unpublished essay, "The Fusion of African and Amerindian Folk Myths," Jan Carew, professor of Afro-American literature at Northwestern University, indicates that this tale is told by the Maroons in Jamaica and by the Amerindians in Guyana.

3B Dat's Pe-e-r-fick

This story is saying that the reason why some people are black or white is that some people stayed in the oven too long, so they baked a bit blacker and some brown, but the white ones came out before they were able to get brown or black.

Collected in Kingston on October 30, 1978.

4 Why the Black Man is Black

This is a story about why the Black man is black and the white man is white. The story is that God made man from the dust of the earth, and then he told them to go and wash off. And the white man was greedy and used up all the soap and water, so that the Black man just had a little bit of soap and water left to wash the palms of his hands and the soles of his feet.

Collected in Kingston on October 11, 1978.

This is Motif A1614.2, "Races Darkskinned from Bathing after White Men," in Baughman, *Type and Motif-Index.* Versions of this tale appear in Harris, *Uncle Remus,* I, 33; *American Stuff,* An Anthology of Prose and Verse by Members of the Federal Writers' Project (New York: Viking, 1937), pp. 150–51 (reprinted in Botkin, *Treasury of American Folklore,* pp. 428–29); and Perdue, *Weevils,* pp. 232–33.

5 The Creation of the Negro

This is a story about why Negro became Negro. Because in the beginning God didn't make any Negro; he just made straight-hair people, right? So a set of people went to the zoo and saw the monkey with fire on his tail, and they were laughing at the monkey and the monkey just thrashed the tail, around in the air. The fire burned the hair [and made them] black.

Collected in Kingston on October 30, 1978.

6 Why the Black Man Has to Work Hard

When God was giving out talents and giving out gifts, he put two barrels out in front. He had the people up dere and he told the white man, "Go and choose a barrel." And he went and he tried the barrels: one was light; one was heavy. He took the light one.

And when he called the Black man, and said, "You go and choose a barrel," he tried this one—it was light. He tried this one—it was heavy, and he felt that, well, this one was full of money, so the Black man took the heavy barrel. The heavy barrel was full of *pure* stones and iron, and the light barrel was full of all the checks.

So that is why white man is rich and Black man is so poor. They took up the heavy barrel out there; they always love heavy *weight,* you see, thinking it is money—not money at all. They went there and they made the choice themselves; they took the iron and the work.

[Member of the audience] Yes, they tek up the load and till today Black people have the load dragging, have to work very hard. The white people dem cut ten[1] and order the Black all day long to work for them, for they have the money and the poor Black tek the load, so they have to drag the white man load.

Collected in Mandeville on September 16, 1978.

This is Motif A1671.1, "Why the Negro Works," in Baughman, *Type and Motif-Index.* Variants appear in Dance, *Shuckin' and Jivin',* No. 5; Dorson, *Negro Folktales in Michigan,* p. 76 (reprinted in Dorson, *American Negro Folktales,* pp. 172–73; Hurston, *Mules and Men,* p. 102 (reprinted in Botkin, *Treasury of American Folklore,* p. 427); and Madeline Kerr, *Personality and Conflict in Jamaica* (London: Collins, 1963), p. 152.

1. Cross their legs.

7 Mango and Orange

He tells us one bout . . . bout fruits . . . some fruits. Well when Adam and Eve and deh were in di garden, they name up all di fruits. *Two* fruit leave that didn't get any name, which is mango and orange.

So 'im go to Christ and ask 'im, "What dese fruits name? What dese fruits lef' that don' get any name?" 'Im say, "Man, go and arrange."

So dat's di reason why dem call di fruit mango and orange.

Collected in Kingston on October 6, 1978.

8 Congo and Nago

This story I heard in Westmoreland, Jamaica, and I think, if my memory serves me right, it was an attempt to explain how the names *Congo* and *Nago* came to be. And if I remember rightly the lady said that it was as if Africans were in Africa, and some of them said to the other as they were parting, about leaving Africa to go somewhere else, and some said, "Caan' go! Caan' go!"

which in Jamaican creole is "Come go," and the other said, "Me nah go, me nah go."

Those who said "Caan' go!" were the Congos, and those who said, "Me nah go, me nah go," were the Nagos, Nago being another name for Yoruba. But of course I don't know how it came that the Congos and the Nagos in Africa landed in Westmoreland in Jamaica.

Collected in Kingston on August 25, 1978.

9 Sorrel

Once upon a time Christmas a come, so everybody a go a town fi go sell tings for dem Christmas now, get dem Christmas money, you know, buy up dem Christmas tings.

So Brer Anancy never have one Gawd ting fi go sell because you know him a man nuh work field. When everybody *gawn* a market him siddown and him consider himself, "Everybody gawn a market wid someting fi go sell and me nuh ha none." When him go over Brerer Tiger yard, Brerer Tiger clean out him field and gone a market; everybody gone leave him one. So him go and take Brerer Tiger bush. When him go a Brerer Tiger bush him see a whole heap a red bush stan' up in a di field. Dat's all because, you know, all the yam and everyting else which can sell, gawn a market. Him say: "Me nuh have nuttin fi go sell, but me a go sell dat red bush yah today." And him cut the red bush and him carry it go a market.

When him go in deh *everybody* frighten fi see Brer Anancy come wid something fi sell, so they ask him, "What is that?" Him say, "Humn, try it and you will see it." So the rumor start to go round the market say Brer Anancy come a market wid someting and him nuh know a what, and dem start to run and everybody a run fi go see Brer Anancy now; and Brer Anancy catch him fraid and start to run, and him run wid di bundle a someting and him run and him run, and you know the people dem who cook in a di market have a pot of bwoiling water pon the fire and di someting drop in a di water, you know, and it just turn *red* same time. So everybody come and look down in a di pot and say: "I' look so *real*, i' look *real*." So Brer Anancy say, "If you want it more real put little sugar in deh."

But dat time Brer Anancy a fret, you know, because him nuh know if a poison, yes or no, and dem put the sugar in deh and when dem taste it, it taste nice. Him say, "If you want it to taste more real put ginger in deh." And dem put ginger in deh, man, and when dem drink, when dem taste it, it taste *good*. And Brerer Anancy start to sell quattie[1] a cup, fippance[2] and thrupence[3] a cup, and everybody taste it, "It *so* real, it *so* real," and from that it get the name *Sorrel.*[4]

Collected in Kingston on November 8, 1978.

A version appears in Bennett, *Anancy and Miss Lou,* pp. 48–50.

1. Three farthings.
2. Six pence.
3. Three pence.
4. Sorrel is an extremely popular Christmas drink in Jamaica. For an interesting account of the origin of this word (French *surele*), the history of the plant, its varied uses as a herb and a punch, and recipes for the Christmas drink, see Myrtle Marcelle, "Sorrel: A Truly Jamaican Tradition," *Jamaica Journal, 2* (March 1978), 60–61.

10 Why Satan Did Not Learn to Blow Breath

This story is telling why the devil did not learn to blow breath. In the Creation it is said that Satan was with God while he was making man. In the process he was sent back to heaven for something and when he came back God had already blown the breath, so he did not learn how to blow breath.

Collected in Kingston on October 30, 1978.

II

Anansesem

Introduction

Animal tales have long been popular in Jamaican folklore and continue to be so. They make up by far the largest group of folk materials that have been published there, and I find that they remain a significant aspect of daily life for a number of people. Practically every one of the numerous Jamaican writers and artists whom I have interviewed told me he grew up hearing Anancy tales from his parents, grandparents, nurses, or school chums. Indeed, the popular Anancy, who is the subject of a number of these animal tales, commonly appears as a character or a symbol in the poetry and stories of numerous Jamaican and other West Indian writers, including, most notably, Louise Bennett, Andrew Salkey, Philip Sherlock, and Edward Brathwaite.

Certainly one of the items of their folk culture that the African slaves brought with them to the New World and that they have preserved in its most uncorrupted form is that indestructible and irresistible spider, Anancy. Robert D. Pelton's description of the Ashanti Ananse is an apt description of his West Indian counterpart as he survives in contemporary lore. Pelton writes, "He is both fooler and fool, maker and unmade, wily and stupid, subtle and gross, the High God's accomplice and his rival."[1] Like the American Brer Rabbit,

11

another African survival found only rarely in Jamaican lore, Anancy is generally a figure of admiration whose cunning and scheming nature reflects the
indirection and subtletiès necessary for survival and occasionally victory for the
Black man in a racist society. Though most of the storytellers rejoice in his
victories over the stronger animals with whom he is frequently in contest, they
also recognize his immorality, his greed, his stupidity, his deceitfulness. Thus,
as Louise Bennett points out in her introduction to *Jamaican Song,* after she
and her childhood friends reveled in the antics of Anancy, "At the end of each
story, we had to say, 'Jack Mandora, me no chose none,' because Annancy sometimes did very wicked things in his stories, and we had to let Jack Mandora,
the doorman at heaven's door, know that we were not in favor of Annancy's
wicked ways."[2] Thus it is that some contemporary Jamaicans look with dis-
favor on Anancy. H. P. Jacobs observes in a recent *Gleaner* article a prevalent
concern that "the admiration of unscrupulous cunning is encouraged by Anancy
stories and that they express an unhealthy trait of character."[3] And Eddie Burke,
folklorist and storyteller par excellence, told me that he doesn't tell Anancy
stories because Anancy's rascality and deceit are bad for the national character.[4]
Despite these distractions, my own experiences in Jamaica in 1978 convinced
me that Anancy is alive and well and as beloved now as ever. Mocking her
countrymen who proclaim, "'Oh, the Anancy mentality bad!'" Louise Bennett went on to relate her early delight in the Anancy tales—a delight that
I found reflected over and over in my interviews with contemporary Jamaican
youths:

> But the way I learnt Anancy, I knew Anancy as a child, and it was a *joy-y-y*!
> We *loved* to listen to the stories, we loved to hear about this little trickify man,
> you know, and one thing we knew, that this man was magic, and we could
> never be like him. You know—he is a magic man. He could spin a web and
> become a *spider* whenever he wanted to [laughter]. You can't do that, so you
> better not try the Anancy's tricks, you know, but it was fun![5]

As Bennett's comments suggest, Anancy takes many shapes; at times he
seems to be a man, and at other times he is an insect, running up his web and
taking refuge in the ceiling. Another point of interest in the character, and one
that marks the distinguished teller of the tales, is Anancy's distinctive speech,
which is characterized, as Jacobs notes, by "a peculiar form of dialect . . . [that]
consists of old-fashioned pronunciations, but may point to some recollection
in Africa of the original Spider having his own language,"[6] and which is also
marked by a notable nasal quality and lisp. As Miss Bennett observed, "'Im
tawk wid a lisp tongue. 'Im tongue tie."[7]

Another character that appears frequently in the Anancy tales is Tacuma,
who is sometimes Anancy's companion, sometimes his spouse, sometimes his
son, sometimes his neighbor. Harold Courlander suggests that *Tacuma* is the

local pronunciation of *Intikuma,* the Ashanti name for the son of Ananse.[8] In most of the tales Tacuma is duped and victimized by Anancy, but occasionally he is the victor and succeeds in outwitting Anancy.

In Jamaica the term *Anancy story* is often applied, as several other scholars have noted, to any storytelling, riddling, and singing.[19] Likewise in Africa, Helen L. Flowers informs us, "the term 'Anansesem' (spider stories) is used to refer to all stories."[10] Within this chapter I employ a more limiting connotation, including herein those tales treating any of the animals—Anancy, Rat, Mouse, Puss, Dawg, Alligator, and John Crow.

As we look at the Anancy stories, we will find that they appeal to us not only because of their drama, excitement, and humor but also because we quickly perceive that, like most animal tales, these are not really about animals but about human beings, and we realize that a part of our attraction is that we recognize ourselves in the antics of these creatures.

1. Pelton, *The Trickster in West Africa: A Study of Mythic Irony and Sacred Delight* (Berkeley: Univ. of California Press, 1980), pp. 28–29.
2. Bennett, Introduction, to Jekyll, *Jamaican Song,* ix.
3. Jacobs, "Who Was Anancy?" *Gleaner,* August 16, 1982, p. 3.
4. Interview with Eddie Burke, Santa Cruz, Jamaica, November 4, 1978.
5. Interview with Louise Bennett, Gordon Town, Jamaica, September 15, 1978.
6. Jacobs, "Who Was Anancy?" p. 3.
7. Interview with Louise Bennett.
8. Courlander, *Treasury of Afro-American Folklore,* p. 129.
9. See Beckwith, *Jamaican Anansi Stories,* p. xi.
10. Flowers, *West Indian Types and Motifs,* p. 5.

11A   Cork di Pot, Man

One time you have this Brer Anancy and Brer Dawg. Brer Anancy and Brer Dawg say—the two of dem trying to outwit each oder. So Brer Anancy cooking a pot now; so Brer Anancy say, "Quick, Dawg, go inna di pot, and mek I show you how dis ting work, man." Brer Dawg say, "You tink you can outwit me, Anancy, *you* go inna di pot firs', man."

Brer Anancy jump inna di pot first because di water cool; it nuh start bwoil up yet. Brer Anancy: "When I knock, you open it." When Brer Anancy feel di water start boil, you know [dramatizing Anancy reaching up, knocking on pot]: "Bum, bum, bum!" Him jump out a di ting: "Yes, man, nice, nice, nice! Is you time now, Brer Dawg."

Brer Dawg jump in. Hear him nuh: "Cork di pot, man." When Anancy fire start tek him now, him say [dramatizing Dog frantically knocking on pot]: "Bum, bum, bum!" Hear Brer Anancy now, "No, man, not time yet. I stay in dere longer dan that." "Bum, boom, boom, boom!" "Not time yet. I stay dere longer dan dat." "Bum, boom, boom, boom!" Hear dis knocking. Hear Brer Anancy: "Yes, man, dat is di game, you don' come out until teeth skin and batti shoot."[1]

Collected in Kingston on September 21, 1978.

See Motif K710, "Victim Enticed into Voluntary Captivity or Helplessness," in Baughman, *Type and Motif-Index*, This is Motif K851, "Deceptive Game: Burning Each Other," in Flowers, *West Indian Types and Motifs*. Two versions of this tale appear in Beckwith, *Jamaican Anansi Stories* (Nos. 16 and 37).

    1. Bottom pushes out—this will indicate that he is dead.

11B   Cork di Pot, Man

    Brer Rabbit and Brer Tacuma a go fi hot water, so Brer Tacuma first go in and say, "Water hot." And Brer Rabbit lif' it up and tek him out. Brer Rabbit go in dere, and Brer Rabbit say, "Water hot," and a push up di sump'n. Him just hole it down and say, "Mek water bun yu 'kin,[1] mek water bun yu' 'kin!" And when di water bun 'im up, bwoil 'im up till 'im a laugh, hear Brer Tacuma nuh: "All you eat mi meat, you still a laugh after me." And eat him off. And that is the end of the story.

Collected in Kingston on September 15, 1978.

    1. Skin.

12A   Bird Cherry Island

    This is a story about Brother Anancy on Cherry Island and some birds. Once upon a time long, long ago Bredda Anancy and some birds decide to go to Cherry Island. Bredda Anancy wanted to go, but he didn't have any feather nor no wings, so he made a deal with the birds. If the birds will lend him their feathers, he will go to Cherry Island with them and pick all the cherry he could pick and share it even. Bredda Anancy got together with the birds and each bird took out some feathers and give Bredda Anancy. Bredda Anancy fix up himself and they both went to Cherry Island now. They all pick cherries, picking cherry, picking cherry, so, till the bag got fill. Bredda Anancy decide to move away with the bag of cherries.

    When the birds saw that, they decided to take back their feathers, so Bredda Anancy decide to keep the feathers, and the birds they took away their feathers and leave him under the cherry tree at Cherry Island.

    Bredda Anancy didn't know to reach home back, so he got near to the seaside, he saw a boat, but he didn'. have any row stick, so he went nearby. He looked in. He saw Bredda Alligator. Bredda Alligator came up and say,

"Well, Bredda Anancy, what happen?" He say, "Well, I want to reach home, but I went to Cherry Island and the birds, they took away their feathers, so I don't know how I going reach home." He say, "Well, then, Bredda Anancy, I believe I can tek you across, but you have to do something for me. Right? I have some eggs down the bottom; I want you bring them up for me and put them in the hut." Bredda Anancy go down dere and start to bring it up, but Bredda Alligator say to him, "Won't you count all of dem before you bring dem?" Bredda Anancy go down and he count one egg two time, one egg two time, so he had six egg. Right? Count one egg twice. Anyway Bredda Anancy come up and Bredda Anancy bring up the egg them and while bringing up the eggs Bredda Anancy burst the eggs and suck them out. Each time him go down him tell Bredda Alligator is one egg him see. When him go back, him see one. When him suppose fi have six eggs down deh. Anyway Anancy eat off all the eggs, so Bredda Alligator start to chase him and Bredda Anancy head for the sea, man. Alligator jump in and start to swim behind Bredda Anancy. Bredda Anancy couldn't swim good as Alligator. So Bredda Anancy saw two fish, one was deaf and one was dumb; one deaf, one caan' hear, one could hear, one caan' hear, and one could talk, but him caan' hear. Anyway Bredda Anancy went in the boat and told the fish them say to row, and Anancy say, "Row fast, row fast. Storm deh pon sea. Row fast." Fish said, the one weh deaf say, "What you say?" Bredda Anancy say, "Mi say fi row fast. Storm deh pon sea." The one weh caan' hear, him deh pon all the while, "Wha you say?" And the other one say, "Row fast. Storm deh pon sea." Alligator behind the boat, man, and the fish a row. Anancy say, "Row fast, storm deh pon sea, man." That is, this alligator deh behind me, you know. "Row fast. Storm deh pon sea. Row fast. Storm deh pon sea, man." And Alligator ah cut water, man, and fish a row, you know! Anancy say, "Row fast. Storm deh pon sea, man. Row fast. Storm deh pon sea!"

Recorded in Kingston in November 1978.

See Motif Q597.2, "Birds Take Back Their Feathers from Ungrateful Wolf to Whom They Have Lent Them," in Baughman, *Type and Motif-Index*. This is Type 225, "The Crane Teaches the Fox to Fly," in Flowers, *West Indian Types and Motifs*. Variants of this tale appear in Courlander, *The Drum and the Hoe*, pp. 179–81, and Beckwith, *Jamaican Anansi Stories*, No. 39. Versions have also been collected in Grenada and the Cape Verde Islands.

12B Bird Cherry Island

Anancy and Tacuma again — they are always friend. They go to a place the name of Bird Cherry Island. That is the island have a lots of cherries, and when it ripe up is only bird that eat it. So Anancy go and invite Tacuma to this Bird Cherry Island. Him say, all right. Them straggle out together and dem get there, and them feed fi di day until Anancy stomach fill now and night is coming on. Anancy say [nasal voice], "Bredda Tacuma, I am going now, you don't ready?" Hear Tacuma, "No, Bredda Anancy, I don't ready yet. You go on. Leave me. I will catch you."

And when him tink Anancy reach home, him start, because him know night goin' tek him. And he go to Anancy gate. He call in: "Bredda Anancy, the night tek me. I caan' reach home tonight. Could you put me up till in the mawning?" "Oh yes, Bredda Tacuma, come in."

Tacuma go in and have him dinner and they go to bed now. Now poor Anancy have a hundred eggs one side in him fowl-nest. Every mornin' him get up and him check him egg. So the mawning now; Tacuma sleep las' night and get up in the mawning now. Dat time him suck out *every one* of Anancy egg, get up in the night and suck it out. In the mawning now, and they wake up. Anancy say, "Oh, let I go and check my egg before I get someting to eat." Tacuma know him suck out all the egg already. Tacuma say, "Bredda Anancy, you get the tea. I will check the egg."

And you know what Tacuma do? Him go in di house and 'im tek up *one egg trash*[1] and 'im count di one egg trash to a hundred; "One, two . . ." and is di one trash 'im is countin' until he goes to di one hundred. And Anancy say, "All right, Bredda Tacuma, come and have your breakfast." Dem have breakfast together and after breakfast Tacuma tell goodbye—him gone.

When him gone away, Anancy say, "Let me go and check my egg." When him go di hundred egg suck out and jus' throw down one side. Den him *make* after Tacuma. When him reach to the shore him see di boat was pulling out. Him say, "Bring back me egg, Tacuma."

Hear Tacuma to the two man that run the boat: "Sail fast. Storm on sea!" Anancy say, "Bring back, Bredda Tacuma." "Sail fast. Storm on sea!" "Tacuma! Bring back Tacuma!" "Sail fast. Storm on sea!" And him stan' up and watch the boat out of reach and Tacuma don't come back. Him have to turn back in tears—no Tacuma and all him egg done. He was smart.

Collected in Mandeville on September 16, 1978.
1. Shell.

12C Bird Cherry Island

Once upon a time a Monkey who lived among some bird decided to visit Bird Cherry Island. Naturally the Monkey could not fly, so he was lent some feathers by his bird friends.

And thus he began to fly with the birds to Bird Cherry Island. When they reached, they all began eating cherry. When they were ready, Mr. Monkey was not ready. Even when night fell he was not ready, so they took back their feathers and fly away, leaving Brother Monkey stranded.

As it would be in any case the high and mighty, hoity-toity Brother Monkey became tired of the cherries that made his inside ache with discomfort.

He wanted to go back home, but he could not fly. Eventually he threw a bit of stick in the water and it floated, so he decided that if the stick floats, he would float, and [he] jump into the water. Instantly he began to sink, and had it not been for Brother Alligator, he would have drowned.

Nevertheless Brother Alligator told him after saving him that his old wife need monkey liver soup or she would die. Brother Monkey told him that his wife was dying in a tree. Being foolish, Brother Alligator decided to take him home as it was late and bring him back to fetch the liver the other morning. This he did.

At home he gave Brother Monkey the task of washing his eggs. Ten eggs. Brother Monkey on the morrow ate nine eggs and wash one repeatedly before Brother Alligator and his wife.

However, Brother Monkey was lucky. He was taken back to shore by the foolish but kind Brother Alligator. Then and there at the shore Brother Monkey swing onto a branch in a tree and vanish as he was never born.

This is the end of my story.

Received in writing on October 11, 1978, from a Kingston resident.

See Motif K961, "Flesh of Certain Animal Alleged to Be Only Cure for Disease: Animal to Be Killed," in Baughman, *Type and Motif-Index.*

12D Bird Cherry Island

One bright mawning, a whole heap of birds fly go a Brer Anancy yawd. And Brer Anancy was sleeping. He said, "Birds, why you waking mi?" Deh seh, We are goin' to Bird Cherry land. Brer Anancy say, "Let's come with you." Dem say, "You caan' come for you caan' fly." And dem tek out some of dem fedder and dem fit inna Brer Anancy, and everybody fly go a Bird Cherry Island.

And when dem go a Bird Cherry Island to eat and when dem a come way now, 'im no wan' come way. Say, "Brer Anancy, we ready." Him sey, "Very nice to stay here. I am not coming wid you." And dem tak out dem fedder now, take out dem fedder now and dem gawn wid i'. And when evenin' a come now, him fi go home, den him mus' haffi go home, and 'im cutlis is in a river. And him sink himself wid bamboo stick, . . . him wi' sink and him cutlis, 'im dash it in a di river, and him float way. Him say, "Me a go pon dat." And 'im go pon i', and when 'im go in a di river now, him buck up Brer Alligator. And Brer Anancy say to Brer Alligator, say, "Evenin', Godfader." Brer Alligator say, "Who tell you sey you a mi godson?" "A mi ole parent, sah." And him tell him say him ole parents tell him.

And 'im say, "I goin' to pull you as you is mi godson." And Brer Alligator now draw one pot a porridge and give Brer Anancy, say, since 'im a him godfader. Anancy mek one sup and drink it out. And Brer Anancy say, "Godfader, it no hot now; put i' a sun fi hot more." Dat time a cool him want it fi cool, you know. And when Anancy feel i', and when 'im mek one big drink and 'im done it, Brer Alligator say, "You is my godson, you is my godson." Dat time him no reach a yawd yet. And when 'im go a yawd now, Brer Alligator have nine nephew, nine pickney, and him left 'im wid Brer Anancy. And when him gone, Brer Anancy eat off eight, leff one. And when Brer Alligator come now, Brer Anancy say, "Godfather, I get letter sey mi moder dead and mi fader dying and I ben well waan go." "Awright." And Brer Alligator say now, "Bring di children dem come." And 'im tek di egg and 'im go, and 'im wash it off and 'im say, "One, Godfader"; so tell 'im reach nine. And dem put in a one ship[1] and when di two fish start 'old,[2] when di two fish start 'old one . . . and dem say, "Boatman, oh-h, bring back Brer Anancy." Dat time 'im eat off egg and only lef one. And dem say, "Boatman, bring back Brer Anancy." Him sey, "Whe you say, heavy wind deh pon sea. Sail fast." And dem sail and dem sail and dem sail and dem sail and dem sail till dem land di two fish. . . .

'Im get one pot and 'im put in Brer Anancy in deh. Him put in Brer Anancy in a di big pot and when di water warm, him say, "Brer Alligator, water warm. Tek mi out." Brer Alligator tek 'im out. And when Brer Anancy now put Brer Alligator in a di pot now, and when di water hot now, him say, "Brer Anancy, water hot." Him say, "Tan in deh you too bad. You ben keep mi miles down a bottom." Dat a di fish you know. And Brer Alligator mek di water hot till di fish cook and 'im eat 'im. Eat off di whole fish. And that's the end of the story.

Collected in Kingston on September 15, 1978.
1. They all got into one ship.
2. When the fish bite the bait on the hook.

13 Why Dawg Hate Puss

Brer Dawg and Brer Puss buy one pan a butter and dem hide it and a time run out. Brer Puss say, "Brer Dawg, I have three sister and one a go married and Parson say mi fi come." Brer Dawg say, "Gwan nuh." And Brer Puss go. And when Brer Puss go, him open di butta and 'im eat off di butta top out a di kerosene pan and 'im come back a yawd, and 'im say, "Evening, Brer

Dawg." Brer Dawg say, "Evening, Brer Puss." Him say, "How di wedding go on?" Him say, "Di wedding go on nice."

And a period of time run out again. Dat time 'im a go back di second time. Him say, "Brer Dawg, mi second sister a go married and I ben waan' go." Brer Dawg say, "Go on, Brer Puss." And Brer Puss go and 'im open di pan and 'im eat off di whole of di butter, lef haf now. Dat time a di second time. And him come back, him say, "Evening, Brer Dawg." Brer Dawg say, "Evening, Brer Puss. How di wedding go on?" "Di wedding go on nice." Him say, "Den what is your second sister's name?" Him say his second sister name is Half-done.

And when him go back di las' time now, him say, "Brer Dawg, di las' sister ah go married, and ah ben well waan' go." And Brer Dawg say, "Go on, Brer Puss." And by the time him go him eat off the butta clean now and cover up the pan. Dat time di butta done now; three time him go and come back a yawd. Him say, "Evening, Brer Dawg." Brer Dawg say, "Evening, Brer Puss." Him say, "How di wedding go on?" Him say, "Di wedding go on nice same so." Brer Dawg say, "Brer Puss, mek we go look pon di butta weh we hide." And when dem go now, Brer Puss no open di butta. Him waan' Brer Dawg fi open it, and Brer Dawg open di pan. And when him look him say, "Yes, Brer Puss, all di weddin' you was a come a yahso,[1] you was a come come eat out di butta!"

And from that day, Dawg hate Puss.

Collected in Kingston on September 15, 1978.

This is Motif K401.1, "Dupe's food eaten and then blame fastened on him," in Baughman, *Type and Motif-Index*, and Type 15, "The Theft of Butter (Honey) by Playing Godfather," in Flowers, *West Indian Types and Motifs.* Versions appear in Courlander, *The Drum and the Hoe,* pp. 176–77; Beckwith, *Jamaican Anansi Stories,* No. 9; Parsons, *Folk-tales of Andros Island,* No. 5; Parsons, *Folk-Lore of the Sea Islands,* No. 3; and Dorson, *Negro Tales from Pine Bluff,* No. 1. Versions of the tale have also been collected in Antigua, Trinidad, Grenada, St. Vincent, Dominica, St. Croix, the Dominican Republic, Guadaloupe, Nevis, India, and Japan.

1. You came here.

14A The Bone Sweet

This is a story about Anancy and his big fat goat. Anancy and his wife lived together and they had a big goat, and Anancy want to eat it all off. But he never want his wife to get any. So one day he formed sick, and while he was at home he asked his wife to go and call the Doctor. So while the wife took the long road to the Doctor surgery, Anancy dress up quickly like the Doctor and went and sit in his surgery.

When the wife came up she told him all what happen, and then Anancy say, "Don't you have a big goat at home? All you have to do, go home and cook it and give him *all* of it."

The wife said, "Yes, sir."

And then she took back the long road and Anancy took the short cut and run back home, lie down in the bed. When the wife reached, he was groaning as if he was in pain. "Wha di Doctor say?" "Him say mi fi cook di goat and give you all of it." Anancy say, "Mek haste wid it." So while the goat was cooking Bredder Tacuma came in and Anancy was there in bed, and the wife said that it was ready. Anancy get up, ready to eat, and Bredder Tacuma took away the meat from Anancy and cover up Anancy underneath a basket. And so he eat the meat; he throw the bone underneath the basket and give Anancy. Anancy say, "Out a mi big big goat a dis me get!"

Tacuma say, "What you say, bwoy?"

"Mi say di bone sweet, sar."

Collected in Kingston on October 30, 1978.

This is Motif K352, "Theft by Posing as Doctor," in Baughman, *Type and Motif-Index,* and Type 1372, "The Woman Feigns Periodic Attacks of a Disease That Can Only Be Cured by Eating a Great Number of Delicacies: Her Husband Feigns the Same Disease," in Flowers, *West Indian Types and Motifs.* Versions appear in Beckwith, *Jamaican Anansi Stories,* No. 30; Harris, *Uncle Remus,* I, 17; and Bennett, *Anancy and Miss Lou,* pp. 59–60. Others have been collected in Suriname and Antigua.

14B The Bone Sweet

Once upon a time Brer Rabbit and Brer Tacuma. So Brer Tacuma says he is sick. So Brer Tacuma gawn a 'im bed. So 'im wife have a cow. So him sey to him wife, sey, "Go a Doctor, go hear wha dem say what me can get fi ease di pain." Him a eena bed [groaning]: "Uhmmmm."

And di Doctor gone out and tek off fi—him run gawn through the short cut and put on Doctor clothes and dress up, man.

"What you say now, lady, what 'appen to you 'usband?"

"Him sick."

"All you have to do, give him a cow and sen' him down a river wid it."

And she go up and Brer Tacuma run through the short cut and come in a bed, a groan, and she send him a river wid di cow, and 'im a cook, 'im put in di cow in a pot now. So guess wha now? Him put in di cow in a pot and a breadfruit drop—Brer Rabbit up in a di tree a bust di breadfruit, and a drop pon di groun'. So him a bus' breadfruit. Every minute him go pick up one: "Dis nice to go in a di pot, man." Him run go put it inna di pot.

So dis time Brer Rabbit—BUFF! [dropping from tree] pon ground. Him lif' up Brer Tacuma. So Brer Tacuma say, "Let me go, man! Weh you hole me fah?" Brer Rabbit say, "Ah wah dat a cook?[1] A Wha dat a bwoil out so?"

Hear him nuh: "A dem people down a bottom a scald clothes."
Hear Brer Rabbit nuh: "Mi say fi carr' mi down deh, man."
"No, man, no . . . rocky down deh. A people down deh a scald clothes."
Hear Brer Rabbit: "Carry me down deh fi *blow* fire pon you behind."
Rabbit put him over him head top yah so and carry him go straight down.
Brer Rabbit say, "*You a tell me lie!*" Brer Rabbit mek him stay outside and go
on in a di house and start to eat now, and Rabbit trow di bones outside. Di
man [Tacuma] grumble and a say [grumbling to himself]: "Dat a my bones,
after my cow ga-ga. . . ." Rabbit say [threateningly]: "Wah you a say?" [loud]:
"The bone sweet, sah." "Wah you a say, sah?" "The bone sweet sah."
That's the end of it.

Collected in Kingston on September 18, 1978, from an eleven-year-old.
1. What is that cooking?

14C The Bone Sweet

Once upon a time Brer Anancy had a hog at him home and he wanted
to eat it alone so he formed sick. He formed sick and him tell him wife say
him going a Doctor because him feel sick, but she must walk through long
cut and him will walk through short cut, so the wife say all right. Anancy
put on him jacket and walk through short cut, go to the Doctor. That time
he become the Doctor, and when the wife come now, Anancy say, "What happen now?" Him wife say, "Me husband sick and him send me go ask for. . . ."
Him say, "All right, I know what is wrong. Him have one hog a yu yawd?"
"Yes, sah." "All right, if you want him fi get better, kill it, give him it, but
you must not go with him. Let him go to the butcher and he alone must eat
it." Him[1] say, "Me one one hog, sah?" Him say, "Yes, you don't want him
to get better?" So him say all right. So Anancy wife go outside now, and Anancy
run through short cut gone back into bed, start to grunt, "Ummm-mmmm.
Me Wife, wah Doctor say?" "Him say mi one one hog me have me fi give
you." Him say, All right, get the hog; follow me go half way, and then you
can go back." And the two of them now were going along, and when they
reach half way, him say, "All right, you can go back now."
While Anancy was in the bush cooking, when he kill the hog and were
cooking it, he hear something drop from the tree. So Anancy believe it was
a coconut, so when him look, him saw this man with a dry head, and Dry
Head[2] say to him, "If you come and look at me, you have to pick me up, and
you have to pick me up and carry me with you." So Anancy tek up that Dry
Head, and when Dry Head go now and see the hog, he want to eat it too.
So he put Anancy to bed. Anancy gone to sleep now. He boil one side of the

hog first and eat off all the meat and leave the bones, and then he wake Anancy. "Anancy, pot ready." When Anancy wake and saw the bones, he say, "Out a mi whole whole hog a di bone me get!" So Dry Head say [threateningly], "What you say, bwoy?" He say [meekly], "Lawd, sah, di bone sweet." When him gone back now, him say, "Out a mi whole whole hog is bone me get!" "What you say, bwoy?" "Lawd, sah, it sweet so till."

The other side leave[3] now, so Dry Head got him back to bed and start to eat the other side, leave only the bones and wake Anancy, and Anancy say, "Out a di whole whole hog a di bone me get!" "Wah you say, bwoy?" "Me say, it sweet, sah, me could a eat more," and it go on and go on until him finish. When Dry Head ready to go home now, him say, "How must I get home?" When Anancy look up him see Bro Pichary[4], so him ask him fi carry home Bro Dry Head. When Pichary tek up Bro Dry Head now and start going on, Dry Head started to pick Pichary. Pichary said, "If you pick me again me goin' drop you." So Dry Head pick him, and him drop him, and him drop him and the whole of him mash up. So Anancy eat off everything and say, "Dis a mi whole whole hog!"

Collected in Kingston on November 8, 1978.

1. It is not uncommon in Jamaican patois for *him* to refer to a female.

2. My informant described Dry Head as a crow. Beckwith says he is an old man in the Anancy stories (*Jamaican Anansi Stories*, p. 27).

3. Is left.

4. The petchary bird is noted for attacking the crow and other birds.

15 Bredda Anancy and Bredda John Crow

Once upon a time there was Bredda Anancy and Bredda John Crow.[1] So Bredda Anancy and Bredda John Crow was mouthin' each oder, said which one can stay longer without eating, you know. Anyway Bredda John Crow say him can stay longer than Bredda Anancy. Bredda Anancy say him can stay longer than Bredda John Crow. So they both get together, got two rooms. Bredda John Crow went in one, and Bredda Anancy went in the oder. Bredda John Crow, everytime him go inside he will call out, "Bredda Anancy, are you there?" Bredda Anancy say, "Yes." Bredda Anancy said to Bredda John Crow, "Bredda John Crow, are you there?" Bredda John Crow say, "Yes, I am here still."

Keep up for a long while, they calling each other; they are answering, answering. Anyway Bredda Anancy said to Bredda John Crow, "Bredda John Crow, I am tired to answer now, man. Gon' tek a nap of sleep, so anytime you call me, I no goin' bother say, 'yes.' I now say 'pup'; that mean you know I am alive still. Right?" Bredda John Crow say yes. Meanwhile Bredda Anancy get a goadie, pour a hole and put some water in it. By this time Bredda Anancy waan' to go and look food because Bredda Anancy a man can't stay hungry, but him want to get food and outlast Bredda John Crow. Bredda Anancy put the water in the gourd, bore a hole and get a piece of string and — and tie it upon on the ceiling. Meanwhile Bredda John Crow say, "Bredda Anancy!" The water drop out of the gourd on the floor and say, "pup." So Bredda John Crow know say Bredda Anancy is still around. That time Bredda Anancy gone to get food. Bredda John Crow call Bredda Anancy, hear "pup." Anyway, Bredda Anancy go out and look food for a long while, full him belly and him come back. Him come; him say, "Bredda John Crow, Bredda John Crow!" Him don't hear no sound. Him say, "Bredda John Crow, Bredda John Crow, are you there still?" [Pause] He hear no sound. Bredda Anancy go round and bus' down the door and go inside. When him look, Bredda John Crow stone dead. So him take a stock. John Crow only have one tripe, only wha could a las' him for a day. That's why we know say John Crow only have one tripe. Yeah, one tripe Bredda John Crow have, man.

Collected in Kingston in November 1978.
See K81.4, "Contest: Who Will Eat Least," in Baughman, *Type and Motif-Index.*
1. The crow, frequently called John Crow in Jamaica, appears in numerous folk tales.

16 Anancy and Monkey

Well, there were once a man, a white man, that bought a property. So Mr. Anancy said to him, as he heard that the man bought the property, and him want to make certain that he is close to the property that if anything, him can tief it. So him run and go to the boss, who is the white man.

Mr. Anancy meet him by the gate, for the property wire round, so him meet him by the gate when he was coming in: "Hi, Boss."

Well, the white man says to him, "Hi, sir."

"I hear sey you a buy dat piece, piece a place over yah, over property yah, sah."

The white man say yes.

Him say, "You get anybody fi you headman yet, sah?"

He say, "Well, really, no."

"Hmmm. Well, you see I come out yah, not doing nuttin now. I say mek I come ask you fi get the job from you sah."

Him say, "Will you?"

Him say, "Oh, yes sir, yes sir, that's what bring me here."

Him tek on Bredder Anancy and him carry him back in. So him carry Bredder Anancy now far far to show him, and Bredder Anancy say him know (h)all[1] about the property, him was working on the property here already. The work him was working, you know what him was doing—killing it! So as the poor gentleman don't know, him tell him that him was working there. Well, the gentleman was very glad to know that he getting a man that was working there already. Himself carry him and show him sheep, goat, and pig over by his [Anancy's] place where he live and tell him say he must get some men to help him to protect them, to drive them over, to drive them to where him property, him say to let them back in the property.

Bredder Monkey and Bredder Anancy were good friends, and they both went. And Bredder Tiger went with him, and they drive in sheep, they drive in goat, they drive in cow. And after everything was set, Bredder Anancy and the gentleman come to price.

Bredder Anancy kill the poor man sheep dem and him cure the skin. So den, when the poor gentleman couldn't bear it any longer, him say. "Mr. Anancy, I want to take over, for these sheeps are moving on very fast and *you* is the headman here. I tink I'll have to seek a nex' headman."

Him say, "Backra Massa, you 'low mi, 'low mi, I goin' fine out who dat take yu sheep . . . you 'low me."

The gentleman say, "Well, all right, I will give you a little time."

Him say, "Now, you know wah you do, Backra Massa. Mek a little get-together and call in all a you friends, dem come and dem have a little dance. Me a musician; mi play fi you fi nuttin."

Him say, "Awright."

"And you have a little nyaming-up[2] up a yu yard, and den now I gwain bring de man come right in."

The white man say, "All right."

Mr. Anancy went to Bredder Monkey because he knew that Bredder Monkey was a poor man, him naked. Him say, "See yah, Monkey, I see a man wah go ha a nyaming-up feas' up a 'im yard, and him get mi fi play di music, and I want you fi a play music with me. You can play you mout' orgin."

Bredder Monkey say, "Yes, Bredder Anancy, dat is true."

"But yu will need a shirt. If yu go round yawd now, mi wife tek measurement off a you and mek dose shirt."

Poor Bredder Monkey go round; Bredder Anancy wife tek measurement off a Bredder Monkey. Bredder Anancy tell him wife that him wife is to mek a suit of clothes out of sheep's skin wah cured and give Bredder Monkey, and when he go to the white man Bredder Monkey will know wah him go for. Dat is what him say. The wife do it. The mawning of di party the night, the morning Bredder Anancy call Bredder Monkey and say to walk up a yawd an' go try on di ting. Bredder Monkey say to Bredder Anancy, "I goin' come up deh in a di day."

Him say, "All right."

The wife cut out di suit and stitch it up. When poor Monkey go up into the day, Anancy come: "Hi, you an' Monkey deh yah?"

Bredder Monkey say, "Yes, yes Bredder Anancy."

He call him wife: "Go try on di someting pon Bredder Monkey nuh, dat ting—you know."

She come out and she try the thing on to Bredder Monkey. When she try on the suit on Bredder Monkey, Anancy say, "Lawd a marcy, see yah, Monkey, di suit fit you like a how jackass fit jawbone. Nuh tek i' off, nuh tek i' off! Keep i' on, for we soon go wey." Poor Bredder Monkey so glad in a him new suit him just a wave up and down. Anancy wife cook and Bredder Monkey eat and Bredder Anancy eat. All Bredder Monkey do was go roun' to his house to take up his flute, and di both of them start and go (h)up. In the evening Anancy says to Monkey, "Bredder Monkey, we have to start to serenade on the road. We caan' jist a galong so. When you a play you fife a go long so, is time I have to talk, I have to sing."

Bredder Monkey say, "Yes, Bredder Anancy."

Bredder Anancy pick up him violin and him start off the tune:

> All mi tell mi ah tell Bredder Moneky fi mine backra sheep, oh!
> All mi tell mi deh tell Bredder Monkey fi mine backra sheep, oh!

Poor Bredder Monkey deh pon [blowing the flute]: "Wee-e-wee-e-wee-e-wee-wee-wee-wee-o-wee-o-wee-o-wee-wee-wee." He is not listening to what Bredder Anancy da say:

> Him do and him do and him do and him do,
> Till him a wear di ting go a prove yah.
> Him do and him do and him do and him do,
> Till him a wear di ting go a prove yah.

And him go on and go on and go on till him reach the gate. Then him stop. And when him stop by the white man gate, when he look up, boy, him see friends like whirlwind on the verandah.

Bredder Anancy [playing]: "Tinki-tinki-tinki-tinki-t-i-n-g, tinki-tinki-tinki-t-i-n-g."

Bredder Money [playing]: "Wee-wee-wee-o-wee."

And they start now: "Tinki-tinki-tinki-tink-tink-tink . . ."

Bredder Anancy:

> All mi tell, mi deh tell Bredder Monkey, fi mine backra ting, oh.
> All mi tell, mi deh tell Bredder Monkey, fi mine backra ting, oh.
> Him do and him do and him do and him do,
> Till him nuh wear di ting come up a prove yah.

> Him do and him do and him do and him do.
> Till him wear di ting come, come prove yah.

That time him reach on the verandah. All that happen now is, well, they pon poor Bredder Monkey and tie him up. Bredder Monkey say, "Lawd a marcy, ah weh mi do?"

Bredder Anancy say, "Ah weh you do! Weh you tek Backra sheep mek? You tink a cockroach? Tan deh, tek you punishment!" And away they sent for the police and lock up Bredder Monkey for the sheep that he knows *nothing* about. Anancy is the thief and they put Bredder Monkey into jail.

And that is the end of the story. That's why it is said, man to man is so unjust that we knows not who to trust.

Collected in Kingston on July 8, 1978, from a resident of Cassava River.

This is Motif K1066, "Dupe induced to Incriminate Himself," in Baughman, *Type and Motif-Index.* See also Motif K346.2, "Herdsman Slaughters Animals Entrusted to Him," and Motif K401.2.3, "Surreptitious Transfer of Stolen Object to Innocent Person's Possession Brings Condemnation," in Baughman, and Motif K435.3, "Child's Song Incriminates Thief," in Flowers, *West Indian Types and Motifs.* Versions appear in Beckwith, *Jamaican Anansi Stories,* No. 4; and Parsons, *Folk-tales of Andros Islands,* No. 33. Other versions have been collected in Africa and the United States.

1. This speaker has the not uncommon tendency among Jamaicans to put an *h* sound before some words beginning with a vowel.

2. A little feast. *Nyam* is an African word meaning to eat.

17 The Tar Banana Tree

One time there was a landowner; he have a property wid some bananas. So every night a tief go in di field and tief out di bananas, and in the mawning him wake up him find some a him banana missin'. So him say, bwoy, him haf fi ketch da man deh wah a tief him bananas. So Anancy went to him and said, "Well, Boss, gi mi di job as a watchman, nuh, we mus' ketch di banana tief."

So Anancy him now—he was di tief. But he do it so, you know. Steal the banana and carry it, you know. The nex' mawning him report to him Boss: "Boss, banana still a go, but mi caan' ketch di tief." So the Boss plan pon him and say, "Well, I goin ketch di tief." So the Boss him went ahead and put some tar, or pitch, or what you call it, on the banana tree.

The night Anancy went and work so, him saw this pretty hand of banana, so decide to steal it. So him hole on di bunch a banana and try to pull it, but instead of pulling it his hand stuck. So him kick the tree . . . with his right foot, and it stuck. So him kick the left foot now and it both stuck. Him thump the tree wid him right hand and the right hand stuck, and him thump it with di lef, but di both stuck. So on the way him saw Brer Nanny Goat coming. So him bawl out to Brer Nanny Goat and said: "Well, Brer Nanny

Goat, you waan' see, bwoy, mi a try pick a banana and mi hand stuck on. So try to help me nuh!" Brer Nanny Goat him go ahead now and try to pull him off. Brer Nanny goat him now, instead of pull off Anancy him both stuck too. So Anancy manage to get off, and tie up Brer Nanny Goat and go to the Boss and show the Boss, say right now him ketch di tief. The Boss come now and say, "Yes, so you did a tief my banana all this good while!" Anancy hit him wid di whip now. So him say, "Brer-bre-bre . . . !" "Anancy," him trying to say. So from that day deh until now them say ram goat say, "Brer-bre-bre!" you know, that kind of sound deh.

Collected in Kingston on September 15, 1978.

Another version in which tar is put on the banana tree appears in Bennett, *Anancy and Miss Lou,* pp. 32–34. This is a variant of the popular Motif K741, "Capture by Tarbaby," in Baughman, *Type and Motif-Index,* and Type 175, "The Tarbaby and the Rabbit," in Flowers, *West Indian Types and Motifs.* See also Motif K401, "Blame for Theft Fostered on Dupe," in Baughman. Versions of this tale appear in Beckwith, *Jamaican Anansi Stories,* No. 21; Parsons, *Folk-tales of Andros Island,* Nos. 10, 11, and 12; Johnson, "Folklore from Antigua," Nos. 53–56; Harris, *Uncle Remus,* I, 2; Dorson, *Negro Tales from Pine Bluff,* No. 3; Courlander, *Treasury of Afro-American Folklore,* pp. 75–76; Brewer, *American Negro Folklore,* pp. 4–5; Parsons, *Folk-Lore of the Sea Islands,* pp. 25–26; Parsons, *Folk-Lore of the Antilles,* Pt. 2, pp. 6 and 325–26; Bacon and Parsons, "Folk-lore from Elizabeth City," pp. 256–60; Parsons, "Folk Lore from Aiken," pp. 4–6; Fauset, "Tales and Riddles," pp. 532–33; Dorson, *Buying the Wind,* pp. 248–49; Perdue, "I Swear," pp. 24–25; and Dance, *Shuckin' and Jivin',* No. 349. Other versions have been collected in Japan, the Philippines, Africa, India, Spain, South America, Alaska, Indonesia, Trinidad, St. Vincent, St. Lucia, Martinique, Dominica, Guadaloupe, Montserrat, Nevis, St. Martin, St. Croix, and Barbados.

In his study of 152 versions of this tale collected from all over the world, Aurelio M. Espinosa concludes that it originated in India, passed into Europe, and then to Africa. He contends that the American versions are of European and African origins ("Notes on the Origin and History of the Tar-Baby Story," *JAFL,* 46 [April-June 1930], 130–209).

18 Mi Waan' Bulla

Once upon a time Brer Anancy and Brer Tacuma did a walk. So dem see a shop now, and them did have money, and dem a go buy bulla. So dem go buy bulla and Brer Anancy eat off 'im ten bulla, Brer Tacuma a save him own. Brer Anancy tink of a plan and go outside and push 'im 'ead ina one tree-e, and him start bawl out, and people in a village dere a run come and a try drag 'im out. And 'im say, "Mi 'ungry, mi 'ungry." And Brer Tacuma push a bulla troo part a di hole and 'im eat and say, "One bulla?" Brer Anancy say, "Nine bulla lef'." And dem gi' 'im one more and say, "Eight bulla!" And den Brer Anancy start bawl out again and dem gi' 'im bulla, and gi' 'im bulla. Only one more leave. 'Im say, "Wa, mi 'ungry, mi waan' bulla." And dem push in one more, and when di people dem a try to drag 'im, 'im a push in 'im 'ead. And den him say, "Wa, wa, mi 'ungry, mi 'ungry, mi 'ungry! Gi' mi bulla and mek me get strong." And den dem gi' 'im bulla, and gi' 'im bulla until 'im drag out 'im 'ead.

And when 'im drag out 'im 'ead now, and Bredder Tacuma find out say is a trick 'im play 'pon 'im, him never talk wid Bredder Anancy again.

Collected in Kingston from a nine-year-old informant on September 10, 1978.

19 Anancy is Riding-Horse

Another story— the same Tacuma—Anancy is always a stupid and 'im always mek Tacuma turn him a fool—both of them—and they always love one girl togedder, and both of them get in love with a nex' girl, and Tacuma go behind Anancy back one day and tell the girl don't marry Anancy because Anancy is him fader best riding-horse. Well, that is what Tacuma tell the girl about Anancy.

Anancy go di oder evenin'. Di girl said, "I don't think I will marry you because Tacuna say you is him fader best riding-horse." Anancy say to him "Tacuma will have to prove it." Him said, "Yes, bring him and let him prove it."

Anancy now in temper, go home and say: [nasally] "Bredda Tacuma, how you carry a news like that to my girl?"

"What! [innocently] What you say, Anancy?"

Anancy say to Tacuma that "You go and tell the girl that I am your father best riding-horse!" Hear Tacuma: "Oh no, Bredda Anancy, I could never say that. I could never do you that dirt. I will have to prove it."

Anancy say, "Yes, you will have to prove it."

At that time Tacuma *play sick*. And Tacuma say, "Yes Bredda Anancy, if you are even[1] to give me a ride on you back?"

Anancy say, "Yes, I will ride you." (Stupid, so stupid!) And him dress, and him get outside now, and he: "Come on Bredda Tacuma, get on mi back." And 'im ride 'im right into the yard.

When him reach partway, him say [plaintively], Bredda Anancy, don't go too fast because you know I am a sick man, and I don't want the girl to find out I am so sick. Could you give me a little stick, dat if I am going to fall I can rest on it?" Anancy give him the stick, dat time to a whip to beat him, you know.

And him give him di stick, him ride off a little way: "But mi foot is getting down off you back every minute, Bredda Anancy. What can I do?" Anancy say, "You wait." Get rope, him tie it to him side and put him two foot in it—that were stirrup. My dear, him gallop, riding! When him get to the gate, hear Tacuma to Anancy: "Don't walk so poor; the girl will think that I am dying. Mek a little trot off, make a little trot off. Trot off, Bredda Anancy!"

Anancy gallop right into the house. Tacuma hold up him hand: "Don't I tell you, you prove it? Don't I tell you Anancy is my fader best riding-horse!"

And from that day Anancy go up in a house roof and him live in the roof of the house till today.

Collected in Mandeville on September 16, 1978.

This is Motif K1241.1, "Trickster Rides Dupe A-Courting," in Baughman, *Type and Motif-Index,* and Type 72, "Rabbit Rides Fox A-Courting," in Flowers, *West Indian Types and Motifs.* Versions appear in Beckwith, *Jamaican Anansi Stories,* No. 3; Parsons, "Barbados," p. 269; Parsons, *Folk-tales of Andros Island,* No. 19; Harris, *Uncle Remus,* I, 6; Parsons, *Folk-Lore of the Antilles,* Pt. 2, pp. 424–27; Dorson, *Negro Tales from Pine Bluff,* Nos. 3 and 7; and Bennett, *Anancy and Miss Lou,* pp. 19–20. A discussion may be found in Levine, *Black Culture.* Other versions have been collected in India, Africa, the Virgin Islands, Trinidad, Martinique, Guadaloupe, and St. Croix. I collected a version from Guyanese poet A. J. Seymour in 1979.

1. Would you even . . . ?

20 Tacuma Wins the Girl

Anancy and Tacuma were very good friends, and they always fren' *one girl*—both of dem friendly with one girl. Anyone that the girl love most, well, she will get 'im. So they went on and went on, every evenin' visiting this girl, until di girl said to dem, "Any one of you that have the mos' money, I will marry."

Anancy scrape up every farthin' dat him have put in him jar—*big jar* of pure checks. What you tink Tacuma do? Full his jar of mess, dirt, mess! Because he didn' have any money. And the two of dem start out now, and when they journey, hear di Tacuma to Anancy: "Bredder Anancy, I would like you to marry dat girl, you know, [plaintively] for I can't support him."

"[nasally] Certainly."

"You give me your jar and tek my jar."

The idiot Anancy go ahead and say all right, give Tacuma his jar of pure check and tek Tacuma jar of mess! And them go in the home now, and when dem go in the home and dem put down dem jar on di table, and them come to business now, fi check money; di girl tek Tacuma money first what he took from Anancy, and open it: oh, pure check! She *laugh* and so pleased, and she put it one side. And when she came to Tacuma's, she say well this must be gold, it is so heavy. When she open, pure *mess*! She flash it outside, My dear! And dat was Tacuma money, you know; and she laugh now over Anancy money, thought that Tacuma would have more, and she didn' know that a swap dem

swap by the way, and she dash it outside, and run out poor Anancy, and tek
Tacuma now wid Anancy pot of checks.

So Anancy go outside, and Tacuma married the girl—with his money.

Collected in Mandeville on September 16, 1978.

21 Gashany Bull

There was a bull by the name of Gashany Bull, and he had seven heads.
He lived near a river. And he had seven wives. But one of the head is a golden
head. So this woman now—she expect a baby, and she went to the river to
go for water, and the bull buck her and cut the baby out of her belly. So this
other lady take up the baby and nurse it until it grow up *big* boy, and was
going to school. So after him going to school now, the other children start
to tease him and call him a-hit-mek, a-hit-mek.[1] Him go home and tell his
stepmother, him say, "Everytime I go to school, Mama, them tell me, say 'a-
hit-mek.'" Mother say, "Awright, and I buy a knife gi' you and anytime them
tell you say 'a-hit-mek' stick them with the knife, and then they will tell you
what, what a-hit-mek." Anyway, he went to school, and then the children say
"a-hit-mek, a-hit-mek." And the boy stick him with the knife. And him say,
"Ah, it mek Gashany bull buck you outta you mamma belly." He went home
and told the mother. Mother said, "Yes, my pickney, true. Is really a riverside
me pick you up, because the bull down yah bad you know," and tell him 'bout
the bull.

Say, "Mama, I *kill* 'im."

She say, "No, my pickney, you can't kill 'im."

Say, "Yes, Mama, gwine kill 'im."

She say, "Awright, you must make seven cornmeal dumplings and seven
duckonoo.

"And me gwine down, me gon' kill 'im."

And there was a little mango tree there. The boy go down and climb
the mango tree and go in there and see those seven wives around the bull
head combing it. But the King say anybody kill Gashany Bull and cut out the
golden tongue will get his daughter to marry too.

The boy climb the tree and start singing:

> Gashany Bull o-o-o,
> Gashany Bull o-o-o,
> Ah, you buck me out a me Mumma belly.

Gashany bull stop and him say, [gruff voice] "Somebody's calling my
name." The wife said, "No."

The little boy started singing:

Gashany Bull o-o-o-o
Gashany Bull o-o-o-o
Gashany Bull a you buck me out a me Mumma belly.

The bull get up and him listen. Boy started to sing again:

Gashany Bull o-o-o-o,
Gashany Bull o-o-o-o,
A you buck me out a me Mumma belly.

The bull *run* to the tree and look up, and the boy drop down one corn-meal dumpling. The bull catch it. The bull *send* up one steel, steel something up there like rod, and the bull "Hu-hu." The boy catch it, and the boy send down one next duckonoo until the seven. That mean that the bull don't have anything more now. Everything gone from him. And the boy aim fi him and knock him into the head with the steel and drop him. And knock him again and him drop, and him kind of stagger. And the bwoy come down and cut his throat, cut off the golden tongue. Carry up to his mother.

Brer Anancy now passing and see that the bull dead. (The boy did only cut out the tongue.) So Brer Anancy now cut off the head and present it to King, and King now no look fi see if any tongue in deh — only want fi get the head.

But it's the tongue that him really want. And decide say, must mek feast and everything to marry to daughter and fix up Bredder Anancy. So when everything going on now, only ready to put on the ring and thing, the little boy come, say somebody tek him (the little boy) to the king. But Anancy say: "Yeah, yeah, yeah, yeah, a mi ki—, a mi ki— the cow, a mi ki—Gashany Bull. You yie, you yie, you yie, she-e-e di head deh!"

The boy say, "Mi have the tongue." So the boy present the king with the tongue.

And them find out say a lie Bredder Anancy telling, and them carry him into kitchen and they hot a iron, and tie him up into the pole into the kitchen weh a hanging down, and they hot the iron, and they push up into Bredder Anancy bottom, and him go up a pole, and from that day that is why you find Anancy into the kitchen.

Collected in Woodside on September 6, 1978.

This is Type 300, "The Dragon-Slayer," in Flowers, *West Indian Types and Motifs*. See also Motif H335.3, "Suitor Task: Killing Ferocious Animal," in Baughman, *Type and Motif-Index*. Versions of this tale appear in Beckwith, *Jamaican Anansi Stories*, No. 89; Parsons, *Folk-tales of Andros Island*, No. 21; Jekyll, *Jamaican Song*, No. 17; and Bennett, *Anancy and Miss Lou*, pp. 3–4. The tale has been collected in Cape Verde, the Dominican Republic, Puerto Rico, Trinidad, St. Lucia, Martinique, Dominica, Guadaloupe, St. Kitts, and St. Martin.

1. According to Carlos Nelson, this literally means "it is because." The phrase has been used in a popular song recorded by Desmond Decker and the Aces.

22 Escaping Soldiers

Once upon a time there was a doctor into a small village in England, and he was walking, walking up a likkle road, and some animals started to follow him. And 'im and di animal dem was started to fren', so 'im walk go into 'im house and di animal dem follow 'im go into 'im 'ouse. Some parrot and owl and goat and all kinda animal and some duck too.

And he pick out his favorite animal dem and give dem name. He give di monkey a name by the name of "Sh-h-h." And the parrot a name by "Pyaa-Pyaa,"[1] and the dog a name by "Shoo-shoo."

And di parrot and 'im was walking and some monkey too. So di monkey dem was di wisest one. So dem went behind a big tree and went into a cave. So some soldier was coming to the cave now, and di monkey 'ear di footstep and di monkey say to di doctor: "Sh-h-h, I hear footstep outside." And the doctor said, "Go and look." And when the monkey go and look den, soldier stick dem up with some spear, so di monkey run and lead dem di way, and dem run go up on a 'ill and jump right over from a nex' stone. So di monkey 'old 'and[2] wi di doctor and di parrot dem fly, and dem walk go—dem 'old 'and and go right over and di soldier was flinging spear at dem. So di soldier go down and climb up and looking for dem, and deh were into a tree, a long tree, like what cut out and dem was into it, 'iding. And di parrot come out and go roun' dere and see di soldier dem and tell dem two badd word [Pyaa-Pyaa]. So the soldier dem was after di parrot and di parrot fly away.

Collected in Kingston on September 19, 1978.
See Motif B520, "Animals Save Person's Life," in Baughman, *Type and Motif-Index*.
1. Weak, cowardly person.
2. Hold hands.

23 Dis Yah One Ya Bal'

One day they were having this party, so this blind man was supposed to be at the gate. So when the people came in he would feel their heads and take their tickets or whatever they had to go in.

So Brer Anancy he was willing to go inside, but he didn't want to pay. So when Brer Anancy's time came to go in, he walked on his head—took off his pants and walked on his head. And when he was going in now, the blind man was feeling his way all around, you know, and he reached a point where, you know, the ball of the head is. So the man felt all around, and then he said, "Bwoy, dis yah one ya bal' till it split!"

Collected in Kingston on October 30, 1978.

24 Town Mouse and Country Mouse

Town Mouse and Country Mouse. Once upon a time Country Mouse come to town a look work, but Town Mouse say to Country Mouse, "You can a look work and a chuck badness[1] dem from a way deh, man, and even waan' come steal up all I and I[2] nuts and I family food and ting. Dat bad, you know. You caan' come a town come do tem ting deh."

Country Mouse say to Town Mouse, "If you come a country, eat food till you belly *bus*'!"

Town Mouse say, "A lie you a tell, man, for mi can stay up yah and more time mi hungry, but my family half fi eat food."

Country Mouse say to Town Mouse, "You a eediot, man, look how country stay well green, well fertilize, well vegetable-up and ting, and you a come tawk bout town betta dan country."

Collected in Kingston on September 18, 1978.
1. Stop doing bad things.
2. Rastafarian substitution for several pronouns, including *my, I,* and *we.*

25 Dem Caan' Call Me Rat

Once upon a time you have two rats, one from the country and one from the town. Well, the town one tell the country one, say, "I bet you dem caan' call me rat." Him say, "Gway, man, you a fool, man. Dem mus' can call you rat, because you a rat." Him say, "No, man." And him say, "Awright, come mek we go down King Street."

So di two of dem go down King Street, and di Town Rat tell the Country Rat, seh, "You fus', go across the road." Some schoolchildren were passing, and the Country Rat run across di street. And the schoolchildren say, "See a rat deh!" And him say, "Awright, my time now." And him run cross the road. The school children: "See anoder one deh!" Him say, "Seet, ah show you," say, "dem nuh call me rat; dem say, 'See anoder one deh!'"

Collected in Kingston on October 6, 1978.

26 The Ugliest Man Mus' Wash Up

Out of all the animals, the Monkey is really the ugliest. You must admit that. Well, I understand that one day the animals met him in the forest with the other beasts. Any animal you can think of was there. But the Lion, of course, that's the king of animals. So after they had their drinks and they had their food and they had their storytelling. Things to be washed up now. So the Lion said, "Well, now that we are finish, the ugliest man mus' wash up." Ups came Mr. Monkey: "Not me!"

Nobody called his name. The Lion only said the ugliest man mus' wash up, and Mr. Monkey said: "No, not me!"

Collected in Mandeville on September 16, 1978.

This is one of a number of tales focusing upon the hypersensitivity of the monkey (as well as of other primates other than man) regarding his looks. In *Where Animals Talk: West African Folk Lore Tales* (Boston: Gotham, 1912), R. H. Nassau mentions an African tale in which the gorilla is sensitive about his looks. Variants appear in Fauset, "Tales and Riddles," pp. 533–34; Sterling, *Laughing,* p. 184; and Dance, *Shuckin' and Jivin',* No. 449.

III

Duppy Tales

Introduction

Some of the most interesting, unusual, fascinating, and frightening inhabitants of Jamaica are the duppies. Duppies are spirits, but they are very different from the ghost spirits with whom most of us are familiar. Unlike the rather drab, colorless ghosts that float around in European lore, Jamaican duppies take on many interesting and different forms and personalities.

The word *duppy* is an African word that is still, according to MacEdward Leach, found today in West Coast African languages.[1] Sometimes, as Leach observes, duppies take "the form of a dog with red eyes, a rolling calf, a three-legged horse, a sea mahmy, or a Bubby Susan."[2] The rolling calf is a dangerous duppy who goes around spitting fire and making a hideous noise with a clanking chain. The Bubby Susan is a frightful woman duppy with inordinately large breasts. The sea mahmy is a mermaidlike creature.

Most often, however, duppies appear as the souls of dead people that retain their human forms. They are a pale white color, which makes them difficult to see in the daytime since, as Eddie Burke observes, "the sun shines right through them."[3] They usually roam at night, and during the day they go back to the cotton trees, where it is believed they make their home.[4] Leach points out that the belief that duppies live in the cotton tree is clearly an extension of the African belief that "the spirit of the dead takes refuge in cotton trees."[5] It is believed that duppies generally travel in groups—often noisy groups, as they are fond of singing and are sometimes heard laughing or talking loudly in their peculiarly nasal and occasionally unintelligible fashion. They move about in a floating, whirling manner, their feet two feet above the ground.[6] They sometimes ride donkeys and horses, in which case, as Leonard E. Barrett observes, the duppies' heads are turned backwards and they use the tail of the animal as a bridle.[7] Duppies are frequently in quest of food. They seem to have a particular fondness for sweets, but they harbor a well-known aversion to salt.[8] Duppies may often be seen going about ordinary "human" activities:

> In the days before there were a lot of motor cars in Jamaica, duppies were seen rather more often than they are today.
>   People used to see them sitting in churchyards nursing their babies, running behind the cane cart to pick up bits of juicy sugar cane, and going off to market on Saturdays to buy their yams and sweet potatoes.[9]

Duppies are sometimes playful, sometimes helpful, and sometimes cruel and vengeful, but since one never knows whether the duppy is a good or a bad one, the sight of a duppy usually inspires fear. The duppy may simply be a nuisance, as Eddie Burke notes:

> A man riding a mule along a country road at night may suddenly feel two arms go round his waist. A duppy is having a free ride on the back of his mule. Sometimes when boys are swimming in the river duppies go and sit on their heads and push them under the water. They also like to pull people's noses to make them longer.[10]

At other times, as the tales in this chapter illustrate, the duppy may threaten actual physical harm, or even death, to people.

The living being is not, however, absolutely helpless in the face of the threat of duppies. At times, as some of the tales indicate, the individual may physically defeat the duppy. Generally, however, the human being must call upon some special knowledge or cunning or powerful agent to help him escape the duppy. The problem may be circumvented beforehand, as Leach notes, by following certain rituals during the burial of a dead person to prevent his duppy from returning, including throwing parched peas into the grave, placing the limb of a cotton tree on the coffin, and carrying on one's person shavings from the coffin or sod from the grave. The wife can prevent the return of her husband by renouncing him at the burial. Leach observed such an instance where the widow approached the coffin and "looking intently at the dead, she said, 'John, I'm trou we you; I'm trou we you. Don't ever come back.'" Then she placed in his hand a handkerchief said to contain strands of her pubic hair.[11]

If, however, a duppy does return and confront an individual, the person may escape by running from him while making the sign of the cross, or he may seek help from the Obeah man.[12] It is also believed that dogs, especially black ones, can frighten duppies away and that duppies may be smoked out.

A few of the tales in this chapter focus on spirits that are more closely related to the traditional ghost than to the Jamaican duppy. A couple of songs treating duppies may be found in Chapter 10.

---

1. Leach, "Jamaican Duppy Lore," p. 207.

2. Ibid., p. 208.

3. Burke, *Water,* p. 45.

4. Carlos Nelson told me that the old army barracks at South Camp Road in Kingston is called Duppy Gate because there is a big cotton tree there (interview, Richmond, Virginia, December 14, 1982).

5. Leach, "Jamaican Duppy Lore," p. 214.

6. Jekyll, *Jamaican Song,* p. 176.

7. Leonard E. Barrett, *The Sun and the Drum: African Roots in Jamaican Folk Tradition* (Kingston: Sangster's Book Stores Ltd., 1976), p. 43.

8. This is clearly another African retention. Maureen Warner Lewis pointed out in a lecture at the University of the West Indies, Mona, July 1982, that in African beliefs anyone "with a spiritual dimension" does not eat salt.

9. Burke, *Water,* p. 43.

10. Ibid.

11. Leach, "Jamaican Duppy Lore," p. 211.

12. *Obeah* comes from the Ghana word *obayi,* meaning witchcraft. The Obeah man sells charms, casts or removes spells, and heals. His work is frequently, though not always, viewed as negative, sinister.

27 Tumpa-Tail Mare

One night he rode to a church and when him come to the church, he saw it light up, and he hear a lots of music going on. Him say, "What happening in this church?" And him ride down. Church a little way off di road, and him ride down, and when him go down *hundreds* of ghosts dancing. *Music!* Oh, the sweetest music! Grandma said, if the man ever hear, is dat night; and the ghost dem *dancing* as dem like, and him *watch* until him belly full. And di only two dat him know out dat bands of ghosts, the name of them was: one is Cutty Saw and one is Tom Shanta.

And him was riding off and him say, "Oi, Cutty Saw and Tom Shanta!" And him ride off. And dey lay down music and *everyone* follow him, and dem *run-n* him and him *ride,* and all di way he is riding, and tap up di mare [illustrating]:

Go, Meg, go, the running stream we are near,
Go Meg, go, the running stream we are near.

And him *ride,* and the rest of ghosts *tired* and stop, and the Cutty Saw and Tom Shanta wid dem cutla[1] in dem hand to kill the man would *never* stop. And when dem go to the stream, the mare tek up himself and go right over the stream; and all they could do is fling the cutla in deh hand and chop off di mare tail, but the man was laying one side of the stream and watching dem over dere. Deh could not trouble him because they can't cross the stream, and so they had was to turn back. And him come home wid him tumpa-tail mare.

Collected in Mandeville on September 16, 1978.
See Motif E261.4, "Ghost Pursues Man," and Motif E434.3, "Ghosts Cannot Cross Rapid Stream," in Baughman, *Type and Motif-Index.*
   1. Cutlass.

28 Baad Sarah

When I was a boy, we had a girl working with us by the name of Sarah. Sarah like to tell us stories at night. So one night Sarah told us this story. Sarah's job was to close a gate when she was in another place. She had a gate to close at a railroad station. Every night she close the gate around six o'clock. Well, as the days got shorter and shorter, six o'clock came earlier, and one evening when Sarah went to close the gate, she heard a singing. She look up the road, and she saw *one heap-a* duppy comin'—*real* good duppies—some o' dem tall, some short, and the tall ones were carrying a dead duppy in a coffin. So they come on, and they singing, [nasal] "A-a-a-a-bide with me-e-e-e, fast falls the e-e-e-vening tide . . . dah, dah, ah dah, ah, Lord, with me abide-e-e." Just at that time as they come to the word *abide* and Sarah seen dem coming, coming nearer and nearer to the gate, Sarah clap the gate, BOOOOM [dramatizing the slamming of the gate], and the duppies dem frightened. Dem never knew was that Sarah so brave for shut de gate pon duppy. When the gate clap so, duppy run to the left, duppy to the right, duppy up, duppy down. The one in the coffin drop down, nearly pon top o' the gate, but him catch up himself just in time. Him move away. Hmmmmm. Sarah laugh till she nearly died. Sarah laugh till she nearly died. All right. Sarah say next evening she go out to close the gate—six o'clock again. Hmmmmm. So this night—it was around quarter to six. She look up the road. She don' see no duppy. She look down. She don' see no duppy. She say, "Awright, I teach him a lesson last night. This gate is not a *duppy* gate, and whoever walk past here must be living somebody like meself. I don' waan' see no duppy *pass* here."
Round five to six Sarah feel her head begin raise [voice continually increasing in intensity], Sarah feel her head *twice* the size, *tree* times the size, *four* times the size! Her leg begin tremble. Sarah knee begin tremble. Father King,

the uncle born them![1] Worse than all, Saran tongue—when she look before her, she see her own tongue. She never know her tongue so long. Her tongue nearly drop out of her mouth. That time Sarah say, "But what is a happen to me?" You know. Well, she look about her. She see one duppy bandaged up. She say, "Jesus Christ!"

She hear a voice say, "Hummhun, humnhun, hummhun [duppies speak in a nasal tone throughout], so you are Sarah, nuh? I hear so, you are *baad* Sarah, nuh? Humn. Humn. You're bad Sarah!"

She say, "But I no trouble yu, suh."

Say, "Nuh trouble me!" Say, "You remember what happened here last night at this same gate around six o'clock? You remember how you close the gate? Heh? You remember how you close the *gate*! And if I wasn't a very agile duppy, if I wasn't very smart, if I didn't do me athletics when I was a young man alive, I would have dropped dead pon the top o' de gate."

She said [pleadingly], "Lawd, suh, I won' do it again. I won' do it again." Say, "Do suh, do, suh, do suh, do, Mr. Duppy, give me a chance."

He say, "All right." Say, "Since you go pon your knees. Since you go down pon your knees and beg me pardon, I wll be merciful. Though I'm a ghost, I'll be merciful. But you know what you'll have to do, girl!"

"No, suh. Me no know, suh. Me no know, suh."

"You have to boil a pot of rice. Tomorrow night I coming back right at this same gate here again, and you boil me one pot o' rice, one big pot o' rice—no salt, you know, you know duppy don' eat salt."

[Humble, whimpering voice] "Yes, suh, I know it, suh, duppy don' eat salt."

"Well, you boil the pot o' rice, and you bring it here. And when you come, and you see me, you throw the pot o' rice. Scatter it. And me and me duppy friend I will get it, and after you scatter it, you can go bout your business, but don' let it happen again!"

"All right, suh. All right, suh. All right, suh." Sarah say, man, she went home and she take out for Chapelton. She bought *two pounds* o' rice. She come, she wash it clean, man, squeeze lime pon it and sibyl orange.[2] Then she put on the big pot. She boil the rice, and the rice swell. She carry it to the gate, man. And at quarter to six, she look up the road. She see nothing. She look down the road. She see nothing. Ten to six—not a thing. Five minutes to six, her head raise [voice increasing in volume], her head *raise*, her tongue *swell*! Sarah feel the knee begin buckle underneath her and the ankle bone them begin shake, and she hear the voice: "You bring the rice, girl, you bring the rice?"

She say, "Yes, I bring the rice."

"All right then, all right. Scatter it."

Jack Mandora, me no waan' no more.

Collected in Santa Cruz on November 4, 1978.

See Motif F405.6, "Grain Scattered as a Means of Dispersing Spirits," in Baughman, *Type and Motif-Index*.
1. A folk exclamation.
2. Seville orange, a large, sour orange with a rough skin.

29 Don't Go Out Late Time of Night

I always go out at night. Those old-time people never have them tilet[1] on the house; they always buil' tilet outside of the house. And my parents them always tell mi not to go out late time of night, it is not good; but I wouldn' hear them. I always go out. And one night, I get up and was goin' out, but I go to the window first, and I look outside. And when I look outside the gate, a donkey was tying, feeding, and I saw a tall man stan' up before the donkey. I said, "Cho, it is not anyting because I always hear my people dem say when animal saw a ghost they gallop and makes a lots of fuss, blow dem nose and all dose kind of tings, so if it was ghost or anyting to hurt dem, him wouldn' be feeding and dis ghost stand up before him." I go on straight out, and as I go to the door of the tilet, to step up, I hear a thrash break behind me and when I tun round, dere was the tall man was moving off like to di place dere and I am dere stepping up. And I mek: "Whaa-a-a, Wha-a-a!" And I run! And when I run and *shut* de door and run back in and *lock* it, I go back to the window and look; and the same place I run and leave the ghost, him stood up same place. I go to mi bed; I never say anyting. And next day mawning when I woke up I was telling mi grandmoder what happen to me las' night, and she said, "Is the owner of the donkey, and that is why the donkey never make any fuss." The owner of the donkey was *dead,* you see, and so, although he was coming in—ghost all over—he is coming in, and him stood at the gate watching the donkey feeding, and mi granny say is di owner of the donkey, dat's why the donkey never bray, "and you are lucky he didn' *kill* you because I always tell you not to go out."

Collected in Mandeville on September 16, 1978.
1. Toilet.

30 A Sign from Daddy

And when I came in the church road there, it was very late, two of us, me and my bradder. So we sort of walk pious like that in the road. Met a big bush in the topside, see a big thing just—just flash and drop in between the two of us to the bottomside, and I say I goin' knock 'im back, and me bradder says, "No, you leave it alone!" Well, we came to the gate, and I see mi [dead] daddy. It was mi daddy. Yes it was mi daddy. Him do so to me, three time. It was very late. It was very late, and that's why him do it so, just give me a sign like that.

Collected in Woodside on September 6, 1978.
See Motif E327, "Dead Father's Friendly Return," in Baughman, *Type and Motif-Index*. This tale is similar to one collected by Leach in which a duppy parent returns when her child does what he had been told not to do ("Jamaican Duppy Lore," p. 210).

31 Tiger Work on Rolling Calf

Going to mi yard—we did live round below the church there. A shower of rain comin' and wet up mi guitar, but di guitar, di guitar start to pull me on mi shoulder, same time di rain stop, and a rolling calf, Mam, believe you me, follows me! I have to go wake up a man out a his bed, him name Toach, bring me home. He woulda kill me pon the way! He woulda *kill* me pon the way! Anyway, when I go home, I had a dog, big black dog, name of Tiger. Tiger work pon him di whole night, work pon him di whole next day clean, eh-heh, tek him out a di yard completely.

Collected in Woodside on September 6, 1978.
See Motif B785, "Animal Wards off Spirits," in Baughman, *Type and Motif-Index*. Similar tales appear in Leach, "Jamaican Duppy Lore," pp. 208–9.

32 If I Ketch 'Im I Kill 'Im

Once upon a time rain did a fall, an' one man waan' shelter an' 'im see one hole an' go down in deh; and one rolling calf run and go down in a di hole weh di man did deh, and put 'im bottom in a di man face. The man say, "Mine you poop pon mi!"

And den di rolling calf come up an' say, "A ooo-oo dat! Mi gone!"

And nex' mawning di rolling calf come back and look in a di hole and say, "If I ketch 'im I kill 'im!"

Collected in Kingston on September 10, 1978, from a nine-year-old informant.

33 I Am Not Going to Play Tonight

You know I play music, yes, I play a guitar. Sometime late in the night, I came in and when I come in, sometimes I has to walk far, and when I coming

on, one night especially, I saw a black dog—high about that—and just . . .
had a little piece of chain around its neck. And I passed him and turned and
looked back. His eyes like furnace of fire, and I walk to that bottom side, and
I walk . . . and I cross a bridge. I turn back and I see him just sobbing like
. . . and I walk around a chain or two. Here is a big bamboo root come right
down on me. Say, "What's dat you doing, man?" And I had the guitar 'tan[1]
behind me, and all this children just making a lot of noise, just making a lot
of noise. I say, mi fingers dem curling, you know; I know I am not going
to play tonight. And believe you me, I had was to tek it round and start to
play, and that thing follow me nearly three-quarter mile. And when I come
off on a level up turning Woodside Road coming on this way, I see a *tall* man,
and I get one little piece of the bamboo, and he hail to me to give him piece.
I don't see him again! And in time I reach right where Margie is. I look down
the road. I saw him right below Margie's gate—that is Miss Lixie's gate. I saw
him right below Miss Lixie's gate. I look down the road; I saw him, full suit
o' black, and I turn in a di gate, in a di church gate.

Collected in Woodwide on September 6, 1978.

See Motif E421.3.6, "Ghosts as Dogs with Glowing Tongues and Eyes," in Baughman, *Type and Motif-Index*. Tales of dog spirits are popular among Black Americans, as indicated by the fact that there is a collection of such tales, Brewer's *Dog Ghosts*. Similar tales also appear in Dorson, *Negro Tales from Pine Bluff*, No. 27; Perdue, "I Swear," pp. 16–17; and Dance, *Shuckin' and Jivin'*, Nos. 30, 31, 32.

1. Standing.

34 Duppy Incident

Over and over it done me dat. I go to play at (you don't know the place)
—they call the place Chumoso. Late the night, very late, coming home, and
come out a di main, and turn on the road; and I never know that a woman
dead up there. There is a high banking and a river was on top of the banking,
and I never know that a woman was dead—died childbirth. I never knew it.
Night *dark*, but I had a flashlight. I see di woman just stan' up, lean right so,
lean right so pon di bank, and hold the baby same way so; and I go *bang* pon
her wid di flashlight, and I see di baby natural. Mi grab him up and hold him . . .
and lean pon di bank same way so. And I hold di flashlight pon her, look pon
her good. Is a tall, big, young woman. Look pon her good and still, step off.

And do you know that it follow me *all* the way, *all* the way, actually
the whole way!

[Dance] The woman and the baby?

Yes, the woman, yes, see the natural baby, but 'ow she wrap him up,
you know.

[Dance] How long had she been dead?

I tink she been dead, I tink a three months she been . . . but she lean pon di bank. Now this side of the road the bank is high, and then on *top* of the bank, over, is a big river up dere, and is up dere she died.

[Dance] Will the duppies do you any harm?

No, they never done me any harm, never hurt me, never hurt me.

[Dance] Everybody doesn't see them?

No, is not everybody see dem. No, I sit down right here, just in March . . . before Easter week, before Easter week, and I see one right here, just come out the man room, and sit down right here, put on shoes. Tall woman, she come and she have on a straight dress, and is a *big* size woman, *good* size woman, good height, and she comes in and she stops, she see say mi see her, natural someady.[1] So mi say, "But you lass[2] the way?" Same way so mi say to her, I say, "But you lass di way?" And she just turn face 'gainst di ting, and as quick as she turn way, she gone a bottom; I don't see her. Is a big-size woman into a full dress.[3] And it was with plaid something, something brighter than this [pointing], *deep* plaid. See her come right on yah, she just turn to the cassava and I don't see her anymore.

Go out one day and coming in back, go out sport and coming in back, so it never know that I would see her; I see her right dere [pointing]. Remember the day I sit down right deh so and look right at the mango tree there so, I see one—him was coming deh so, and him find seh me see him; him turn down deh so and cut out at the mango tree, and me glimpse him right at the mango tree deh, and she gone dat way.

Collected in Woodside on September 6, 1978.

See Motif E425.14, "Revenant as Woman Carrying Baby," in Baughman, *Type and Motif-Index.*

1. "She see say mi see her, natural someady" means that "she saw that I, a natural somebody (a living person) saw her."

2. Lost.

3. The emphasis on size here suggests that this may be a form of the duppy known as Bubby Susan, whom Leach describes as "truly a grotesque creature. She is a tall woman whose breasts hang down below her knees. When she chases her victims, she throws those pendulous breasts over her shoulders. She kills characteristically by blowing her hot poisonous breath on her quarry" ("Jamaican Duppy Lore," p. 209).

35 Dis Man Look Like a Duppy Man

You waan' see one time mi go a town, go shoppin', same time I shoppin', you waan' see dis ghost. . . . You nuh seet? So I say, "Cho, I will walk it," you nuh seet? So I walk and I walk and through[1] I feel tired, so I see a big shop; so I go up on dis shop and I waan' ice cream upstairs. So I go up on

top a deh and lie down, man, because I feel *hot.* "Mi say you caan' sleep." So
one time mi pick up and mi look down and mi see a head a juk and a come,
you nuh seet? So mi say,"Ooo you?" And 'im say, "Ah mi." So mi say, "Mi
ooo?" Him say, "Ah mi."[2] Mi see some wings . . . see di head push out and
mi jus' see it and a draw back. Him say, "Who you?" Mi say, "Mi." You no
seet? When mi look, is a duppy man, you nuh seet? A duppy man stay a deh
watch me tru di wood hole. I lie down a sleep. Mi say, "Rahtid! Dis man look
like a duppy man!"

Mi double back now, man, but you haf two gate—one di walkway and
you haf a nex' one, you nuh seet? But mi stand up a one gate a walk, when
the next door gate in a di back now, so mi a go tru deh so now. So when
I running di gate *lock,* you nuh seet? Mi say, "Rahtid!" Mi say, "Watch yah
now, how mi a go pass dis man yah now!" So when mi come a gate, mi see
di man stan' up at di gate, same way. Mi say, "Watch yah, man, I ah goin'
jump dis fence," you nuh seet? Stand up same place and a watch him, you nuh
seet, but di man still deh a push out 'im head, and a draw . . . mi jus' mek
one bitch noise and fly out and di man . . . in a di road, you know. Him come
up pon de road, man, and I walk same . . . and a woman was a come on to
me now and say, "Please you can show mi di Catholic church?" Mi look pon
di woman; di woman nuh have in no eye, you nuh seet? Me say, "Rahtid!"
Mi say, "Get away from here! Who you asking bout Catholic church?" You
nuh seet? Mi jus' say, "Cho," and mi just turn mi back and *run* down mechanic
shop deh a di place now, dem know I, you nuh seet? And I go in dere and
di duppy woman start go fi stone and fling pon I, but him nuh know if a
duppy or what. but through I know a duppy, I just *wings.*[3] And she stayed
and threw and threw stones until daylight fi save me.

Collected in Kingston on October 6, 1978.

1. Because.

2. This conversation with the duppy is similar to one in "Fling-a mile," No. 33 in Beckwith's
Jamaican Anansi Stories.

3. Just stay in one place, frightened.

36 Young Gal Will Carry You in a Trouble

This is a duppy story, right. Once upon a time there was this man and
him loved walk street a nighttime and look sweet girl. So one night him coming in one o'clock in the night, him see this pretty girl (there was a basket
of clothes pon her head) going river. So him say, "All right, man, going check
that chile yah tonight."

So him say [exaggerated friendliness]: "Young lady, can I help you?" No
answer. Him say, "Young lady, I sure the basket heavy," you know. "Let me

help you nuh." No answer. He asked her the third time, and she don't answer. So him say, "Cho, no pasture nuh de so."[1] So him a go home. As him go fi enter through him gate, the lady just throw her frock tail round the gate and say, "You nah go in deh tonight. Teach you fi 'top look young gal!" So him deh deh, man, and him start to sweat from *head* to foot now. So the young lady say, "You nah go home tonight. You a 'tan out yah." So one dawg come now, and the dawg go under the woman foot, and the woman run away. So when the dawg gone now, him dash in a di house and him go under the bed. When him go under dere, him hear one [voice] just a go: "Let that be a lesson to you. You won't go back go look young gal, because young gal will carry you in a trouble."

Collected in Kingston on November 8, 1978.
Motif E425.1, Revenant as Woman," and Motif B785, "Animal Wards off Spirits," in Baughman, *Type and Motif-Index.*
1. "There is no pasture here": he won't get what he wants.

37 Too Kind, Too Cruel

Well, there were once a woman traveling on Spanish Town Road. She had a *big* basket on her head *full* with load. She had a big pumpkin underneath her (h)arm, and she had three *long* canes tied together on one shoulder. And while going along, a cartman from Guy's Hill, coming on and seeing her — his heart wrench to see what a woman have. He hang over the cartwheel and said, "Stop the cart." Him drive up to her and said to her, "Can I help you?" And she was very glad and she stopped. She don't answer him. She just stopped, and him said to her, "Put it here." And she put in the pumpkin and afterwards she put in the three canes that tie together, and after she lift the big basket, she alone. By the time the man come to help her, she get the basket inside long time and get in. The man says to her, "Come right beside me up here." And while they were going down and talking, the man talking, she not answering. When she reach May Pen Cemetery, she say to the man, "Drop me off right here." She just said, "Right here." And the man *stopped,* and after the man stopped, she take the three cane, she hold them and she sail them out, and she tek the pumpkin and she hold it and sail it over in the burial groun'. Afterwards she take up the basket and put on her head. And after putting the backet on her head, she don't come off the cart. She stand in the cart, and step from the cart right over May Pen fence and right into the burial ground. She stroll right down the walkway, and the poor man just stay into the cart and watch her like this . . . [unbelieving and falling back into a faint].

Just fall back, like he was in pains and what really happened, the mule stand eating on the bank while *he* lying in the cart *roasting* with fever. They had a res' of men that stay back late to come in from Guy's Hill, came along and saw his cart, and they just stop and take him off and put him into a nex' cart to lay down. And a nex' man from a cart come in and drive him to the hospital. They say nothing is wrong with him, but he was *roasting* with fever. And the doctor gave him something, just rub him up with something, just rub him up with something and tell them get him home. And by one o'clock he was a hearty man again like (h)everybody.

Collected in Kingston on July 8, 1978, from a resident of Cassava River.
See Motif E332.3.3, "Ghost rides in carriage, disappears Suddenly at Certain Spot," in Baughman, *Type and Index-Motif.* A variant appears in Dance, *Shuckin' and Jivin',* No. 46.

38 Right Now, Right Now

All the lonely hours at night. I tell you something. One night Busha,[1] Busha love off a young girl, and Busha say to the girl, "All the while I come to your house." "Ah can't come out; mi granny a tell me say ah nuh fi come out a di house." So Busha say to the girl, "Just tell her one night (I goin' come out deh), you must tell you Granny sey, 'I goin' to the toilet.'"

And the girl come out dere and say, "Granny, I goin' to de toilet." Granny say, "Don't stay too long, mi darlin'." And she come and she and Busha out dere, and she and Busha hug and say, "Busha, dawling, I love you Busha, dawling." And Busha say, "When we goin' get married?"

[Speaking hurriedly] And same time Busha see a duppy, and Busha [ran], and the duppy hug her up. And she say, "Busha, don' hug me, mek married."[2] And the duppy say [rough but enthusiastically]: "*Right* now, *right* now, *right* now!"

And that is the end of it.

Collected in Kingston on September 11, 1978, from a fourteen-year-old informant.
1. The overseer of a plantation is frequently referred to as Busha. Bushas have a reputation for taking advantage of the young girls on the plantations, who obviously are vulnerable to their advances.
2. Let's get married.

39 Nobody Res' Here

A man was traveling once, and when he reach to di place dat dem always rest, you know, him feel tired; and him say him going to rest here. And while he was leaning on the tree resting, he hear a *large* singing coming from far away. And him waited and waited till dem come up. It was bands of ghost with a *coffin*. And they come to the tree, for they did not see di man. Dem say, "Let us rest the body here."

And the man: "Nobody res' here! Nobody res' here!"

And *everyone* of dem tek up di coffin, and they *run* away and leave the man sitting down dere.

Collected in Mandeville on September 16, 1978.
See Motif E592.2, "Ghost Carries Coffin on Back," in Baughman, *Type and Motif-Index*.

40 Wait for Mi Now

One time dis likkle youth, him father have a donkey cart. Every night him fader a pass in di sugar yard, you have some duppy go in deh, eat it out and filth.[1] And so him fader say, "You know wah I goin' do?"

Say, "Wha' you are gon' do, sah?"

"Smoke a weed now."[2] So one night dem deh in front of di donkey cart again, and 'im 'ear a ting: "One come in a it, you nuh." And he hear him: "A two dat you know."[3] So 'im jus' go so and *BAP-P-P* [hitting duppies]! And start beat dem now. So di duppy go so now and start run now. So dem have a one-foot duppy in a di crowd now. So hear di one-foot duppy nuh: "Bredder Tom, wait fi me now!" Hear Bredder Tom: "If you know you have one foot, wha' you come tief sugar fah?" And start run lef' him now, you know, so him start get some lick now with the whip. And a so it go.

Collected in Kingston on October 6, 1978.
See Motif E593, "Ghost Takes Things from People," in Baughman, *Type and Motif-Index*.
1. Defecate.
2. Smoke marijuana to keep away duppies.
3. This is a conversation between the duppies—not very logical.

41 Pretty, Pretty Moon a Fell Down pon Me

This is a story about a market woman. Now they used to go to Old Harbour to market—Old Harbour Bay, from this place name Point Hill. So this woman was coming. It was *very* late 'cause market break up and have to walk on foot—not the days when you have motor vehicles. So when she was coming on, she reach a place named Florry Bridge, and she see a *duppy*. The duppy on the bridge *jumping* up:

> [Singing] Pretty, pretty moon a go fell down pon me,
> What a pretty, pretty moon a go fell down pon me,
> Pretty, pretty moon a go fell down pon me,
> What a pretty, pretty moon a go fell down pon me.

She want pass, but she fraid cause she realize say it was a duppy. And she stand up and she look. So she had one *big* pudding pan — shine! She carrying fish into it. So she let down her basket. She throw the fish into something, and she sail up the pudding pan up in the air. And when the duppy see the pudding pan coming down, him said, "Pretty, pretty moon a fell down pon me," and just jump back down into the water.

Collected in Woodside on September 6, 1978.

The duppy's reaction to the moon in this tale is similar to that in one of Beckwith's duppy stories (*Jamaican Anansi Stories*, No. 7).

42 The Automobile-e-e-e a Come

In the days when we didn't have motor cars. So this man dead *before*. He didn't know *what* is motor car or truck or things like that cause he didn't see it. So this duppy now, this one died now when motor cars and trucks and things come in. So the two duppies meet up now and was talking. So this one that dead long before everything said to this one, say [nasal tone], "Man, what happened? Is long time me gone way."

The other one say [nasal tone], "Yes, man, one something come in here — the auto-mo-bile-e-e-e. If you ever see it, man, it have four foot and carry a lotta pe-o-ple and got two-o-o big yeyes.[1] Me say, when you see it, man, it b-r-i-g-h-t!"

Same as them talking now, you hear it blow around the corner, "Bwoop, bwoop, bwoop, bwoop!"

Hear the duppy: "Same Ford, same Fo-o-rd! The automobile-e-e-e a come!" And him just run down the gully.

Collected in Woodside on September 6, 1978.

1. Eyes.

43 It Come Out, It Go In

Once upon a time, two duppy sit upon a wall. So when dem look up, dem see the moon a come out and go in. Dem say [nasally]: "It come out, it go in; it come out, it go in; it come out, it go in."

Hear one man now pass pon him bicycle, man, and hear dem. And him jus' tek him hand and knock dem over di wall.

Dem say [nasally], "A nuh lick mi get, but a di wet me wet."[1]

Collected in Kingston on November 8, 1978.

1. Me didn't get hit, but me got wet.

44 Tilli-Lip

One day there was two duppy, one good one and one bad one. So there was a man selling sky juice.[1] So when him go, the bad duppy say, "Man, ah tilli-lip."[2]

So the good duppy say, "Man, nah tilli-lip."

So the bad duppy say, "We can get tilli-lip and to-dal-tweed."[3]

So the good duppy say, "Man, nah tilli-lip."

So the bad duppy say, "Man, ah tilli-lip."

So him go up to the man sky juice cart and him dip him hand in a di syrup and say, "Man, tilli-lip and to-dal-tweed."

So the good duppy say, "Man, nah tilli-lip."

So the bad duppy say, "Man, ah tilli-lip."

So him go back again, and him dip him hand in deh. And di good duppy say, "Man, nah tilli-lip."

So the bad duppy say, "Man, ah tilli-lip."

So the good duppy say, "Man, nah tilli-lip, man."

So him go back di third time, and when him go back now, the man now draw him whip, and give him *one* lick! And him say, "Jesus Chris'! Mi dead one time and now mi dead two time, and a tilli-lip, man, a tilli-lip."

Collected in Kingston on September 11, 1978.

A version of this tale appears in Beckwith, *Jamaican Anansi Stories,* No. 5.

1. Juice used in snow cones.

2. It's possible that this undecipherable phrase is "I'll get a sip."

3. I'm not sure what this phrase means. It again reflects the duppy's often unintelligible speech. I suspect *tweed* is his attempt to say *sweet,* because the juice is sweet and duppies are especially fond of sweets.

45 Never You Sleep in Dead Solomon Room

A gentleman was sending a letter to a man one day, and him call him yardboy and give him the letter and tell him to take it to dis estate, like him say to Mr. Clark on the estate: "But you must be very careful because he have a cross dawg. When you go to the watchman hut he will tell you." And the fellow go to the watchman hut and him show the watchman the letter and told him what his boss tell him, and the watchman say, "Yes, but if you don't have to go into the yard, the dog won't interfere with you; but remember this what I am telling you: if you are going to sleep, never you sleep in dead Solomon room, because a man dead over dere the name of Solomon and he jus' bury today, so don' sleep in his room."

He go and he hand the letter and it was late and he could not come back, so him ask them if they could put him up until nex' day mawning. The servant dem say, "We don't have anywhere." The other one answer, *spell* dead Solomon; he didn't call dead Solomon name and he didn't know that the fellow could read. So they spell the name of the dead man room and say they would put him in dere. The fellow pronounce it right away and say: "I am not sleeping in dead Solomon room." And they laugh and say, "No, we are not putting you in dere." And that was the same room they put him in. And no sooner, my dear, everybody gone to bed and he lay down, the ghost raise the night, and him come in and him draw him right offa him bed, and him *fling* him outside. And him *run* with all his life back to the watchman hut, and tell the watchman what happen to him. The watchman say, "I told you wasn' to go in dead Solomon room. You should never say anyting; you should wait until them put you in dere, and you come out."

That was the end of the story.

Collected in Mandeville on September 16, 1978.
See Motif C611, "Forbidden Chamber," in Beckwith, *Type and Motif-Index.*

46 The Incident at Albion House

I guess you would call it the incident at Albion House. Tourists used to visit Mandeville years ago. On one occasion the hotel owner was asked if there was a old house or any slavery houses nearby that he could visit, and they were taken to Albion House, which is about five miles from Mandeville, on a property, the house is situated on a hill. So after they were shown around the place and shown different sections that had slavery names: one section was Chainpiece (they used to chain the slaves there); one was Niggerhouse (that's where the slaves lived); and they had different sections that have different names according to how they used to run the slaves.

They were offered a drink, so they went inside, and whilst this visitor was sitting in a chair, he felt somebody pushed him; and he *looked* behind him. And on the third occasion he asked if anybody was living in the house and described this person that he saw: long beard and a eighteenth-century outfit. The owner of the house said, "Yes, that was my husband's grandfather, but do you know him?" He said, "No, but he's trying to push me out of this chair."

And he asked if anything unusual happened, and they told him that the grandfather was a surveyor. He ordered some instruments from England years ago, but he took sick before he could use them. So he asked his family to repack the instruments, send them back to the firm in England as a *gift;* they weren't to collect any money for it. Well, they couldn't afford it; and getting transport from here to Kingston, you would have to go by horse, and take them days to Kingston in those days. So they packed the instruments and simply put them under the cellar.

Well, one of his granddaughter got married to a young surveyor, and they came to Albion House. And the chap was relating to them how difficult it was to get instruments and he couldn't afford it and he didn't know how he was going to manage, and they remembered that they had this box of instruments downstairs, which they sent for and told the chap that, well, he could look if anything was in there that was of use to him. He found quite a bit and put them one side on the table and left the rest in the office to be placed back under the cellar.

They all retired to bed. In the *middle* of the night they heard as if the roof was coming off. Everything in the place was being broken or flung away. They didn't know what was happening, but everybody was afraid, so nobody would come out. And around daylight, around seven o'clock, each person decided that, well, we all go out in one body. When they reached the drawing room, they didn't see anything unusual, nothing was moved, nothing was wrong with the furniture. And then this chap realized that, well, let me look on my instruments.

They were all broken beyond repair, and bent, and then all the pieces were thrown around this chair that this visitor was sitting in. Then he was told what happened and why these things were in the chair. Well, maybe he didn't like him sitting in the chair, because, funny, even though the chair was there and dusted every day, nobody used to sit in it because it was Grandpuppa's chair and it was just there as an ornament, something to remember him by.

Collected in Mandeville on September 16, 1978.

See Motif E421.1.1, "Ghost Visible to One Person Alone," and Motif E236.4, "Return from the Dead Because Last Will Was Not Fulfilled," in Baughman, *Motif and Type-Index.*

47 I Am di Ghost of Crickety-Crocket

Once upon a time three men — dem go inna hotel room. So di hotel chef say to dem dat, "One room leave but 'aunted." So di three of dem tun roun' and say to him dat, "Ooo, mi nuh fraid a ghost."

So dem go up to the room. The first one go in is a Chineyman. So 'im go inna di room, man, and see a five dollar pon di table. Him a go tek up di five dollar, 'im 'ear [chanting]:

I am di ghost of Cain and Able,
Dis five dollars stay on di table.

When him look roun', 'im nuh see nobody, him *move*.

So a white man go in now, man. And him see di five dollar pon di table too. So 'im a go tek it up. So him only 'ear:

> I am di ghost of Cain and Abel,
> Dis five dollar stay on di table.

Him *move* too.

Black man go in now, man. See di five dollar pon di table. Tek it up and a go push i' inna 'im back pocket. Him hear:

> I am di ghost of Cain and Able,
> Dis five dollar stay on di table.

Di Black man tun roun' and look and nuh see nobody. Black man say:

> I am di ghost of Crickety-Crocket,
> Dis five dollar go in my pocket.

Collected in Kingston on September 19, 1978, from a twelve-year-old informant.

IV

Big Boy Tales

Introduction

One of the best kept secrets in Jamaican folklore is the popular Big Boy. No published collection of Jamaican folk materials even mentions this figure,[1] and yet I have found during my quest for Jamaican folklore that he is one of the most popular of all Jamaican folk heroes. I had been in the field collecting for a couple of months before I even heard his name mentioned. Jamaicans are inclined to give collectors the Anancy tales and a couple of other traditional pieces. They tend not to even mention to outsiders some of the more popular contemporary tales, particularly if they are at all ribald. I recall my first introduction to Big Boy came from a little six-year-old girl whose tale I was recording simply to humor her (I thought). I was having an enthusiastic session among a group of youngsters in a Kingston yard. When they realized the fact that they would have an opportunity to hear themselves on tape, there was increased excitement, and everybody wanted to participate, even those who were not "storytellers." Thus it was that I was recording this young girl, and not really paying too much attention to what she was saying until the group started giggling and shushing her. Despite the efforts to restrain her, she stubbornly persisted, and the one thing that at the time I recalled from her more or less unintelligible account was the frequent mention of Big Boy. My efforts to learn more about Big Boy were at first met with some snickering and hesitancy, but after a while the group overcame its initial reluctance and began to enjoy exchanging tales about what I discovered was the most popular subject of folktales among Jamaican schoolchildren. Wherever I went, once I was able to penetrate the initial protective devices that children maintain in the presence of adults, I found Big Boy popular. I was surprised also to find that he has been popular among Jamaican children for *years*. When I asked Louise Bennett, who was born in 1919, about Big Boy, she laughed:

> *Bennett:*   OH-h-h. Well, I used to hear Big Boy from I was going to school, you know.
>
> *Dance:*   Oh, really?
>
> *Bennett:*   Yes-s-s! Big Boy a' di back say, "Teacher-r-r. . . ." Something terrible to teacher all the time.
>
> *Dance:*   Yes, but I have never seen these in collections. Why is it that they . . . ?
>
> *Member of audience:* Too rude!
>
> *Bennett:*   Yes. Them too rude!!! [Laughter][2]

Indeed the Big Boy tales are "rude" (by which Jamaicans mean obscene), but that is a part of what makes Big Boy typical of the trickster-type figures that are popular in every culture in various guises, particularly among children — the figure who audaciously mocks the society's restrictions and moral values. It is no surprise then that the butt of the humor in most of the Big Boy stories is the teacher or the parent. Big Boy, who like most of these typical heroes is absolutely lacking in moral and social values, is motivated purely by his own desires, appetites, and passions. Thus it is that much of the humor in these tales comes from Big Boy's seduction of the teacher, or his mother, or even a playmate whose purity society attempts to protect, or from Big Boy's robbing, tricking, or outsmarting everyone from his playmates to the school inspector. Big Boy is often pictured as very much the fool, the moron; but even in his ignorance, he usually triumphs over his enemies. We would perhaps not love Big Boy so much if he were not such a moron; for if he were more intelligent, we might not be able to forgive him some of the transgressions for which a more responsible person would be condemned. Indeed, his irresponsibility allows the schoolchildren the opportunity to enjoy vicariously the antisocial behavior which they must repress.

---

1. There is a folder of Big Boy stories in the unpublished Folklore Research Project at the Institute of Jamaica, which has versions of several of the tales in this chapter.

2. Interview with Louise Bennett, Gordon Town, September 15, 1978.

48A E-G-G

One time Big Boy went to school and the subject was spelling. Eventually it was his turn to spell *egg*, but he could not spell it.

However, his donkey G. G., who was outside the class window, was walking away, and Big Boy cried out, "E-G-G!" Teacher and student began to applaud Big Boy.

Given to me in writing by a resident of Kingston on October 11, 1978.

Several tales in which Big Boy accidentally is perceived as correctly answering the teacher's question appear in Folklore Research Project.

48B E-G-G

One day Big Boy go a school. So Big Boy stay in a school. So Teacher say, "Which of you can spell *egg*?" Big Boy start look pon 'im book dem. 'Im come back; 'im go straight over. . . . Big Boy caan' spell it. Big Boy a look now. So di teacher say, "Which one of you can spell *egg*?" Big Boy stay so, "Uhmmmm." So Big Boy donkey did name E-G-G. Big Boy donkey name E-G-G now. So Big Boy donkey have to run now. So Big Boy say, "E-G-G! E-G-G!" So Teacher say, "Oh, oh, spell it again" And him spell it again, and him get the prize.

Collected in Kingston on October 6, 1978.

48C E-G-G

One time Big Boy go school. So Teacher ask him to spell *egg*. So him sit right beside the window. So down by the street him saw him donkey, and him call him donkey E-G-G. So Teacher ask the classroom to spell *egg*. No one couldn' spell egg. So him see him donkey a run, man. So him say, "E-G-G! E-G-G!" Teacher say, "Right, Big Boy, that's how it spelt—e-g-g."

Collected in Kingston on September 15, 1978.

48D E-G-G

Once upon a time Big Boy have a donkey, him name E-G-G. Big Boy carry di donkey go a school. And Teacher said, "Big Boy, spell *egg*." And a

boy outside was fassing around Big Boy donkey, and Big Boy say, "E-G-G!"
And den Teacher said, "Come up here, Big Boy. Spell *egg*." Big Boy said,
"E-G-G!" And then Teacher said, "Go and sit down." And from that day Big
Boy can spell *egg*.

Collected in Kingston on September 18, 1978.

49 Big Boy Spells Ink

One time Big Boy go to school, and Big Boy teacher say, "Who can spell
ink?" And Big Boy say, "Well, I caan' spell *ink*." Everybody in a di class caan'
spell *ink*. So a man say, 'Big Boy, wha' appen? Spell *ink* nuh!" Him say, "I
ain' kare."
Teacher say, "What you say?"
Him say, "I *ain' kare*."
"Yes, Big Boy, spell it, him say I-N-K!"

Collected in Kingston on October 6, 1978.

50A Miami

One time Big Boy go to school, man. And Big Boy go to school, the
bwoy them telling Big Boy that he not going to get a girl if him caan' answer
the question the teacher tell him. So Big Boy come in. Awright, Teacher give
out question, say that must tell him which, after the plane leave Jamaica Airport, which place it first. So Big Boy nah answer, nah answer. So the girl dem
a laugh after Big Boy, and say if Big Boy nah answer him nah get. . . . So Big
Boy say, "Nuh bodder me!" And Teacher say, "Not nuh bodder me, Big Boy,
Miami."

Collected in Woodside on September 6, 1978.

50B Miami

Big Boy was in school. Right? So Big Boy's friend gave him a chewing
gum to keep or something like that to keep, you know. So Big Boy have it
now. Big Boy *eat* it. The teacher asked a question in the class and said, "Which
country does [the plane] stop when it leaves Jamaica?" At the same time Big
Boy's friend said to him, said, "Where my bubble gum? Where my bubble

gum?" Big Boy say, "Mi nyam it. Mi nyam it."[1] So the teacher say, "That's good, Big Boy, that's good!" Because the state that she was talking about was Miami.

Collected in Kingston on October 11, 1978.
1. *Nyam* means "eat." Jamaicans often pronounce *Miami* as me-am-me.

50C Miami

Once upon a time Big Boy go school. So Big Boy moder give him fifty cent to buy five bulla fi him lunch. So Big Boy go school, man. Big Boy get break and by di time lunch now, Big Boy fren' give him ten cents fi buy one bulla fi him too. So Big Boy buy di six bulla and eat it off, man. Bell ring back.

Big Boy go in a class. So Teacher say, "Which is the country dat produce the most sugar?" The bwoy juk Big Boy wid him pencil, and the bwoy ask Big Boy weh him bulla deh. And juk Big Boy wid di pencil, and Big Boy say, "Mi *nyam* it!"

Hear di teacher now: "Yes, Big Boy, you are right. But nex' time is not so loud. Is just Mi-ami, not Mi*nyam*mi."

Collected in Kingston on September 18, 1978.

50D Miami

Once upon a time a boy fren' beg him to buy ten bulla for him. Well the teacher send dem for break, so 'im give Big Boy ten cent, and Big Boy buy the ten bulla and eat off di whole of it. And when dem come in back, inside back, di fren' took Big Boy wid im . . . and say, "Whe mi bulla?" Hear Big Boy: "Mi nyam i'." And the teacher say, "Dat's right, Big Boy, dat's right, but you nuh fi say, 'Mi nyam i'; say 'Mi ha mi.'"

Collected in Kingston on September 10, 1978, from an eight-year-old informant.

50E Miami

One time Big Boy moder give him dollar say to buy bulla for him. So when him go to school now, a boy give Big Boy ten cents to buy bulla for him. And when recess now, Big Boy go out and buy the bulla and eat off the whole of the boy bulla, and eat off the bulla now.

When him come back in a class, Teacher say, "Big Bwoy, pronounce *Miami*." Boy juk Big Bwoy in the face and say, "Big Bwoy, whe mi bulla deh?" "Mi nyam i'."

Teacher say, "Big Boy, dat's not how you pronounce it; its' Mi-am-i."

Collected in Kingston on September 10, 1978, from a ten-year-old informant.

51A Jesus Christ

This is another school situation in which the Inspector was visiting, you know, questioning the children to see really what they know. And he was doing religious knowledge this time. So he asked, you know, "Do you know who died for you, for your sins?" *Nobody* in the class knew, man. So the teacher was so ashamed now, was going up and down looking on the faces; nobody still didn't know. So she had a pin. So she just stick the person behind—the closest person to her, you know—and the person bawl out, "Lawd, Jesus Christ!"

So you know that was the answer. The Inspector praise the boy, *brilliant* boy. And not knowing really what brought about the answer.

Collected in Kingston on November 8, 1978.

A version appears in Box 1 of Folklore Research Project. For a similar tale see Legman, *Rationale*, p. 75; and Dance, *Shuckin' and Jivin'*, No. 130.

51B Jesus Christ

One day Big Boy went to school, and Teacher asked Big Boy who was crucified on the Cross. So Big Boy didn't know. So Big Boy had a big sore foot, and the same time another girl stepped on Big Boy sore foot. And Big Boy said, "Lawd, Jesus Christ!"

Collected in Kingston on October 30, 1978.

51C Jesus Christ

Big Boy went school. It was a Christmas. So Teacher ask the classroom who was born in Bethlehem.

So Big Boy did have a cut pon him foot, though Big Boy always gi' trouble in a school. One a him fren' juk him wid a pencil in a him gut. Him say, "Jesus Christ!"

So Teacher say, "Yes, Big Boy, Jesus Christ was born in Bethlehem."

Collected in Kingston on September 15, 1978.

51D Jesus Christ

In the past, you know, we had a story about Big Boy and Teacher. Teacher was taking up the class, and Teacher decide to ask the children about some religious knowledge. Anyway, Teacher ask in the crowd who know the story about who died to save us all. So the children stood on their feet starting shouting, and the teacher said, "I will have to ask one, one at a time." Anyway one specially sat down. That was Big Boy. He did not put up his hand. So Teacher got curious and wondering what happened why Big Boy didn't put up his hand. Anyway Big Boy sat there picking his finger all along — picking his finger, hold down his head, picking his finger. So Teacher said, "You, young man across the corner there, why you picking your finger like that and your hand isn't in the air?" So Big Boy hold up his head and then hold it down back again. Teacher said, "You, young man that sat down, why is it your hand isn't up?" Anyway, Big Boy said, "Me, Teacher?" Said, "Yes." Said, "Who died to save us all?" Said, "Barabbas,[1] Teacher." And Teacher laughed, "Barabbas?" Said, "No. couldn't be Barabbas. You want to tell me that your parents didn't tell you who died to save us all?" He said, "No, Teacher, I know of Barabbas." Anyway, Teacher said, "I want you to tell me who died to save us all." Big Boy said, "Barabbas, Teacher." Say, "No, not Barabbas." Teacher come a little closer with his strap, and said, "Well, Big Boy, you have to tell me who died to save us all." Anyway Teacher start to put on couple licks, couple licks, couple licks, and Big Boy say, "Jesus Christ, Teacher!" Teacher say, "Yes, man, good, you pretending. I know that you know the story it was Jesus Christ who died to save us all. But you was hiding it from me, huhn?" Anyway, Teacher say, "Well, I want to know if your parents don't have a Bible at home that you should know about the Crucifixion — who died to save us all, who was crucified to save us all." He say, "No, Teacher. No know bout no Bible, Teacher, because we live clear cross the riverside, Teacher. So my parents a no tell me bout that, Teacher."

Anyway, one day Teacher was on his way and met Big Boy parents and stopped them and said, "Mr. Brown and Mrs. Brown, imagine the other day I stood in the class taking up some religious knowledge and asked the children who died to save us all, and your son, Big Boy, sit down as if he didn't know.

Anyway I have to start to put some licks. While putting on the licks he shouted 'Jesus Christ!' but it seemed to me he was pretending." So his mother said, "Jesus Christ, Teacher, but we don't know nothin' bout Jesus Christ. Who you call Jesus Christ?" Say, "You don't know?" Say, "Yes, Teacher, we live way across the river. Jesus Christ no mussi the Governor for we know you ha dem big man deh sometime and dem call dem big name, so maybe a Governor a Jesus Christ, Teacher. Me no ben know say man dead fi save me, Teacher. We nah buy *Gleaner,*[2] Teacher; we no ha radio, Teacher; then how we must know, Teacher? We live away cross the river deh Teacher. Look, see deh we wet up fe cross the river, Teacher. Teacher is a good day when we buck you up,[3] Teacher, for now we know say Jesus Christ dead fi we all, Teacher. Yes, Teacher, we ha fi go buy one Bible, Teacher, let Big Boy read it fi we, Teacher." Anyway, that is the end of Big Boy story.

Collected in Kingston in November 1978.

See Motif J1738.4, "Numbskulls Surprised to Hear That God's Son Has Died," in Baughman, *Type and Motif-Index.*

1. Barabbas was the prisoner released in preference to Christ at the demand of the multitude.
2. Popular Jamaican daily paper.
3. Bumped into you; met you.

52A Half Idiot

One day the Inspector walked into the school and asked, "Who can guess my age?" And Big Boy said, "Me, sir." And the Inspector said, "Yes, Big Boy." And Big Boy said, "Thirty, sir." So hear the man: "How you know?"

Big Boy say, "Because I have a brother at home and he is fifteen, and he is a half-idiot, so you must be thirty.

Collected in Kingston on October 30, 1978.

See Motif J2212, "Effects of Age and Size Absurdly Applied," in Baughman, *Type and Motif-Index.*

52B Half Idiot

This story is told of Big Boy, you know, on Inspection Day, and everybody dress up, man, and come to school ready for Inspector. All who never used to wear shoes and socks wear shoes and socks that day.

So Inspector came in, you know, and asking questions. So Inspector said, "By the way, who would be able to tell me my age?" Everybody put up hand, man: "Sixty?" "No. Wrong." So Big Boy was coming around the corner, man. "Yes, you, Big Boy." He said, "Forty, sah, forty."

He said, "That's a bright boy, brilliant boy. How did you know that?"

"Well, sah, I have a half-idiot a yard, and he is twenty. So you *must* be forty for you is a full idiot."

Collected in Kingston on November 8, 1978.

53 Come On, Baby, Let's Go-Go-Go-o!

Once upon a time, Big Bwoy' teacher tell 'im fi do some 'omework. So 'im go home and ask him madder, "Mama, Teacher say mus' do some home-work." "Get loss!" Him write it down [dramatizing]. She send him to shop and she say, "Go and buy some food." And 'im was passing and 'im 'ear a man say over the T.V., "Dingy-dingy Batman."

Him run go home back and write dat down in a 'im book [dramatizing]. And 'im a walk go supermarket, 'im a come, 'im 'ear a white man say, "Come on, baby, let's go-go-go-o!" And him come back home from shop, him write down [dramatizing].

And when Teacher come she say, "Big Boy, where is your work?"

"Get loss!"

"Who you talking to?"

"Dingy-dingy Batman."

"What????? I carry you to the principal!"

"Come on, baby, let's go-go-go-o!"

Collected in Kingston on September 6, 1978, from a ten-year-old informant.

54 Jesus Going into Jeruselam

One time now, Big Boy now him see him father peter, and him say, "What is dat, Pappa?" And him say, "Jesus!" Him see him moder peter, and him say, "What is dat, Mamma?" She say, "Jerusalem!"

Him a peep now and him see him moder and him fader deh. . . . Him fader say, "Big Boy, what you was doing here? From when you deh here?" Hear him: "I was dere from Jesus going into Jerusalem."

Collected in Kingston on October 6, 1978.

For other tales that play on names for the sexual organs in this way, see Knapp and Knapp, *One Potato*, p. 186; Dance, *Shuckin' and Jivin'*, No. 92; and Legman, *Rationale*, p. 552. A discussion of this type of humor, including illustrations, may be found in Zumwalt, "Plain and Fancy," pp. 348–54. These tales that play on parents' evasiveness in speaking truthfully about sexual organs and acts reveal the child's great joy in turning the parents' own artifices against them when the child not only observes the organs, but also witnesses intercourse.

1. How long have you been here?

55 Gorilla Eat Banana

One time Big Boy old lady and old man a bathe. So Big Boy say to him old man, "Daddy, Daddy, what is dat [pointing to his genitals]?"

Daddy say, "Cho, a big long banana."

"Mama, Mama, what is dat [pointing to her genitals]?"

Mammy say, "Cho, a hairy gorilla."

In a di night right now the two a dem gon' a bed. So Big Boy never a sleep. So Big Boy go prupp-s [roaming around the house] again, and when Big Boy prupp-s him see di old lady and di ole man a gon' wid business. And him just bounce down di door and just say, "Jesus! Jesus! Jesus! Daddy, Daddy! You don' see what? Mammy hairy gorilla eat off you ripe banana!"

Collected in Kingston on September 19, 1978.
A version and a variant appear in Zumwalt, "Plain and Fancy," pp. 349–50.

56 What Yu Want, Big Boy?

Big Boy at school. So holiday coming on. So Teacher giving out presents to children. Teacher give out pencil—all kinds of toys to the children. So Big Boy don't talk what him want. So Teacher say, "Big Boy, what you want?" Big Boy say, "Nah tell you, Teacher." Teacher say, "What yu want, Big Boy?" "Nah tell yu, Teacher." Teacher say, "Awright, Big Boy, tell me, Big Boy." "Teacher, nah tell yu. Yu gon' beat me, Teacher." Teacher say, "Awright, Big Boy, you want cyart? You want bicycle? You want everyting that toys can make of?" Big Boy say, "Nah tell yu, nah tell yu, Teacher." Teacher say, "Awright, Big Boy, come we going in a staff room and yu tell me." Teacher say, "Tell me, Big Boy." Big Boy say, "Nah tell yu, Teacher. Yu gon' beat me, Teacher." Teacher say, "Big Boy, tell me, man. Me nah beat yu." Big Boy say, "Yu gon' beat me, Teacher." Teacher say, "Whisper in my ears, Big Boy." "Teacher, yu gon' beat me if me tell yu, Teacher." Teacher say, "Awright, Big Boy, me nah beat yu. Whisper in my ears." Big Boy say, "Little a di salt ting, Teacher."

And Teacher beat Big Boy.

Collected in Woodside on September 6, 1978.
See Motif P340, "Teacher and Pupil," in Baughman, *Type and Motif-Index.*

57A Red Ackee

Well, say it happen that Big Boy mussi was picking ackee. So well den, di teacher and di oder students, you know, mussi was playing game and so forth. So in picking ackee, Big Boy look up and di teacher was up in di ackee tree and, well, she have on a dress and ting, you know, and she was exposing herself. So Big Boy look up, astonish, and [said], "Ah see a *red, red* ackee!" So di teacher say, "Pick it and. . . ."

"Awright [dramatizing Big Boy reaching under Teacher's dress]."

"AA-OOOOOO [teacher's reaction]!"

Collected in Kingston on October 6, 1978.

57B Red Ackee

Once upon a time Teacher said to Big Boy in class, "We does not have anything to eat today for lunch, you know children." And Big Boy say, "Wait a minute, Teacher, I see one pretty, pretty red ackee outside in the tree. Can I have di permission to go and pick it, Miss?" Teacher say, "Yes, Big Boy, you can 'ave all di permission you need to go and get dat ackee for us to have lunch today."

And Big Boy went for a 'ooker stick and went back in class and use it and push di 'ooker stick up underneat' di teacher's leg and interfere what he was not to interfere wid.

Collected in Kingston on September 18, 1978.

57C Red Ackee

Once upon a time Big Boy go to school. So Teacher say, "Who is the nicest boy into di class?" And Big Boy act like 'im nice. And Teacher say she gon' carry 'im and mek him spend a time at her 'ome. So when Big Boy [got there], Big Boy say 'im no sleep inna pants, 'im nuh sleep inna shirt, 'im no sleep inna briefs. Teacher say, "Me nuh sleep inna none; me no sleep neider inna slip, neider in a baggy."

So di two a dem start to do oder tings inside di house now. And here's came di Teacher 'usband come. And she tie up Big Boy up in a di ceiling, and di man and him wife start do business now. Big Boy up in a di ceiling a cuss, a cuss, a cuss—a grumble and a go, "Ru-ru-grr-grr!" And dat man down pon di lady looking all over di place and caan' see Big Boy. And a parrot is only telling him, and him doan know weh him.

Everywhere di parrot fin' it and show (di man is a dumb man), di man point a different place, and Big Boy stay deh till, from about three o'clock and starve fi hungry till about, till tomorrow mawning. And she look after tea and gi' him when her husband drink fi him tea and gon'. And she carry Big Boy a school. And dem say, "We didn't have no lunch to eat for today." And Big Boy say, "Miss, let me and you go out and pick ackees." Dat time Miss could climb, and when she go up into di tree, Big Boy go up into di tree too. And Big Boy tek di 'ooker stick pon her, and say, "I see a dozen red, red ackee." The teacher push up her foot up in di air and say if she could see it. And Big Boy tek di 'ooker stick and push it up, and do *wrong* tings what he is never supposed to do.

And that is the end of the story.

Collected in Kingston on September 18, 1978, from an eleven-year-old informant.

58 Frying

One time Big Boy go to school. Anyway, dem have a new teacher, foreign teacher just come off a small island, and she decide to tek out di student dem. Everytime dem tek out dem, di boys dem pair off wid de girl. Big Boy never even have no girl, cause all di girl dem fear Big Boy.

Anyway, some of di girl dem deh in front of de teacher, and a bwoy mek a bad move wid a girl, and a move it, and the teacher see and say, "Oh, Big Boy, what is that?" Big Boy say, "Aw, Miss, deh only frying, you can see de frying." The teacher say, "Oh, how they fry?"

Big Boy say, "Let ah show you." The teacher go down and Big Boy de deh a fry, and Big Boy crack a fart. And di teacher say, "What is that?" Big Boy say, "Is di frying pan bottom bus'." Hear di teacher: "I believe you. I can feel di oil running betwixt mi legs."

Collected in Kingston on September 18, 1978.

59 A Nuh So Mama Sleep

Big Boy went to school now and there was a teacher woman, so Big Boy loves Teacher. So Big Boy ask the teacher to let him come and sleep with him. So the teacher say [naively], "Awright." So when Big Boy go to the house now,

Teacher going to put him into the next room. Him say, "No, man, because my mother never let me sleep alone. Mama mek me sle-e-e-ep with him." Teacher say [naive voice], "Awright, you can sleep." When him go in him say, "When Mama take off him clothes, Mama take off him clothes before me." The teacher take off him dress. Him say, "No, man, Mama nuh sleep so. Mama take off him slip." The teacher take off her slip. Say, "Mama, Mama, Mama no sleep so. Mama take off him brassiere." So the teacher take off her brassiere. "And Mama, and Mama, Mama take off the panties too." So the teacher take off her panties. Him say, "A nuh so Mama sleep in a bed." So the teacher go in and sleep into the bed now. "A nuh so Mama stay, you know, Mama, Mama let me sle-e-ep on top a her."

Collected in Woodside on September 6, 1978.
See K1350, "Woman Persuaded (or Wooed) by Trick," in Baughman, *Type and Motif-Index.*

60 Mummy Never Sleep in Clothes

Once upon a time Big Boy go school. So Big Boy teacher carry him home. So night come now, man, night come. So Big Boy teacher put on pajama pon Big Boy and a carry 'im inna di bed fi sleep. Bit Boy start bawl: "Ah-h-h-hanh!" Teacher say, "What is the matter, Big Boy?" [Whining] "Mama never mek me sleep in clothes."

"Awright, go and tek it off, and go back to bed."

"Ah-h-hanh!"

"What is it, Big Boy?"

"Mummy never let be sleep beside her. She always mek me sleep on top of her."

"Awright. Come."

"Ah-h-hanh!"

"What is it, Big Boy?"

"Mummy never sleep in clothes."

"Hmmm! Oh, bwoy!"

Awright, Teacher go tek off clothes, man. Big Boy go back pon top a her: "Ah-h-h-hanh!"

Teacher say, "What is it now, Big Boy?

[Whining] "Mammy never sleep in panties."

"Awright, let me take it off."

And that is the end of the story.

Collected in Kingston on September 19, 1978, from a twelve-year-old informant.

61A The Boys Are Throwing Stones

Well, there was supposed to be sport at school, so the teacher, di head-mistress, told the boys dem wasn' to come because it was girls' sport, no boys wasn' to come. So Big Boy: "I waan' know is wah kind of secret dem haf up dem nuh waan' no man fi come and be dere." So Big Boy go home and put on him sister frock, put on a wig, and Big Boy tie up him prick and put a — tie on a mango seed pon it, you nuh seet, fi gi' di 'pression, you know how it go and ting.

So sport now. Big Boy go in and tek in girls' sports and ting. Dat time dem sit down in a little circle and ting, and doan' know what teacher reely a do, you know, but Big Boy deh and deh and, you know, him a look up under-neat' di girl dem, and a examine all a dem and ting, you know. Him eye get . . . and him prick start to stand up now, and teacher mussi a move round and a examine tings. So it happen dat Big Boy prick stan' up so stiff that it snap di cord now, and the mango seed fly off and lick Teacher, lick off Teacher glasses. She say, "Run, girls, the boys are throwing stones!"

Collected in Kingston on October 6, 1978.
See Motif K1321.1, "Man Disguised as Woman Admitted to Women's Quarters: Seduction," in Baughman, *Type and Motif-Index.*

61B The Boys Are Throwing Stones

Once upon a time Big Boy go to school. So the teacher tell the boys not to come back di oder day. Only pure girl must come back. So Big Boy go home, man, and tell 'im moder say dat, "Mummy, Teacher tell mi dat no boy is to come to school tommorow. So you know what I goin' do. I goin' dress up in mi sister clothes and I goin' borrow you wig. You hear, Mummy?" So Mummy say, "Yes." So Big Boy dress up in a him moder wig and him sister clothes and him sister shoes and everyting.

So him go school di mawning. So Teacher look. So Teacher a show di pickney dem her crawncy.[1] So Teacher a go roun' and ah look pon di pickney dem crawncy now, man. So she reach to Big Boy. So Big Boy wood get stiff. So she go roun' and ah look pon Big Boy, and she draw down Big Boy sister baggy. So Big Boy "buddy" get stiff and lick off di glasses offa her face. Hear her nuh: "Girls, girls, shut the windows! The boys are flinging stones!"

Collected in Kingston on September 18, 1978.
1. Private parts.

62 The New Bell

Once upon a time Big Boy was given money to get a bell in his school because the Examiner was visiting.

On the day of the Examiner visit Big Boy hang his balls and penis through the ceiling. As the Examiner approach what he thought was the bell, the teacher began to boast about their new bell and told the Examiner to ring it. This he did by pulling Big Boy long penis *HARD!* Big Boy said, "Bong, bong, bong, bong!" The Examiner pulled again. Then Big Boy screamed, "Wha' di blood clat! You no hear me say 'Bong!'"

Given to me in writing by a resident of Kingston on October 11, 1978.

63 Gi' Mi di Ting pon di Table

Big Bwoy. Right now you waan' see Big Boy go a school. Teacher say right now, "Big Bwoy, I waan' you fi go home fi someting, just go home and tell mi dawter say fi gi' you the eggs upon the table."

So Big Bwoy jus' go 'ome and look pon di dawter and say, "Teacher say fi gi mi di ting pon di table."

She jus' go pon di table and just start gi' Big Bwoy—anyway, Big Bwoy move it. Mek a juice an' ting.

Teacher come home and say, "God bless, Big Bwoy never even boder carr' all a di egg. 'Im all broke one pon di table. Look where 'im deh waste it." And just scrape it off.

Collected in Kingston on September 18, 1978.

64 A Duck fi a Fuck

Once upon a time Big Boy was walking down the road from school, and he saw a girl by the name of Angela. So Big Boy had a duck in his 'and, and dis girl was passing by di street. And say, say to di girl, say, "A duck fi a fuck!" And di girl say, "Yes, man, come over di churchyard."

And Big Boy say, "Awright, come nuh." And Big Boy go over di yard and bus' couple juice well, and you waan' see di dawter belly start get fat and ting. And when di girl go home now, her moder say to her: "Girl, where you get dat drake from?" And di girl say to her moder, "Mummy, I was comin'

from church, and I saw Big Boy comin' from school. A boy by the name of
Big Boy gave me dis duck for a fuck."

And di moder say to di girl, "What! You tell mi dat dis boy give you
a duck for a fuck! Go back to dis boy's yard and tell 'im tek back him duck
and give you back yu fuck." And [she] jus go dere and say, "Big Boy, Mummy
say to tek back you duck and gi' me back mi' fuck." And Big Boy just carry
it back over the churchyard and just pop it, three juice dis time, and she just
go home and jus' look sad. And Mummy jus' say, "What, dat's 'ow it goes.
You should not tek a duck for a fuck."

Collected in Kingston on September 18, 1978.

This is Motif K1362, "Innocent Girl Sells Her 'love' and Later Receives It Back," in Baughman,
Type and Motif-Index.

65 Ah Worm Is Tickling Me

Once upon a time Big Boy saw a nice, nice girl that he like. And Big
Boy couldn' go at dis girl's yawd, because of her fader who was too ignorant
and bad and was a bully. So Big Boy decide to pay this girl a visit one of the
day, by back door or back fence. So Big Boy jump di fence one a di day and
peep thro' a likkle bored hole in a di 'ouse. And when him look him see di
fader a read a *Gleaner* pon a chair. So Big Boy go round to which part di kitchen
deh, and see di girl a mek some cawfee fi her fader, and start mek some signal
and sign and start talk to di girl, officially, roun' a di forward. And the ole
man caan' know. So after di girl done mek dat fi her fader, and went to give
him, while him drinking his breakfas' and 'aving a read at his daily *Gleaner,*
the girl went around to her room to change off in her school clothes, but Big
Boy could not enter di 'ouse none at all because her fader were too bad and
was a bully, and everybody fraid of him. So it happen dat Big Boy have to stay
outside and push his peng-ge-leng thro' a big bored 'ole, and di girl go down
on it and lay down like dat [illustrating — elbows on floor like reading a book],
and pretending like she is reading a comic or a book someting or di oder.

And her fader come around and say, "Jennifer, why are you doing yourself like dat on the floor?" And she say to her fader, "Daddy, ah worm is tickling me." So Daddy say to her, "Den why you haf a worm tickling you and
you does not tell me about it and let me tek you to a doctor?"

She say, "Daddy, dis worm dat is tickle me, I like it very much. I would
just lie here and tek it all day."

And her father say, "Come here a minute and mek mi some sugar and
water." And it 'appen dat when di girl git up, di fader saw dis big peng-ge-leng

pointing up thro' di house flooring bottom and went for him pick-axe—him axe dat him use and chop wood and ting like dat—and go so—WHAM! after Big Boy peng-ge-leng, and Big Boy draw it down and push it up again and him go so—WHAM! again and chop out him flooring. And when him look him see Big Boy. Big Boy jus' draw up 'im pants and jus' run through the gate and run up di street. And the ole man screw[1] fi dat, beat 'im dawter all day.

Collected in Kingston on September 18, 1978.

1. Angry—as one who has been, in the vernacular, screwed or fucked over.

See Motif K1344.1, "Girl Seduced from beneath Ground"; Motif T41.2, "Communication of Lovers through Hole in Floor;" and Motif T41.1, "Communication of Lovers through Hole in Wall"; in Baughman, *Type and Motif-Index*. Two versions that focus upon having sexual relations through the hole are cited by Stith Thompson in *Motif-Index of Folk-Literature*.

66A Can I Drive My Little Mini?

One time Big Boy go inna him moder house now, go inna di house and ketch him moder a tidy up and ting. So him say, "Hey, Mom, what's that?" Hear her nuh: "Big Boy, you not suppose to see it. It's your dad's garage." So Big Boy: "Have a little Mini here. . . . Mom, can I park my Mini dere?" Hear her: "No, son, your Dad's Chev."

Collected in Kingston on October 6, 1978.

A version appears in Zumwalt, "Plain and Fancy," p. 349.

66B Can I Drive My Little Mini?

Once upon a time Big Boy saw his moder bading into a bathroom. So it 'appen dat Big Bwoy getting jumpy thro' 'im see 'im moder bading in di bathroom. So 'im say to 'im moder, "Mammy, can I drive my little Mini Minor into the garage?"

She say, "No, dis garage belongs to Daddy's big Chev."

Collected in Kingston on September 19, 1978.

66C Can I Drive My Little Mini?

Once upon a time Big Boy and his mother was bathing. On observing his mother vagina, he asked her what it was. And she said it was his father garage. Big Boy then ask her, "Can I park my little Mini Minor in it?" She reply, "No, it is for Daddy's big limousine."

Given to me in writing by a Kingston resident on October 11, 1978.

67 Keep On Buying Missa Mac Candle

Dem have a woman deh, you know, every night she send her son go buy four candle. So Big Bwoy notice, so Big Bwoy say, "Wait, wah she a buy candle fa?" Is [for] him moder. Big Bwoy say, "Awright, gi mi di money fi buy di candle." But Big Bwoy know wah a gon',[1] and Big Boy him a jinnal. So Big Bwoy jus' go stand up deh now, and see, and Big Bwoy say, "Ah-o-o, dat?"[2] Big Bwoy no boder buy no candle nuh. Big Bwoy jus' go and 'tan up so and him moder come now and 'tan up so. So him moder start use Big Bwoy now, but she nuh know say a Big Bwoy. She tink a di candle now. Hear her nuh: "Big Bwoy, weh you buy dat candle?" And Big Bwoy say, "Ah Missa Mac, you nuh." "Keep on buying Missa Mac candle." Hear Big Bwoy, "Yes, Ma." "You keep on buying Missa Mac candle."

A Big Bwoy deh, you nuh, but she tink say di candle, but the candle— "Dis yah candle yah caan' done. Keep on buying from Missa Mac, Big Bwoy, keep on buying Missa Mac candle." Is Big Bwoy di deh.

Collected in Kingston on October 6, 1978.
1. Knows what's going on, i.e., that mother is using candle to masturbate.
2. What is that? (He is peeping through hole.)

68 It Have Teeth

Big Boy went to school, and the children telling him 'bout girl, say he was go get a girl friend and so forth. So he went and telling his mother about they teasing him about fish, fishes. Big Boy's mother say to him, say, "Awright, Big Boy, when I go to town and come back I will make you taste fishing, fish." So Big Boy's mother go to town now and come back and get them big fish, you know, them big fish, and Big Boy's mother come outside that night. And Big Boy's mother lay down and put it in front her and call Big Boy. And Big Boy go in and Big Boy doing it, Big Boy doing it! So Big Boy bawl out, "Mamma, Mamma, it have teeth, it have teeth!" And Big Boy run!

Collected in Woodside on September 6, 1978.
See Motif S1222, "Woman Tricks Importunate Love with the Head of a Pike," in Baughman, *Type and Motif-Index*.

69 When You a Fuck My Moder . . .

Big Boy come home early from school one evening and see him fader—
in dere language, you nuh—fucking him moder. So Big Boy look and Big
Boy laugh. And Big Boy go weh now, and Big Boy go weh now, and Big
Boy go fuck him fader moder now.

So him fader come on and come ketch dem now, and rail! And Big Boy
look pon him fader and say, "How when you a fuck my moder mi nuh screw,
and jus' tru mi a fuck your moder, now you a . . . ?"

Collected in Kingston on October 6, 1978.

A version appears in *Rationale*, where Legman notes, "This exact story will be found in the *Cent Nouvelles Nouvelles*, written in Burgundy, between 1456 and 1461, to entertain the Dauphin of France" (p. 96). Other versions may be found in Abrahams, *Positively Black*, p. 98, and Dance, *Shuckin' and Jivin'*, No. 258.

70 Big Boy Bruk Him Behin'

Once upon a time when Big Boy were a swine,
Him jump over Caroline
And bruk him behin'.
And jus' in time
To run up di 'ill
For two green lime
To rub 'im behin'.

Collected in Kingston on September 19, 1978.

V

Tales about Religion

Introduction

Jamaicans, like every other group, derive much pleasure from lampooning their religious leaders, especially those who hypocritically set themselves up as exemplar. Thus it is that the tales in this chapter focus on the minister and other churchmen, relishing revelations of their sin, their greed, their inebriety, and their impiety.

A considerable number of the tales focus upon the love of the churchmen, and the preachers in particular, for liquor, especially rum. Carlos Nelson insisted that this was to be expected, since "rum and sex are the two dominant symbols in the society."[1] Several tales also focus upon food—either the worshipper's sneaking food into the church service or the minister's inability to concentrate on his sermon because of his preoccupation with his waiting dinner. These tales (and many Black Americans can attest to this) are naturally generated in a community in which special services may run for three or more hours, especially in the Pentecostal churches, as Carlos Nelson vividly recalled.[2] Other tales deal with many familiar themes: the misinterpretation or the literal interpretation of the minister's words or the words of a song, the ostentatious efforts of church folk to avoid saying any word that smacks of an obscenity, the utterance of profanities by or in the presence of the minister, and the efforts of an individual to answer overheard prayers to God.

One of the best known subjects of religious tales and legends in Jamaica is the Prophet Bedward, apparently a popular preacher in the early days of this century in August Town, near Mona, Kingston. Bedward decided to enhance his popularity by flying with his congregation to heaven. In preparation, his followers were required to sell their earthly possessions and give the money to the prophet. When they all gathered together on the anticipated morning, Bedward climbed the tree, but his wings malfunctioned, and he fell to the ground. Legend has it that he was then confined to Bellevue, the local asylum. It is still possible today to find Jamaicans who recall Bedward. Carlos Nelson told me about a yardman he knew at the University of the West Indies at Mona, Kingston, who had sold his possessions to fly away with Bedward and had been a witness to that legendary attempt at flight. This man, according to Nelson, still believes in Bedward. There continue active religious sects that stem from the Bedward movement in Jamaica today. Nelson also insisted that the song "If I Had Wings Like a Dove," recorded by Byron Lee and the Dragonaires, was motivated by this incident.[3] Several literary pieces have been inspired by Bedward, most notably Sylvia Wynter's *The Hills of Hebron* (London: Jonathan Cape, 1962).

---

1. Interview with Carlos Nelson, Richmond, Virgina, December 14, 1982.
2. Ibid.
3. Ibid.

71A Flying to Heaven

There was a man, a preacher, who used to go about. They call him Bedward. He used to be mostly in Kingston up by Mavis Bank—there is a river up there. And he started to collect money. He told the people that he was going to fly, he was going to fly up to heaven, and if they wanted to go with him, they all should pay. And he collect quite a sum.

In the morning when he should fly now, he put on his white gown, and his head band is white, and he went by the river and *everybody* in lily-white, waiting now for Bedward is going to go up. So Bedward climb on a tree and told them to sing and pray and he would take off from the tree. When he goes up, they would come up with him. They were there singing and Bedward in the tree. Poor Bedward put on all kind of attachment, that he could make a wing, and believe that he could fly out. When Bedward leave off the tree, and to make a landing, my dear, he just crashed. No landing. He only wanted the money. So he got the money—and a beatin', because they all nearly killed him to get back their money.

Collected in Mandeville on September 16, 1978.

A version of this legend appears in Burke, *Water,* pp. 5–10, and in Jekyll, *Jamaican Song,* No. 140. Legendary tales of the preacher who promises to fly to heaven are widespread. In Trinidad such legends persist about two preachers, Taffy and Brackley, who offer themselves up for crucifixion prior to their ascent; those legends are treated in novels by Samuel Selvon, V. S. Naipaul, and Earl Lovelace. A similar legend treating the Prophet Jordan is popular in Guyana and has been treated by Jan Carew in *Black Midas* (London: Secker and Warburg, 1958). A comparable event is presented by Langston Hughes in his short story "Rock Church" (in Herbert Hill, ed., *Soon One Morning: New Writings by American Negroes, 1940–1962* [New York: Knopf, 1968], pp. 231–41).

71B Flying to Heaven

Now there lived in Jamaica in the early part of the century a preacher called Bedward. We never heard his first name, nor his second name. We only heard of him as Bedward. When I say "we," I'm referring to the children who grew up with me in the lower part of the town of Chapelton. We went to school in the day like other children, but when evening came and we had finished the duties around the house, the time was our own. And at that time we would meet, listen to stories, tell stories. Particularly we like to hear *big* people tell us stories at night because most of us were very afraid of—we were afraid of the dark, except when the Peenie Wallies[1] and the winkies were flying around—we liked that. We also liked the moon when the moon was up full, but we didn't like the dark. So when we heard about Bedward, who lived somewhere behind the capital city, Kingston, anybody who went there and could bring us back news, we were so delighted! In the case of Mass Tom, Mass Tom worked on a truck, and he went to Kingston from time to time on his truck —not on *his* real truck, you know—the truck belonged to a *big* man, but he worked on it as a sideline. But when he came back, boy, he brought back all sort o' stories. He told us about going to visit Bedward's church. It was a little church in a place called August Town. Well, we children knew about August, the *month* August, but we never heard of a town called *August* Town. He told us that August Town was in a valley, and it was behind a *big* property called Mona, where they reared cows. Well, this man Bedward kept services in August Town. And he didn't keep services like those we kept in Chapelton. His services had a lot of drums and a lot of shouting and a lot of *noise.* One night he demonstrated to us how things went. He made us form a circle and after we formed the circle, he went in the middle, and then he began to sing:

One day me go down a August Town, but me never go down a Mona.
One day me was invited by an old man dere called Jonah.
And when me go down a August Town, me hear about Bedward singing.
Him take on to Mary and dip her in the healing stream.
Dip them, Bedward, dip them.
Dip them in the healing stream.
Dip them sweet, but not too deep;
Dip them to cure bad feeling.
(Everybody) Dip them, Bedward, dip them,
Dip them in the healing stream;
Dip them sweet, but not too deep;
Dip them to cure bad feeling.[2]

So when he got there, we'd stop and ask him what did they dip the people in. He said, "There's a river up there called the Hope River. It runs behind August Town. It runs from the Hope Gardens, and that was done usually on Sunday mornings. He would take his followers — we would call sisters and brothers — and he would dip them in the stream. So we asked him what was this dipping for. He said it was what they called baptism, baptism. When they got baptized, the Holy Ghost came down on them and made them jump up and down. So all of us would form the ring as I told you, and boy! We got in the spirit. And we jumped up and down, and we all sang the same chorus Mass Johnny taught us, you know:

Dip them, Bedward, dip them,
Dip them in the healing stream;
Dip them sweet, but not too deep;
Dip them for cure bad feelings.

And we asked him, "Now what happened to this man Bedward? Did he and the police came in collision?"

He said, "Well, maybe was so. I don't think anything was wrong with that, but I think he was a good man. But the police didn't like him, and when he went up in a tree. . . ."

We said, "Went up in a tree for what? To pick breadfruit?"

He said, "No, there was a time when Bedward said he was going to heaven."

Oh boy, we crept up near to him, and we said, "Tell us about that, man."

He said, "Well, Bedward decided that he was going to heaven in a certain day, and on the day, people came from all over the island, sold off all their hogs, their pigs; they didn't have many cows, but they sold what they had; they sold their land; some people even sold their *houses*. And on the day they all came and met under this *big* tree. He couldn't remember what type of tree it was, but he said it was a *big* tree, bigger than breadfruit, bigger than coconut, bigger than starapple, *big* tree. Bedward decided to go up, but one of his members said, "Brother Bedward, you know what you do, sir, go up in the tree, go *right* to the treetop to the ticky top, way out on the top limb. Then jump! Then jump! And after we see you jump and nothing gon' happen to you, then we go up there too and jump. Then after that we'll fly, we'll learn to fly from the treetop. So Bedward went on the top of the tree. [Obviously the ending is so well known that the storyteller did not consider it necessary to continue.]

Collected in Santa Cruz on November 4, 1978.

1. Lightning bug.

2. This song obviously arose from Bedward's practice of mass baptisms, both for salvation and for healing. According to Eddie Burke, it is sung during a ring game in which a ring is formed around two individuals, one imitating Bedward dipping the other at the appropriate time (interview, Santa Cruz, Jamaica, November 4, 1978).

72 Every Member to Carry His Own Spirit

There was this preacher who on Sundays when he preaching he carried his flask of whiskey or white rum to church. Without that he couldn't preach.

So one Sunday he took the whiskey as usual. The deacon walked through the other door of the church and stole away the parson's whiskey, so Parson couldn't preach after losing his whiskey. So he went to the pulpit and said, "Ladies and gentlemen, I am not feeling well. On account of that I am going to ask Deacon Jones to do the preaching for me this Sunday, but I have one information to pass around. As of this Sunday, I am asking every member of the church to carry his own spirit to church."

Collected in Kingston on September 21, 1978.

See Motif X445.1, "Parson Takes a Drink of Liquor during the Sermon," in Baughman, *Type and Motif-Index*. Tales about ministers who drink, particularly during services, are popular in the United States as well. For variants see Parsons, *Folk-Lore of the Sea Islands*, p. 127; Brewer, *Worser Days*, pp. 49–50; Abrahams, *Positively Black*, pp. 104–5; and Dance, *Shuckin' and Jivin'*, Nos. 78, 79, 80.

73A Now We Will Gather at the River

There was this minister who was preaching. He said to his congregation, "I don't know what is happening of late, but when coming to church this morning I passed a lot of bars well filled with men, and here in the church I can see an estimated crowd of five hundred people of which four hundred and fifty are women. And all the men are in the bars, drinking rum on a day like Sunday, when they should be in church. If I was the prime minister of this country, what I would do, I would give the security force order to dump all the rum in the river!"

Deacon Jones round the back say,"Ladies and gentlemen, let's stand and sing Hymn 127: "Now We Will Gather at the River!"

Collected in Kingston on September 21, 1978.
Versions appear in Dance, *Shuckin' and Jivin'*, No. 103, and Spalding, ed., *Encyclopedia*, p. 514.

73B Now We Will Gather at the River

One New Year's Eve the people in a certain district gathered to have their regular Watch Night service.

While the service was going on, some drunken men entered and started to make a lot of noise. The minister then started preaching about rum and drunkenness. He mentioned that if he had the power, he would throw all the rum that was in the world into the river.

All the drunken men then started to sing and dance around:

> Then we would gather at the river
> The beautiful, that beautiful river,
> Gather for the rum at the river
> That flows from the throne of God.

Given to me in writing in November 1978, by a resident of Kingston.

74 Rum Will Kill Out All the Worms

Father[1] found out that his men were drinking too much white rum, so he decided to use some white rum and experiment on worms to show how dangerous it was. One day he called the men and put a glass of white rum and worms on the table and told them to look carefully at the worms that were wriggling. As he placed the worms in the rum, they died.

The men rejoiced, saying, "That's good, man. Rum will kill out all the worms inside us."

Given to me in writing in November 1978, by an informant from Kingston.
1. The priest.

75A Corner, Parson

[The parson had a parrot that] tawk very religious words, so it happen dat one of di day a Rasta man round pon a gully bank 'ave a parrot weh coulda did tawk nuttin but *pure* bad word. So it happen dat di man go 'change di parson now, tek way di parson parrot and gi' 'im fi him parrot weh can chat bare bad wud!

So it happen that, after church one Sunday, di parson very 'ungry, you know, thru how 'im a did a tawk out him day in a di church and ting, and Parson deh in a hurry pon a street, pon a corner street, a go home a 'im yawd, so di way 'im draw di firs' corner, EH-h-h-y-y! [screeching sound of car] And di parrot say, "Corner, Parson, corner to ras-s-s-s! Parson! Corner!"

Collected in Kingston on September 19, 1978.

Another tale concerning a holy man with an obscene parrot may be found in Dance, *Shuckin' and Jivin'*, No. 117.

75B Corner, Parson

One time there was a sailor man and a parson man. The sailor man have a pigeon and the parson man have one. So the parson man teach the pigeon about Bible. So the sailor man teach fi him own about bare bad wud. So the sailor man and the parson man have a contest. So the sailor man trick the parson man by take away the parson man pigeon.

So when time them went to the church now, the sailor man says. "Is my pigeon first have to recite." So the sailor man pigeon go up now and start to recite. So him recite very nice. And now the parson man put up fi him now, and thought him pigeon caan' lose. So when him put him up now deh now, him reach a part in the Bible and him begin to recite now. And when him reach a certain part, him say:

> Preach me, rass, preach me, rass,
> I'll pop off you fucking head!

The parson man ketch him and throw him in the car, and roll him round a corner. And he says, "A corner, to rass! Corner, to rass! Pop off mi fucking neck! Pop off mi fucking neck!"

Collected in Kingston on September 11, 1978.

76 Abraham, Abraham, What Is in Your Bosom?

When I was a little boy going to church, one Sunday Parson started to preach: "Abraham, Abraham, what is in your bosom? *Pluck* it out!"

A man was there, have a piece of puddin'[1] in his jacket pocket, and he tek it out and say, "What the hell you want me to expect! You want me to come here and sit down all day and die for hunger!"

Collected in Kingston on September 11, 1978.

A version of this tale appears in Parsons, *Folk-Lore of the Antilles,* Pt. 2, p. 452. Tales of sneaking food to church are popular in Black American lore as well: *see* Dorson, *Negro Folktales in Michigan,* pp. 172–73, and Dance, *Shuckin' and Jivin',* Nos. 110–11.

1. The West Indian pudding is very different from the American pudding. Made of cornmeal, potato, bread, and banana, it is firm and more like a cake in its consistency.

77 Shoo!

Dem have a deacon in a church. So every Sunday him go to church, him just sit up a di front bench, because him say him holy, you know. So one Saturday him bake a big potato pudding. So him don't want to give any one o' him family none, so him wrap it up in a tablecloth. And they have a big pimento tree in front of the church, so him put the pudding where him can see it. So him don't worry go up the front bench this Sunday. Him sit down in a di back bench and watching over the pudding.

So you want see a hog coming on and smell the pudding and [dramatizing] a sniff, sniff, sniff, and start smell it. So when him coming near, him say, "Shoo!" So the parson stop. So everybody look round. Him say, "Amen." So Parson start preach again. So the hog coming down and a start smell [illustrating], sniff, sniff, sniff. Him say, "Shoo, you sinner! Shoo, you rass! Shoo, you rass cloth! Shoo, you Bumbo cloth! Shoo, you pussy cloth!"

Everybody just start run and raise up a di church and run him out a di district. Him couldn't stay in di district. Found out say him is a sinner, you know.

Collected in Kingston on September 21, 1978.

A version of this tale appears in Dance, *Shuckin' and Jivin',* No. 111.

78 Puss

This is about the minister preaching in church, preaching on a Sunday in church. So his house, the rectory, was nearby. So the maid cook the food and laid it on the dining table where he could stay on the pulpit and see it. So they have a cat at the house, and the cat—while he was PRE-E-A-CHING! PRE-E-A-CHING! PRE-E-A-CHING to the people, he was watching the food with his eyes [dramatizing worried minister cutting eyes at food], and PRE-E-A-CHING! PRE-E-A-CHING [dramatizing fervent delivery with eyes

on the food]! He see that the cat now jump on the TAble and going to . . .
lifting the towel! Him say, "AND DOWN TO THE VERY . . . PUSS-S-S!"

Collected in Woodside on September 6, 1978.

79 Give Me Even One

Well, you have this parson man now, him have a maid. So 'im goin' to
church de day now, so 'im goin' tell di maid say, "Cook two ducks today for
dinner." Say, "All right." And draw di recipe and ting how she must look after
di duck. So 'im gon' a church now. The maid looking after the duck, man,
and finish, because when di duck smell so sweet dat she say, "Ahhh, wait. Ah
haffi tek a little taste of this duck yah." And she pinch off a little piece, taste
di duck: "Ahhh." Say, "Wha! It taste sweet!" She pinch off a likkle piece, pinch
off a nex' piece, pinch off a nex' piece, till one of di duck finish. She say, "Boy,
dis duck yah nice, you nuh." She jus' turn pon di nex' duck, taste, taste di
duck, till di two duck finish now.

When she realize say the two ducks finish now, she start fret. By the
time when him come home, weh she ah go get duck fi gi him now? So she
hear 'im a come now. So she start fret. Parson come in now, so Parson have
a knife—as Parson come een, I don' know wah get in a Parson. Parson tek up
him knife and start sharpen it like Parson know say someting wrong. So Parson
start sharpen him big butcher knife [dramatizing].

So di maid she go outside, and she see di gardener bredder, and she say,
"Jim, Parson say him waan' you two balls today, you nuh. Parson a cut out
you two balls, you nuh." So Jim say, "Wha! A True?" She say, "Yes, man,
come mek me show you him a sharpen the knife." She just call Jim now and
show Jim and say, "See him deh?" Jim see Parson a sharpen him knife now,
man. So Jim do so and jump through the gate. She just tun inna di house and
say, "Parson, Parson, Jim eat off you two duck. See him a run go down di road
deh. Jim tek way di two duck dem."

So Parson come back out and see Jim run way: "Hey, Jim, give me one.
You can keep one, give me even one, even one!"

Jim say, "Parson, one of my balls, sah! An caan' gi you one!"

Parson saying, "Even one, Jim, even one!"

Poor Jim chase gone down the road, and Parson chase him. Parson running him down for di duck, and him ah run, say Parson want one of him
balls.

Collected in Kingston on October 6, 1978.
This is Motif K2137, "The Priest's Guest and the Eaten Chicken," in Baughman, *Type and Motif-*

Index, and Type 1741, "The Priest's Guest and the Eaten Chickens," in Flowers, *West Indian Types and Motifs.* Variants of this tale appear in Parsons, *Folk-Lore of the Sea Islands,* No. 140; Parsons, *Folk-tales of Andros Island,* No. 36; and Beckwith, *Jamaican Anansi Stories,* No. 130. It has also been collected in Grenada and Dominica.

80 Put Pepper in the Pot

This story is about a lady and a little boy. One day the little boy's mother was going to church. So she put the pot on the fire and told the boy that when the pot is almost cook, he should put pepper in it. But there is a little puppy in the home name Pepper, and while the food was cooking the little boy run and catch Pepper and put it in the pot. And the little dog boil and boil until the teeth skin.

So the little boy run to church and say, "Mama, Mama, you siddown in deh a sing. Come here." The mother still singing, wouldn't come. The little boy say, "Mama, Mama, mi call you. Pepper boil till him teeth skin!"

Collected in Kingston on October 30, 1978.

This is Motif J2462.1, "The Dog Parsley in the Soup," in Baughman, *Type and Motif-Index.*

Thompson (*Motif-Index of Folk-Literature*) notes versions from Lithuania and Russia. A similar tale in which a boy left to watch the pot runs into church to report problems to his mother may be found in Dance, *Shuckin' and Jivin',* No. 123; Parsons, *Folk-Lore of the Antilles,* p. 453, and several other collections from the United States.

81A You Tink a Mi One a Sinner?

One time Parson a keep church and pray. Parson say, "The day of the Lord. . . . And when that day come He's going to blow a trumpet." And white man a pass and hear him now, and go fi a trumpet and blow di trumpet. And Parson say, "God a come!"

And everybody run out a di church, and di Parson run out, you know, and barbwire hole Parson. And Parson say, "Leggo mi nuh, God. You tink a mi one a sinner?"[1]

Collected in Kingston on October 6, 1978.

This is Type 1833.J, "Preacher Says: 'Let Gabriel Blow His Horn!'" in Baughman, *Type and Motif-Index.* Versions appear in Parsons, *Folk-Lore of the Sea Islands,* p. 58; Fauset, "Tales and Riddles," p. 552; Dorson, *Negro Folktales in Michigan,* pp. 169–70 (reprinted in Dorson, *American Negro Folktales,* p. 336; Sterling, *Laughing,* pp. 118–19; Abrahams, *Deep Down,* pp. 207–8; Perdue, "I Swear," p. 33; Irvis, "Negro Tales from Eastern New York," p. 176; and Dance, *Shuckin' and Jivin',* No. 73.

1. Do you think I alone am a sinner?

81B You Tink a Mi One a Sinner?

This one now is bout a parson now. So every day him sit down inna church pon di pulpit [shouting]: "Brothers and Sisters, when you shall hear the trumpet sound! . . . " So them say, "God is gon' come when the trumpet sounds."

Here a sailor man passing, well hungry and nuh have no money. Him spend out him money during the night, and is a man that play trumpet too. So him go pon di church top and put di trumpet inna him mout' and [imitating man blowing trumpet]: "Pop-pop-a-deepee!"

So everybody just get up out a di church and just start ru-u-u-n now. So a one-foot man did[1] in a di church. So since him couldn't run, him sit down, which part the man [sailor] start fi come and start gather up the collection and ting. Hear the one-foot man now: "Lawd, God, you know mi is di only righteous one in here."

[Dramatizing the sailor hitting him] Hear him nuh: "If you never have one-foot you would a run too."

By this time the parson now run, run! When you check out, the parson never righteous, you know. Him one sinner. After him reach at a wire fence, the wire hold back him gown, and him look back and say, "Leggo, me rass cloth! You think a me one a sinner?"

Collected in Kingston on September 21, 1978.
1. Was.

81C You Tink a Mi One a Sinner?

Congregation in church. Parson preaching that judgment is near. Someone went on the church roof and was knocking. The people thought it was judgment coming, so they began to run. One man was there with one leg, so he could not run. Everybody left him in there. He saw a man coming and thought it was God. He said to the man, "Massa God, only me one leave because I have faith." The man hit him in his head and said, "Is because you can't run why you leave in here."

Given to me in writing by a teacher in Kingston in November 1978.

82 Take Me as a Yam

One night there was night service in a certain church, and each person got up to give their testimonies.

Everybody was feeling real good. Soon the choir started singing this song:

> Oh take me as I am.
> Oh take me as I am.
> My only plea, Christ died for me,
> Oh take me as I am.

A man who was sitting at the back of the congregation stood up and testified: "I am glad that my God didn't take me as a coco or a dasheen, but he take me as a yam."

Given to me in writing by a Kingston resident in November 1978.

83 I' Holey Holey, but I' Clean

This is about a woman that went to church, and she have holey, holey panty. While they were singing [dramatizing]: "Ho-ly, ho-ly, ho-o-o-ly . . . ," the woman jump up: "I' holey holey, but i' clean!"

Collected in Kingston on October 30, 1978.

84 I Feel

One day there was a man in a church have a sore foot, and when him have a sore foot so, him go into a church. And a lady was in dere, and the lady step pon him sore foot. And him began to say [chanting], "I fe-e-e-l-l. . . ."

And the parson say, "Tell the congregation what you feel, my bradder."

And him say, "Di rass cloth woman go walk, and the woman nah look weh him put him foot, and the woman step on a mi sore foot. I fe-e-e-l-l, I fe-e-l-l. . . ."

Collected in Kingston on September 11, 1978.

85 Hallelujah

This is about an old lady going to a church, and when the minister preach, the lady always cry out, "Hallelujah!"

So one day the minister gave the lady a pack of rice and told her that she

must stop crying for Hallelujah. But this particular day the lady just couldn'
keep it. So she jump up in the church and say, "Rice and rice, Hallelujah!"

Collected in Kingston on October 30, 1978.
A variant appears in Perdue, *Weevils,* pp. 98–99."

86 A Fly Is on Your Horse' Conclusion

One day a man went to church. So the parson preach a sermon. So the
man like the sermon. So when they come out of the church now, man, they
were shaking hands. So when this man shake the parson hand now, he say,
"Parson, I like your sermon, but I like the tail part best." So the parson said,
"Next time you don't say *tail;* you say *conclusion.*"

So another day he go back to church now, man. So the parson ride a
horse. So the man saw a fly on the tail of the horse. So the man come back
now and say, "Parson, Parson, a fly is on your horse' conclusion."

Collected in Kingston on October 30, 1978.

87 You Have Any?

This is about a gentleman and a lady who went to church to get married, but the lady was sort of deaf. She couldn't hear properly. So the parson
said to her, "You have any ring?" So she didn't answer. The parson say, "You
have any ring?" She still didn't reply. So the parson say, "You have any . . .
[holds one finger up and rubs up and down it with his hand]?

She say, "Two times last night, Parson, and one before the wedding."

Collected in Kingston on October 30, 1978.

88 God, Heaven Post Office

Well, you haf dis man yah weh a suffa. So him say, "Bwoy, mi hear say
if you pray to God, God will gi' you tings." So 'im pray, pray, pray, pray, and
caan' get no answer fi 'im prayer. So 'im say, "Bwoy, mi a go write God a letter
and see weh God a deal wid," because 'im caan' understand how God won'
answer him prayer.

So him write di letter, and say, "Right now, God, I a suffa. I owe sixty poun' fi mi rent and I don' have it, and di people dem out fi tun out mi and mi ten pickney. Asking you fi some help." So him address di letter:

> God
> Heaven Post Office
> Paradise Districk

So him pos' di letter. Now when the letter reach a di Post Office, General Post Office now, di censor a go tru, everybody see dis letter now: God, Heaven Post Office, Paradise Districk. So dem get curious. Dem tek di letter now and open it and see di contents of di letter now. So dem say, bwoy, dis man really in a desperate position, dem a go trump up and help him. So dem trump up, trump up, trump up. Dem a get fifty-eight poun'. Dem couldn't get di sixty poun'. So dem say, *all right.* Dem put di fifty-eight poun' in a envelope and pos' it back to di man. When dem pos' it back to di man now, dis man tek it: "God send back letter!" 'Im open di letter and see fifty-eight poun'. Him say, "Lawd, haf mercy! I'm a write back to God and tell 'im say, dem damn people deh down a di Post Office tief out *two poun'* out a di letter."

Collected in Kingston on October 6, 1978.

89 God Rob Me

I will tell you bout a likkle man now who used to go to church and pray. This man go to church every day and him pray. Him have a little problem, financial problem. So dis man go to church every day and pray and ask God to mek him achieve twenty poun' free to start a business. If him get di twenty poun' and start a business, 'im will 'elp di church. So di parson say, "You must pray every day and God reely assist an' give you twenty pound, start di business and can assist di church." When him go to him bed a night time he mus' pray *hard*." Go to him bed and pray, and the parson go a 'im 'ouse and listen ('im a pray a' 'im 'ouse and ting) and put down twenty poun' in a 'im doorway, and 'im say God sent twenty poun' fi 'im.

Glad! 'Im start di business now. Well, couple weeks afta di business *mash* up. So di business *mash* up now. And 'im go back to di parson and say, "Bwoy, di business mash up, business bad. It mash up. I would like fi get twenty poun' more fi start di business." Parson tell 'im fi go back, go pray again and ting, and God will gi 'im a twenty poun' more. So 'im go back and pray and pray and pray, pray again. Parson put down *nineteen* poun' dis time. When 'im wake up again and him find nineteen poun', him say, "God rob me one poun'!"

Collected in Kingston on October 6, 1978.

VI

Tales about Rastafarians

Introduction

One of the most popular, most widely known, and most influential folk movements in Jamaica is Rastafarianism,[1] which has its roots in the earliest protest movements in that country, going back even to the Maroon societies, and which can be directly traced back to the Marcus Garvey movement. Garvey—the founder of the Universal Negro Improvement Association, who preached Black nationalism and sought to establish a Black state in Africa to which Blacks in the Diaspora could be repatriated—prophesied the appearance of a Black king: "Look to Africa, when a black king shall be crowned, for the day of deliverance is near."[2] The crowning of Ras Tafari as the Emperor Haile Selassie, King of Kings and the Lion of Judah (thus in the legendary line of King Solomon) in Ethiopia in November 1930 was viewed as a confirmation of Garvey's prediction as well as a fulfillment of Biblical prophecy.

Though there are many different Rastafarian sects with varying beliefs and practices, most of them are characterized by a rejection of Babylon (which may be viewed as Jamaica, especially the government and the police, and more broadly as the Western world); by an acceptance of the divinity of Ras Tafari; by a belief that Ethiopia is the home of the Black man, to which he should be re-

Social

86

patriated; and by an assertion of the superiority of the Black man, who shall in the future rule the world. Some of the Ras Tafari are characterized by their wearing of dreadlocks and by their use of ganga both for its therapeutic effects and in religious rituals.

The Rastafarian movement has spread to several other islands, to the United States, and to England. No contemporary aspect of Jamaican life has been more widely studied and reported on than Rastafarianism. Rastafarian musicians have achieved worldwide acclaim with protest songs in a distinctive beat combining ska and rock steady and known as reggae; Rastafarian art is unquestionably one of the most vital and influential aspects of contemporary Jamaican art, and Rastafarian speech is one of the most significant contemporary folk influences on West Indian writers, having motivated a whole group of poets known as the "Dub Poets" and exerted an impact on the language of practically every Jamaican poet (as well as numerous other West Indian poets) writing today.

The selections that follow represent folk reactions to Rastafarianism — parodies of prayers and other rituals, tales about Ras Tafari that satirize some of the aspects of the brotherhood that have been frequently criticized by detractors: their criminality, their use of ganga, their sense of their divinity, etc. While some sense of the speech and practices of the Ras Tafari may be garnered from such selections as those that follow, anyone interested in a serious study of the philosophy/religion, its rituals, its achievements, and its contributions to Jamaican life and culture should consult some of the many studies of the movement, such as Joseph Owens, *Dread: The Rastafarians of Jamaica* (Kingston: Sangster's Book Stores, 1976); Leonard E. Barrett, *The Rastafarians: The Dreadlocks of Jamaica* (London: Heinemann, 1977); Barrett, *The Rastafarians: Sounds of Cultural Dissonance* (Boston: Beacon Press, 1977); and Ernest Cashmore, *Rastaman: The Rastafarian Movement in England* (London: George Allen & Unwin, 1979).

---

1. Although the members of the religion are popularly known as Rastafarians, they prefer to be called Ras Tafari.

2. This oft-quoted statement is attributed to Garvey during his farewell address when he left Jamaica for the United States in 1916. It is found in varied forms in the many studies of Rastafarianism, and I have reproduced it here as it appears in the seminal study of Rastafarianism: M. G. Smith, Roy Augier, and Rex Nettleford, *The Rastafari Movement in Kingston, Jamaica* (Kingston: Institute of Social and Economic Research, 1960), p. 5.

90A Hearken unto My Voice

A man was smoking mariguana,[1] and he was praising the God that he worship, start to say:

Hearken unto my voice,
O Lord, God Almighty,
Have mercy also upon I and answer I.
Bend thy face unto me,
Hide not thy face
Far from I.
Put not thy servant away
. . . .
Leave I, O God,
But forsake I not.
Sette Messgana,[1] Cheddidee,
Emanuel, Hallelujah,
Almighty. Dreadlocks.
Omnipotent.
Selah. Selah.

This obvious parody of a Rastafarian prayer was collected in Kingston on September 21, 1978.
1. The informant's pronunciation of *marijuana.*
2. Rastafarian interpretation of the Coptic language, meaning the ruler of the earth.

90B Hearken unto My Voice

'Earken unto my voice, my King and My God,
For unto Thee will I flee,
Sette Messgana,
Mio Chezedee,
Emanuel, Hallelu-Jah, Almighty Dreadlocks.
I call upon di Lawd God Almighty,
Selassie-I,
Wid my whole heart,
Who is wanted to be praised
As di supreme God of the (H)I-niverse,[1]
God of all Gods,
King of all Kings,
And Lord of all Lords.
Behold di Divine God
Of the Secret of Life,
King of Eternity-y-y-y,
Immm-or-tallll, In-vi-n-sible,
The only wise God to be praised,
A-l-lah, Swaneye.
And Him only shall I bow down

And worship
Sincerely
As di I-rator²
of di (H)I-niverse.
And him only shall I give my sacrifice of Joy
And burnt offering
And thanksgiving
In His tabernacle,
A-a-ah-h-h,
I will sing, I will sing,
Praises unto di Lord,
Blessed of all those have put dere trust
In Nebuchadnezzar, di Emperor,
King of Kings, and Lord of Lords,
His Imperial Majesty,
The Conquering Lion of the tribe of Jud-ea,
Jahovah Humble High,
God Almighty,
RASS-tafari,
Selassie-I,
POWER of the mighty Trinity,
God di Father,
God the Son,
And God the Holy Spirit of I-raa-tion,³
T'ree in One,
Or One in T'ree,
Divine Divinity.
A priest come to you at the Bar,
Sette Messgana,
Mio Chezedee, Emanuel, Hallelu-Jah, Almighty, Dreadlocks,
Ominipotent,
He honor
SELAH, SELAH,
LABA SABBAT TUNYAEE
MAGROCK, SHADROCK, NABROBRA⁴
NEBADALESE, SECAANA, CANNA
Upon Hope Road,
IKKANEE, NARA, KASHA.

Collected in Kingston on October 6, 1978.

1. This is an example of the Rastafarian's frequent substitution of *I* for the initial syllable in a word. Here *universe* becomes *I-niverse*, with the speaker imposing the initial *H* sound.

2. Following the same principle, *Creator* becomes *I-rator.*
3. Creation.
4. Much of the humor in this parody of a Rastafarian prayer comes from the speaker's distortion of Biblical allusions, such as, in this case, Shadrach, Meschack, and Abednego.

91 Love Selassie-I

[*Chanting*]	So if I lie
	God cry,
[*Other*]	Love Selassie-I-e-e
[*Other*]	Et-et-oh-oh.
	If you 'ate 'Im you will die.
[*Other*]	No cho.
	Love 'Im you will live.
[*Other*]	Rasta-fa-ri.
	Love Selassie-I-e-e-e.
	Love humanity.
	In a dis yah community.
[*Other*]	Ridim.[1]
	So mi say fi love of di African berry,
	So mi say it mek you feel God damn cherry,
	So if you love Jamaican berry,
	Man, mi say it mek mi feel for-m, for merry. . . .

Collected in Kingston on September 18, 1978, from a child, exact age unknown.
1. Rhythm.

92 Blessing Chalice

I goin' tell you a story about a Dreadlocks. After 'im done cut up 'im mariguana and ting (weed, man) and put in a kuchy[1] and ting, and den, you know, and den di brethren look pon him and say:

Yi-ye mi tumuck.[2]
Bless the chalice.

So a toast follow, toast di chalice. Di man stand up and,

Oh, Jah,[3] Selassie-I,
God is a Black man.

So him tek way di chalice from the man and say: "A what's dat you a say, man? God a which Black man?"[4] So him tek di chalice and him look on 'im. Hmmmmm. Caan' remember exactly what 'im say now, but 'im say something like:

Bungo nostrilise[5]
Dis country 'Im seet and vomit thru Him eyes,[6]
Selassie-I-I, fire, flame. . . .

Something like that, and when him say *flame* now, the man just draw the stick
a matches, you know, and just put over di kuchy, and 'im just suck i', tek it
een, you nuh, still drawing di air. Them have all different kind of way of bless-
ing chalice.

Collected in Kingston on October 6, 1978.
1. Vessel of the chalice, the elaborate pipe used to smoke marijuana during Rastafarian rituals.
During these rituals, pure, unmixed ganga is taken from a bowl in the center of the table and placed
in the chalice, which is then passed around to individuals seated in a circle around the table.
2. Are you hearing what I'm saying?
3. Haile Selassie's name before he took his title was Jah Ras Tafari. Thus *Jah* means God, which
is synonymous, of course, with Selassie.
4. Negative reaction to the claim that God is Black.
5. Phrase of a very strict sect of Rastafarians—Bobos.
6. Curse of the Bobos: God will see what is going on and punish people.

93 I Feel Like I Want Run

Well, one time three men sitting down and smoking them chalice, you
know, but two is professional chalice smokers, while one is the first him goin'
try it, so. The two men siddown and puff, puff, puff [inhaling deeply], and
he get in now. And him amateur now—so him get in now, and so him a wonder
and say, "Wait, I must try dat now." And him say, "Your chalice." And pass
the chalice to the amateur. Now the amateur puff, puff, puff [inhaling deeply].
So him get in now and him get in now, and him just come so, and just hear
when him pass the chalice to the man and say, "Your chalice. I feel like I want
run . . . and I am going to run."

He did get up and run.

Collected in Kingston on September 21, 1978.

94A Rastafari Drop from Sky

[*Reciting*] Rastafari drop from sky
        Bus' 'im eye
        Tink a lie
        Ask a Rastafari
        From sky.

Collected in Kingston on September 19, 1978.

94B Rastafari Drop from Sky

Rastafari
Drop from sky
Dirty up him brown tie
Tink a lie
Ask di Rasta
From sky.

Collected in Kingston on September 19, 1978.

94C Rastafari Drop from Sky

I drop from sky
You tink a lie?
Look into mi eye
You see pig sty.

Collected in Kingston on September 19, 1978, from a child, exact age unknown.

94D Rastafari Drop from Sky

I drop from sky
Drop in a pig sty
Nassi up mi bow tie
Tink a lie
Look inna mi eye
You see Jah
Rastafari.

Collected in Kingston on September 19, 1978, from a child, exact age unknown.

95 Lucky Me Never Step inna It

One time you haf a Dread, you know, say, Michael, you nuh, so 'im a run down a train, but de train lef' 'im now, so 'im a pass now, and 'im a pass, and 'im a "Whee-ooo" [whistling], and when 'im look 'im see a big load of filth. So 'im step over di filth and go so and pass, and 'im go so and look back and say, "Wait!" And jump back over it and say, "Wait, dis look like filth."

Him go so and dip 'im hand inna it and say, "Dis fava filth, dis taste like filth," and step over back again and look back again, and say, "Chi-chi, but wait, a filth, a lucky say me never step inna it." And gon'.

Collected in Kingston on October 8, 1978.

96 Rape, Rape, Rape

[*Singing*]   Rape, rape, rape,
Lawd, mi say di Rasta man
Rape. . . .
[*Conversation*] Rape ooo?
Rape a nice white girl and. . . .
[*Singing*]   Rape, rape, rape,
Lawd, mi say di Rasta man
Rape. . . .
[*Conversation*] Rape ooo?
Rape a nice likkle white girl down di street.
I would say,
Cho.

social

Collected in Kingston on September 19, 1978.

97 They Shall Stumble and Fell

One day a Rasta man was walking and he was very, very hungry, real hungry that he almost feel like dying. So him went into a market to get some food, but him didn't have the money. Well, him see a man selling some banana and tings like dat, so him beg the man one banana. The man say him caan' give him none because from mawning him don't sell not even one, and it look hard fi him give it away, just like that. So him decide fi tek up one banana and went away. So when him took the banana now, the man start run him down wid a piece of stick in a him hand. Lick after him and him say, "Miss, you fool, you moder never go to school." The man lick after him again and dis time the man drop. Hear the Rasta man in return: "When the wicked, ever my enemy and my foe came up against I to eat up my flesh, they shall stumble and fell."

social

Collected in Kingston on September 21, 1978.

98 Lawd Jesus Chris'!

One time a lady came from foreign as you do. When she came from foreign, you know, them come in Jamaica, and so she get in a Jolly Joseph bus,[1] and she saw a Rasta man. And when she saw a Rasta man she was very astonish. So she bawl out, "Lawd Jesus Chris'!"

Rasta man him turn, say to her, "My lady, go thy way, tell no one that you have seen me."

Collected in Kingston on October 6, 1978.
1. JOS (Jamaican Omnibus Service) bus.

99 Born fi Heng, Caan' Drown

Well, when I was very small, you know, I was a regular yout'. I am at di sea, you know. We have a place weh we call Atom Hole, running water, where in di running stream, we call it Graveyard because many people drown in dat likkle stream dere if you cannot swim, you know. So that every mawning I used to go dere and see a man, a Rasta man, who can swim good good. So 'im have a mark on him neck, and 'im say, "Born fi heng, caan' drown." Any time him ah go chuck off, him say, "Born fi heng, caan' drown." And two somersault and you don't see him fi a long while. And you say, "Weh 'im deh? Weh 'im deh?" And see him come down at di end. And you have a nex' place down at the bottom on the current side go right down, name Red House, and 'im go up pon di top of it, and, "Born fi heng, caan' drown." And him chuck off of a di top and a man swear say him dead, fi swim come up the current well hard, you nuh, not every man can do it.

So me say, "Wait, di man deh look like him reely born fi heng and caan' drown." So it happen dat aroun' two weeks after now, mi go down deh and a fishing pon Red House and, you know, throw over mi line and, you know, catching a few fish. Well, di man go up on di housetop and [yelling], "Born fi heng, caan' drown." Me nuh pay him no mind. So me say, "Cho, him can swim and ting," and him friend dem, "Raah-h" and cheer him and him chuck off! Well, everybody waiting—dem caan' see him come up. Dem say, "Cho, oonoo no know John, man, John caan' drown, man. John soon come up." Dem see little blood float up on di top of di water. Dem say, "Cho, a nuh nuttin' yet man. A mussi a fish under deh a bleed or some dead ting, man. John caan' drown. John born fi heng."

Until now John don't come up.

Collected in Kingston on October 6, 1978.
"Born fi heng, etc." is a common expression in Jamaica.

VII

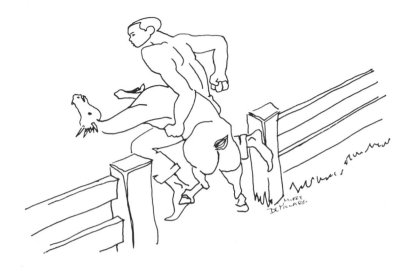

Miscellaneous Tales

Introduction

The tales in this chapter touch upon a variety of familiar subjects in the folk-lore of many nations, as well as a few that are unique to Jamaica.

A few of these tales deal with the problems faced by Blacks during their early years in Jamaica, including particularly their experiences during slavery. They attack the atrocities visited upon the slaves and rejoice in their victories over the masters. Such narratives do not seem to be as widespread in Jamaica as they remain in the United States, possibly because slavery ended earlier in Jamaica, and possibly also because, as Eddie Burke told me, when he was grow-ing up in Jamaica (first quarter of this century), Jamaicans strove to escape the slave consciousness, and thus tales of slavery were not popular.[1]

Some of the materials in this chapter treat very traditional themes that have long been popular in many areas—the girl marrying a monster or animal in dis-guise, the person transformed into an animal, the cruel villain becoming the victim of his own evil deed, the water spirit's revenge on offending mortals.

It is not surprising that in a country like Jamaica, where more of its people live elsewhere than remain there, a great many tales would focus upon the Jamaican abroad. Most of these tales turn upon the ignorance of the Jamaican

95

in a more cosmopolitan and sophisticated environment or upon his efforts to put on airs upon his return, especially his affected speech.

Many of the other tales deal with a variety of physical and mental defects that one frequently finds jokes about: the insane behavior of madmen who sometimes outsmart the so-called sane; the ridiculous antics of the numbskulls; the farcical problems and antics of stutterers, of the blind, and of the deaf; and the hysterical behavior of the coward.

Another large body of materials here may be classified as tall tales. Richard Dorson notes that the tall tale grew out of the seventeenth-century travelers' tales that greatly embellished the strange and marvelous creatures and events they experienced in their travels to America and the Far East.[2] The marvelous exploits of Jamaicans in these tales who stop airplanes and trains with their feet or swim and catch fish are no less wonderful than the exploits of such popular American tall-tale heroes as Davy Crockett. A frequently appearing character in the Jamaican tall tales who qualifies as a legendary figure is Father Forsythe, whose incredible eating feats are the subject of several of these stories and whose authenticity is attested to by numerous informants who recount his exploits.

Several of the pieces here, as in other chapters in this work, derive their humor from their emphasis on forbidden themes. Indeed, the majority of folk materials deal with what are generally considered risque and vulgar subjects. It has been widely observed that the apparently "innocent" children's fairy tales and nursery rhymes frequently have sexual implications. And D. J. Bennett has asserted that even clean jokes, the most innocent kind, are sexually motivated.[3] Certainly Freud has made clear that humor is and always has been largely motivated by the enjoyment of forbidden themes, by the pleasure of rebelling against society's efforts to repress what it considers lewd or hostile cravings.[4] Thus it is that one finds that excessive profanity, sex, and scatology are among the most popular and mirth-provoking subjects in the tales in this chapter and elsewhere, whether they be directly treated, as in "3-F" (Tale 158), or indirectly and symbolically presented, as in "The Groom Is a Snake" (Tale 105).

---

1. Interview with Eddie Burke, Santa Cruz, November 4, 1978.

2. Richard Dorson, "Legends and Tall Tales," in *American Folklore*, ed. Tristram Coffin III (1968; rpt. Washington, D.C.: Voice of America Forum Lectures, 1974), p. 188.

3. "The Psychological Meaning of Anti-Negro Jokes," *Fact*, March-April 1964, p. 53.

4. See Sigmund Freud, "Wit and Its Relation to the Unconscious," in *The Basic Writings of Sigmund Freud*, ed. A. A. Brill (New York: Modern Library, 1938).

100 Nine-Finger Jack

Like Captain Morgan's daughter that captured Port Royal. Di' you learn about it?

[Dance] No.

Well, the first man that captured Port Royal, his daughter—he had a daughter by a Black woman—and he were a white man. You know being here and alone and all that, he see here now is Black people to move with. He go with a Black woman, and get that girl. She were a hero. For imagine (*you* don't know the *distance*, but from St. Elizabeth she walk on *foot*, not on the *road*, in the *bushes*, to Morant Bay, where she met with a man that they call Nine-Finger Jack, you see. And for lifesaving sake,[1] she gots to decide that she fall in love with Nine-Finger Jack, and Nine-Finger Jack, he were on his journey too, you see; he was on his journey, and the both of them meet. And he were a *dangerous* man, and seeing him, she jus' figure to herself who he be. She hide, and as she see that he is going to see her, she look out. And as her eyes blent on him,[2] she just hail out, "I wonder what can this be; it's the first in my life I have ever seen a man that I have fall in love with at the first sight." And he say the same. And then now the both of them start to moving and met with some of her father men. And being Captain Morgan's daughter, they have to obey her as they would obey her father. And as they start to draw sword (for there wasn't anything like guns), she says, "No, if it is to be, it will have to be two, not he alone. It's the first man that I ever fall in love with, and I decide to die with him." And it carry on and on. They walk until—they walk their shoes off their feet, through bush, you know, through the forest—they can't go on the road. That's where Paul Bogle and those men—Paul Bogle was hang by the market square in Morant Bay, and Gordon, all of those men, during those while—they were warring while Captain Morgan were warring for Port Royal over by Palisadoes. And when they was through and they reach their destination, they decide on that they have to kill Nine-Finger Jack. And she decide to suggest to her father, it have to be both of them. And then she hug Nine-Finger Jack, and he hug her. And they just dash, both of them, to death.

Collected in Kingston from a resident of Cassava River on July 8, 1978.

This informant's Nine-Finger Jack is clearly derived from Three Finger Jack, the popular legendary figure whose mother raised him to exact vengeance upon the white master who enslaved and killed his father. In his first attempt he was captured, but he killed his guards and escaped, taking with him the hated slave master, whom he then enslaved. None dared to track the feared fugitive except another Black Maroon, Quashee. During their encounter, Jack lost his fingers, thus the name Three Finger Jack.

1. To save her life.
2. Met with his.

101 Do Good, Do Good

The slave master went to buy some slaves. When he reaches and select his slaves, there were one in the lot of the people that were there that he *wanted*, and then the man [who] was selling the slaves said to him, "You better not take *that* one." And he says yes, he would like to take 'im. He says, "No, if you take that one you will be *sorry,* for he isn't going to do anything; he doesn't work; he don't do anything." He say he will make him work. Him say, "I wouldn't *advise* you." And you know, he t'ought it was—he t'ought the salesman were craffing him den, would want him to get him. So he just say, "Well, if you want him you can take him on your own risk, not mine." And he says, well, he will take him on his risk, and he take him. And after taking him home (they went like today, and the day that he went, it was three days after) the vendor, slave buyer, and his wife were contemplating. She said to him that the boys are out hiking for three days now and they don't come back; and they usual to be back in one day from morning till evening. And they gone now three days and they don't come back yet. He say, "Well, they must be. . . ." He don't feel like anything happen to them, and he try to coax his wife the best manner he could that she might forget. Well, he says the next morning when he was taking out his slaves to work, he call on John. That slave name John Do Good. So he call to John and tell John to come. And when they call him for breakfas', John went in and have his breakfas'. And when he ready now for work and tell him to get out now, in line for work, John says, "Not I." The man says, "You gots to work." John says, "I never tell you dat." And insist on him and he wouldn' leave, and the man leave him that morning. The second morning he came back and insisted on him again to come. And he says no, he isn't goin' to work; he never tell him that he wants to work. And the man get vex and leave him. And then he went and suggest to some other . . . some other vendors like himself, what has happened. One says that he want to tink that that is the very man that he refuse, that the man that sell him, refuse to give him. All right. Him say, "Well, I know what I will do. I am going to hit him some tarrable blows tomorra mornin'."

And the next mornin' he got breakfas', and after breakfas' he says, "Well now, John!" He call him out first. "Come." John says, "*I am not coming.*" And he was still on his drum—"Do good, do good" [illustrating on table]—you know, when each time he hit the drum with his hand, it speak out the words, "Do good, do good." And the man started—the wife were upstairs in her bed—and he started to hit John some *tarrable* blows, and when he hit John and hit him and hit him, the wife *scream* out upstairs. Her husband downstairs tinking that is, you know, sorrowful feelings she keep, she gather now for the slave getting hits downstairs. One of his friend came (h)on and said to him, "You missis is screaming *hard* upstairs." He say, "Cho, you know what—tender heart, man, tender heart." WAP! [hitting John] And John say, "Do good" to every hit him hit John, John say, "Do good." And the *last* blow that he gave to John, his wife hail out by the window: "Oh, God, don't hit him again. If you do I'll die, for every blow that you give to him, it register to me. Is I who getting them up here. I can't take any more." And the man stop from knocking John and run upstairs to his wife. And then the wife *explain* to him, show him her entire body. She was as red, some little blood streaks coming, and that is what blows him giving John she was getting them upstairs. So then he decide then that he isn't carrying John, *but* his wife says to him, "We cannot keep him. He is no good. He is a *horrable* man. We have to send him away." And the husband say, "Yes, I am goin' to put him away. He and the wild beasts of the forest will have some argument." And he told John, said to him, "All right, sir," and him knock his drum again and say, "Do good, do good."

So then after John were ready, for as him tell him him pack his two little pieces of clothes and ready. And the wife got out of bed; she came down to the kitchen and says to the maid, "Please to come upstairs. John is leaving this morning, you know, and I want to get a few journey cakes to give him to carry along with him." And she turn from the kitchen and says to the girl, "When you pour the flour out and finish kneading it, bring it upstairs to me before you fry it." And the girl says to her, yes. And the girl take the dough upstairs to her, and she poison it, put poison to kill John. And after she did that, she tell the girl that the girl is not to eat any of it, and she is to put it, jus' mek that loaf for him alone. And she tell her what she is to fry it in. And she did. And after finish frying it, she came down and pack it out her own hand and gave it to the girl—she make them upstairs and give the girl, and when they finish frying, the girl tell her. And she come downstairs and pack them, wrap them and pack them up and she gave John two—is two that, you know—and a bottle of water for him to travel with to drink. The water were poison, the flour poison. And (h)after John take it from her—for he just had breakfas'; he never wanted anything more—he pack it in his bag, put it on his back, and take his drum in his hand and knocking his drum: "Do good, do good."

So the father told the boys before he leave that he is going for some slaves. They *never* hear anyting like sounds of any drum business before, and while both of them in the bush, they can't find their way home. And then they feel tired and hungry and thirsty, and they can't get any water. And they lay down and were resting, and they hear a drum. And one says to the (h)other, "Praise be to God, we are nearing home. Daddy went to get slaves and is Africa him gone, and him seem to bring them home. . . . Them drum. Lissen, lissen, you hear?" And the brother say to him, "Yes. . . ."

And while they were walking pas' across the desert, the drum coming (h)on nearer to them, and they walk and walk through a track, and the track right out into one track that can come right in. And when the boys came up, John said to them, "Little (h)Arons, little (h)Arons?" And the boys say, "Yes." "Your mummy and daddy is pining for you both. What happen?" And they tell him, and him tell them that he is one of his father's slaves. Say, "We are *dying* of hunger and we are *thirsty*. Is it far from here to my home?" He says,

"Yes, yes, it's very far still, but I have got something here. These are made by your mother own hand, and is she that parcel them. I don't touch them yet; and this bottle of water, your modder gave it to me." And the two boys sit in the grass, and John stay there with them. And the both of them (h)ate the journey cakes, they call them, and after finishing eating, they drink the water, and after drinking the water John say good-bye and them to John. And John tell them to follow the track, don't turn anywhere, just follow the track, don't turn nowhere.

And when John gone, the modder came by the window standing and listening to the sound of John's drum, till she don't hear it again, and she removed; she say he must be eating and she remove from where she was. And as she remove from the windown, one of the boy call out to her, and she *run* downstairs to embrace her son. And she turn and ask him where is his brother. He says to her that we both were hungry and thirsty, and on our way (h)out we heard a drum; and as Daddy say he gone for slaves to Africa, we said then is must one of Daddy's slaves for hear a drum. And we were glad that we heard the drum, for we feel that we were nearing home, and when we reach out on a straight track we met a man. And 'e knows Daddy name, and he says to us, "Little (h)Arons," and we answer and was glad, and he said, "I am one of your Daddy slave." And I told him that I were hungry and thirsty, and I ask him if home is far from here. And he says to me, "Yes, very far—but have something. Here is two journey cake for the both of you. Have it. And here is a bottle of water. It's your mother own hand that bake these journey cake and she parcel dem. I don't touch dem. Have dem." And we (h)ate the journey cake and drank the water, and around a mile from where we finish eating, my brother drop, he fainted, and I turn and hold him up, but I couldn't move him. And he just gasp and died [gesture to indicate corpse]. And I come, I take my own time and walk on and walk on. And I slip down, I slip around three miles from here, and I trow up—some pain! All about me is pain." And he just started trow off again, right in front of his mother. And by the time she hold him up, he was stiff dead.

She says, "Oh, my God! I have killed my sons. I have killed my sons! Oh, God!" The maid run out as she said that. The maid run outside, and as the maid run outside, she just drop dead. And the maid run out and call the husband. And he too came in, and when he look and saw his son lying across the floor, dead, and his wife who fall back in the chair, dead, the man jus' say, "Oh, God, what have I done?" And he were a dead man.

So that's why as the proverb of Jamaica people says, when you are going to dig a hole, dig a ditch for a man, dig two: one for you and one for him; otherwise you is going to drop in the one that he was to drop into, you see, and that's why *everybody* must love each other's children, just as you love yours, for whatever you try to do a nex' woman's child, it's going to reflect to yours, for that's what she did to John, wanted was to *kill* him, and it is the darndest thing, wanted to kill him and kill her two sons, you see. Poison the flour for John, and her two sons dead instead of him. And that's what John been warning them about, to "Do good, do good. . . . " If they will hear!

Collected in Kingston from a resident of Cassava River on July 8, 1978.

See Motif K1613.3, "Poisoner's Own Son Takes the Beverage Intended for Stepbrother," and Motif N332.1, "Man Accidentally Fed Bread Which His Father Has Poisoned," in Baughman, *Type and Motif-Index;* and Type 837, "How the Wicked Lord Was Punished," in Flowers, *West Indian Types and Motifs.* I collected a variant of this tale in Richmond, Virginia, in 1975, which the teller interestingly enough concluded with the same proverb, "You dig a ditch for your fellow man, you may fall in yourself" (*Shuckin' and Jivin'*, No. 219). Versions of this tale have also been collected in Europe and the Virgin Islands.

102 Running to Catch the Tree

The slave them work so hard, and there was no ease for them. So the white men dem always tell dem to go and fall that cotton tree or fall such a tree, and the poor ting dem, feel that if dem *dead* it would be better for dem.

And when dem hear the tree coming down, hundreds of dem will run: "Lawd, backra tree is falling down. We are goin' to catch it!" And is run dem running to catch di tree jus' to see if dem can kill—get kill, you know. So as to ease dem out of the bondage, dem running to catch the tree.

Collected in Mandeville on September 16, 1978.

103 How Black People Got Meat during Slavery

After the slave abolish, white man gone about dem business wid all the cattle and leave the Black slaves out. And they could not buy meat, for they did not have any money, for the white man took everyting and just turn them out because slave abolish. They didn't have anyting; the white man tek up the iron chis'[1] and everyting and own all the cattles. So the Black man dem have to steal at night, and they couldn't *buy* meat. And at night when them put them children to bed, they go and they roll a cotta,[2] we call it cotta; them roll something and them tie it on to the cow feet and lead them out of the pen. And they tek them in their home and they butcher dem, and they cut them up and they have a whole pile tek. And them cut it up and them cover every piece of dose meat wid salt and put it down into dat keg. And dem dig a *deep* hole and sink di keg down in it, cover it over and put di fire over it wid dem stone—you didn't have stove, nor anyting like dat in dose days. We have t'ree block, you know, eider block or stone, and they set it and put a iron across and set dem pot on it. And dat's how them cook, with the meat underneat' in di groun'. And they buy a little salt fish now or a little herring and cook fi di dinner and give di children, and put dose children to bed at night fi sleep. And when di children gone to bed, they tek out the meat and them have *feas'*, but the children don' get it, because the children *chat*,[3] and in those days white people believe in children story. They believe that children don't tell story,[4] so when they come to search for the cow, the first thing they ask the children what they have fi dinner las' night. Pickney say, "Herring, sar," or "Salt fish, sar." Them find that the meat is not dere—them believe the children. But the children don't know that them parents have the meat underneath the ground and eating at night and give them only salt fish and herrin' to go to bed. So they couldn't test them.

That's how the Black people dem get along and live. Yes.

Collected in Mandeville on September 16, 1978.

Tales of stealing food from the master, particularly meat, are legendary in slave anecdotes and tales among Black Americans.

1. Chest.

2. Roll of cotton cloth. The cotta is also used by market women on their heads to relieve the pressure of the basket.

3. Talk too much.

4. Lies.

104 Live Log

Washerwomen washing clothes. . . . And you see, when deh come to scald, you know, the old-time people have a ting we call kerosene tin, and deh always scald dem clothes in it. And them put on di kerosene tin and they fin' themself nice piece of log lie before the river bank, and they get two stone and put dis way and dis way [illustrating] and set the pan on it, and full the pan of clothes to scald. And as the pan start to bwoil up, you only see di smoke in the river and di tin go right up in di air and come down, and di mouth in di sand. . . . Alligator!

[Member of audience] "Alligator. Deh build up the fire on the alligator!" You see they come out to get sun, you know.

You know they have a time to come out for their sun, and that day him come out and lay down on the bank of the river. The river running dere, and he come up and lay down on the bank, stretch out on the bank, big huge ting too! And they thought it was wood log.

[Member of audience] It's so big, so they don't see the head, you know.

And so they get two stone and help it out, one here, one dere, so as to mek the three corner for the tin. And they set it on here, and, my dear, they fill it with them clothes. And as it start to bwoil, them saw the smoke in the river and the tin up in the air, and come right back down. The smoke in the river is the alligator, you know; when the fire *h-e-a-t* him, him spring in the river—and so the smoke. But I don't tink him could live.

[Member of audience] I don't know. I don't think so. Because the skin is so thick. . . . if he stay dere until it penetrate, he couldn't live. . . .

Collected in Mandeville on September 16, 1978.

See Motif J1761.8, "Man Mistakes Dragon for Log," in Baughman, *Type and Motif-Index.*

105A The Groom Is a Snake

A man was friendly . . . with a girl one day. And he always visit the girl home. And the girl did have a sick bradder; him didn' want the man to see him. So everytime as this man visit this home, she always send the bradder into a outroom to hide. And the bwoy have a window looking through all di time, and *dis* bwoy was a sort of old witch, you know. And everytime he go to the window and he see this man come out, for the man always want to tek fresh air from the house. And he have a cane, a stick, we call [it] a "cane," in his hand. He come out wid him likkle stick. And him *walk* around, and anywhere him see a lizard, him strike the lizard with dat stick *and he tek it up and eat it!* Several time the boy have seen that. When it come final for weddin', the bwoy one day sit down and say, "You know, Mumma, I don't tink you should mek my sister marry dat man." And Moder say, "Go away! Why?" "He's a snake," the boy said to his mother. And the mother say, "Oh, go away, you sick bwoy, what you know about snake!" And he said, "Mumma, I am telling you, if you 'low my sister to marry *dat* man, you are going to regret."

And they wouldn' hear what him say. Finally, marry and chariot drive out with the girl the day. But the bwoy was a ole witch. And no sooner deh drive out, little after dat, when the snake reach to the hole where he is living, he shed off *everyting,* and the girl find that it *was* a snake. And him drew down the girl into the hole, where he is living, and him start to lick him, lick him, you know, to bring him where dat he could swallow her. And when him start to lick the poor girl choose a song which say (the father name was Cawley and the moder name is Levy)—and the poor little girl say [singing nasally]: "Cawley, come away, Cawley, come 'ome, Levy. Come, come today, for the s-na-ke is going to kill me."

And the snake now, to answer again, he stop pon lick di spot, and him answer say [singing]: "If him don' come you goin' see a bit of you *bone* today." And him have to go back and lick the same place. So the girl find out that him have to lick one place over and over, so to get his whole body wet, she will continue the singing. And so she continue, so him lick:"Cawley, come away, Levy, come, oh, Levy, come, come, come, for the snake is going to kill me today."

The snake say [singing]: "If him don' come him never see a bit of you bone today." And he gone back and lick the place. And the poor bwoy *feel* it because he is a witch; he know that him word is true.

So di moder den sorta feel some funniness about dem body, dat something mus' wrong. And the sick bwoy step out, and as dem see him step out, deh went after him. And when dem *reach* to di spot where di snake was with the girl and look in the hole, di girl is dere, and he is here [illustrating] and licking. And dem just turn him oneside and *shot* him with a gun. And they *killed* him and draw out dem dawter.

Collected in Mandeville on September 16, 1978.

See Motif R111.1.5, "Rescue of Woman from Snake-Husband," and Motif B656, "Marriage to Reptile in Human Form," in Baughman, *Type and Motif-Index*, and Motif B652, "Marriage to Reptile in Human Form," in Flowers, *West Indian Types and Motifs.* Versions appear in Beckwith, *Jamaican Anansi Stories,* Nos. 85 and 86; Jekyll, *Jamaican Song,* No. 34; Bennett, *Anancy and Miss Lou,* pp. 38–40; Parsons, *Folk-Lore of the Antilles,* Pt. 2, pp. 299–300; and Wake, "Anancy Stories," pp. 288–89. This tale has also been collected in Martinique and Haiti. An African version is Godfrey Brown's *Beautiful Girl and the Snake* (Great Britain: African Universities Press, 1970).

105B The Groom Is a Snake

This one is a story about a beautiful girl. She live into a village. And every man come to ask to marry her. But she don' want them — either some's too tall or some's too short. So one day now a snake with seven heads lived in a cave, and he changed himself into a man and came to this village and to this child's house (girl's house) and asked him[1] to marry him. So the girl looked at the man: he wasn't too tall; he wasn't too short. And she accepted. The people of the village were *very* happy to know at last that she get a husband. So they have teas and things like that. Until the husband and she leave. So when they were traveling, *traveling* and they turned in toward a bush and the snake started to *change,* change — but she didn't realize that he was changing until they reached the cave. After that the house now is a cave, and this snake come with seven heads; and, ya know, she was *frightened* and started to *cry.* And every day the snake now go out and looking food. And she start to sing because she had seven bradders. So they have some birds. And she start to sing-g-g and sing-g-g and sing-g-g! Well, one of the birds (I really don't remember which one) said to her that: "I'm not going to help you because you didn't treat us very well." This other set of birds now decided that they would fly to the village and sing. So they started to sing, sing, and the people in the village calling one another and say, "Listen the birds' song." The song was: "In a cave far away, you sister is calling for you, married to a snake with seven heads." And they sing, sing, sing, sing. So they go and search for the bradder, and the bradder came. And the bird fly before them, fly before them until they reach the cave. And the sister was so *glad* when they came. And hugged them. So while they were in there now the snake came, and the seven bradders have seven sharp knife and tackle the snake. And there was a *fight*, and they kill the snake and went right home with their sister happily.

Collected in Woodside on September 6, 1978.
1. The girl.

106 If You Nuh Gi Mi One (H)ackee

Well, I am going to tell you one now about a woman that had two daughters, you see, and this one is the topic of a person that is *mean*hearted—you don't give away anything, and if a person is kind, you see, the (h)outturn of a kind person and the (h)outturn of a meanhearted person.

That is of a woman with her two daughters—one were kind and one were meanhearted. She says to her daughters, "Now come, I want you two to go to the bush and to bring me some (h)ackees." (This is one with a song go with it.) "Bring me some (h)ackees." The girls says, Yes," and they take two baskets and went for the (h)ackees. And on they way back they reach by the Dry River that they pass and go (h)up. If you are passing the Dry River with you two hands, you don't hear anything. But if you once have something coming wit' and crossing the river, you hear a voice from the river beg you some of what you have. So while they coming on with two baskets of (h)ackees, one of the girl name *Nora*—the meanhearted girl name Nora, but the kindhearted one we never get her name.

So when they reach to the river, a voice (you don't see anybody, but you hear the voice), a voice from Dry River (they call the river) says to her [sings]:

> If you nuh gi mi one (h)ackee you nah pass yah.
> If you nuh gi mi one (h)ackee you nah pass yah.
> If you nuh gi mi one (h)ackee you nah pass yah.
> Dry River da go come down and wash you weh.[1]

The kindhearted girl give one of her (h)ackee; the meanhearted one wouldn't give any. The voice at the River say [sings]:

> If you nuh gi me one (h)ackee you nah pass yah.
> If you nuh gi me one (h)ackee you nah pass yah.

If you nuh gi mi one (h)ackee you nah pass yah.
Dry River da go come down and wash you weh.

The kindhearted sister says to her [sings]:

Gi 'im one, Nora, gi 'im one.
Gi 'im one, Nora, gi 'im one.
Gi 'im one, Nora, gi 'im one.
Mind Dry River go come down and wash you weh.

And she wouldn't give it. The voice from the river say again:

If you nuh gi mi one (h)ackee you nah pass yah.
If you nuh gi mi one (h)ackee you nah pass yah.
If you nuh gi mi one (h)ackee you nah pass yah.
Dry River da go come down and wash you weh.

The kindhearted sister started to cry, for she know. She say [sings in crying voice]:

Gi 'im one, Nora, gi 'im one.
Gi 'im one, Nora, gi 'im one.
Gi 'im one, Nora, gi 'im one.
Mind Dry River go come down and wash you weh.

And she wouldn't give it. And the voice from Dry River keep saying:

If you nuh gi mi one (h)ackee you nah pass yah.
If you nuh gi mi one (h)ackee you nah pass yah.
If you nuh gi mi one (h)ackee you nah pass yah.
Dry River da go come down and wash you weh.

And by that time the river was dry, dry, through the while, but the water come until it reach her to her waist, and *den* the sister started crying again; she say [sobbing even more]:

Gi 'im one, Nora, gi 'im one.
Gi 'im one, Nora, gi 'im one.
Gi 'im one, Nora, gi 'im one.
Mind Dry River go come down and wash you weh.

And she wouldn't give it. And the voice from the river say,

If you nuh gi mi one of the (h)ackees, you nah pass yah.
If you nuh gi mi one of the (h)ackees you nah pass yah.
If you nuh gi mi one of the (h)ackees you nah pass yah.
Dry River da go come down and wash you weh.

That time the water catch her here [indicating breast]. The sister says to her [sobbing even more]:

> Gi 'im one, Nora, gi 'im one.
> Gi 'im one, Nora, gi 'im one.
> Gi 'im one, Nora, gi 'im one.
> Mind Dry River go come down and wash you weh.

The voice from the river say:

> If you nuh gi mi one of the (h)ackees you nah pass yah.
> If you nuh gi mi one of the (h)ackees you nah pass yah.
> If you nuh gi mi (and she in water going so [indicating girl struggling
> to keep from being washed away]) . . .
> If you nuh gi mi one (h)ackee you nah pass yah.
> Dry River da go come down and *wash* you weh!

And she *gone* down the river.

So that is the end of a meanhearted person. Just share what you have.
You have a basket of ackee, and a voice say give one, a powerful voice more
than yours, say "Gi mi one," give it. You wait until the river *wash* you weh before you could able to give it? Well, the river get all. And she lose her life.

That's the end of this story.

Collected in Kingston from a resident of Cassava River on July 8, 1978.

See Motif C41, "Tabu: Offending Water Spirits," Motif F420.5.2.6, "Water-Spirits Take Revenge
on Mortals," and Motif F932.8.5, "Shallow Water Rises up to Drown Man," in Baughman, *Type
and Motif-Index*. Versions appear in Jekyll, *Jamaican Song*, No. 33, and Wake, "Anansi Stories," pp.
280–81.

1. If you don't give me one ackee, you can't pass here.
   If you don't give me one ackee, you can't pass here.
   If you don't give me one ackee, you can't pass here.
   Dry River is going to come down and wash you away.

107 Tek Me, Nuh Tek Me

[This woman] lived in a shoe, and she made two goadies (goadies, you
know, round something, round something). And there was a boy come to her
home, and she send the boy fi one of the goady. She say to him, say, "You
goin' to hear the two goady say—one going to say, "Take me, take me," and
the other one goin' say, "Tek me, nuh tek me." So he 'as to know which of
the goad to tek—one goin' to say, "Tek me, tek me," and the oder one goin'
to say, "Tek me, nuh tek me." Now that is the last one he suppose to tek.
The one that say, "Tek me, nuh tek me," and the other one say, "Tek me, tek
me." That's a story.

[Dance] Why is he supposed to take the last one?

Yes, you mus' tek the last one; that's the right one you is to take. That's the goad what have in the treasure. That's the goad what have in the treasure.

[Dance] So which one did he take?

The one that i' say, "Tek me, nuh tek me."

[Dance] So he got the treasure?

Yes, he got that one.

Collected in Woodside on September 6, 1978.

A variant of this tale appears in Wake, "Anancy Stories," (pp. 282–83) in which a girl refuses the eggs that say "Take me," but takes three others and gets great riches from them. Another girl takes those that say "Take me" and gets bad luck.

108A Big Head, Big Belly, and Little Foot

Once upon a time three children, Big Head, Big Belly, and Little Foot, went to look mango. So they met up on a mango tree, and Big Head decide to climb. As soon as Big Head get up on the mango tree, he picked a mango and he tasted it. So they ask him, "Is it sweet?" And him bow him head. By the time him bow the head, it fell off. So this one, Big Belly, now, started to laugh, and him laugh and laugh until the belly burst. Poor Little Foot, he was the only one left, running home to tell his mother, and it [the foot] broke off, you know [in an] ants' nest.

Collected in Kingston on November 8, 1978.

This is Motif Z13.1, "Catch Tales: Peculiar Name Brings Tale to a Premature End," in Flowers, *West Indian Types and Motifs*. Versions appear in Beckwith, *Jamaican Anansi Stories*, No. 127; Parsons, *Folk-tales of Andros Island*, No. 147; and Parsons, *Folk-Lore of the Antilles*, Pt. 2, pp. 302–3.

108B Big Head, Big Belly, and Little Foot

A mother had three children: one was Big Head, one Big Belly, and one Fine Foot. So that day they were 'ungry, so the mother sent them out to look something. While they were going along they saw a big apple tree.

Big Belly couldn't climb the tree because her belly would burst; Fine Foot couldn't climb it because her foot would break; so Big Head decide to climb the tree. When Big Head climb the tree, Big Belly said to her: "Boy, dem apple ah sweet?" She nod her head, and her head drop off. Big Belly laugh, she laugh, she *laugh* until her belly bus'. Fine Foot now running to tell Mama; grass straw cut off her foot.

Collected in Kingston on October 30, 1978.

108C Big Head, Big Belly, and Little Foot

Once upon a time a lady have three son; one name Big Head, Big Belly, and Mawger[1] Foot. She send the three of dem a shop fi go buy salt. The t'ree a dem buy di salt. When dem a cum back from shop now wid di salt, Big Head look up in a di tree and see one ripe apple. So him one si' down up deh eat di apple now, you know. Big Belly deh down a groun' ah shout up and ask him, say, "Bredder Big Head, di apple sweet?" Him shake him head fi say it sweet now, you nuh; him head drop off. Big Belly a laugh now, fi him belly *bus'*. Mawger Foot deh run go home go tell him moder; him foot drop off in a ants' nes'.

Collected in Kingston on September 18, 1978.
1. Tiny.

108D Big Head, Big Belly, and Little Foot

One day three children went to a mango tree, one name Big Head, one name Big Belly, and one name Fine Foot.

Big Head started to climb the mango tree. He stumbled down and burst his head.

Big Belly laugh and laugh until his belly burst.

Fine Foot run home to tell his mother, and grass straw cut off his feet.

Collected in Kingston on September 11, 1978.

109 Cutthroat, Chawfine, and Suckblood

This is a story about a old witch and a young witch and three dogs. Now this old witch was very, very wicked, and this young boy, now, is a young witch, but he wasn't wicked. So this old witch wanted to kill him, so he knew it. And the old witch invited him to come to a bush to pick some star apple for him. So the young witch has three dogs—Cutthroat, Chawfine, and Suckblood. So he told his mother that he was going to put out a basin out in the yard, and he said, "You must watch the basin because any time the basin, the water turning blood, then he must leggo the three dogs because that mean that he is in danger." The mother in the kitchen beating foo-foo, and the boy follows. So when the boy went to the bush with the witch now, the old witch, he call to him to climb a tree, climb the star apple tree. So when he go on this one, he say, "No, that—that one." "This limb?" "No, that—

that limb." "This limb?" "No, that—that one." And then he climb and climb until the boy reach fa-a-r up in the last point now. And the old woman clap so, clappa, clappa [hitting the sides of her stomach to illustrate], clap, clap, clap, clap, clap. And twelve cutlass men come out, and they start to chop the tree, chop the tree [illustrating], chop the tree, chop the tree, chop the tree. And the boy say [chanting]: "Oftentimes I see my father fall a green tree and a dry tree stand," and the tree come back up and it stand up straight. The old woman clap again, clap, clap, clap, clap, [illustrating]. Twelve sawmen came up, and they started saw the tree, saw the tree, saw the tree [illustrating], and as the tree start topple over, this boy said [chanting]: "Oftentimes I see my father fall a green tree and a dry tree stand," and the tree come up back and stand.

That time the mother in the kitchen beating the foo-foo and don't remember what happen now. Anyway, when it reach about twelve o'clock, she *run* out the door and see the basin turn blood, and she take the mortar stick and she hit the chains and the t'ree dogs run. When the t'ree dogs run and the old woman on the way, the old woman clap again, boop, boop, boop, boop. Twelve axmen came out, and they chopped and chopped and chopped and chopped and chopped and chopped [illustrating], but this was the last time with the boy. He was really in danger. And him say, "Oftentimes I see my father fall a great t'ree and a dry tree stand," and the tree come back up. And the t'ree dogs just rushed down, and Cutthroat jump up and cut the old witch throat. Suckblood suck her blood, and Chawfine chawed her.

Jack Mandora.

Collected in Woodside on September 6, 1978.

This is Motif B524.1.2, "Dogs Rescue Fleeing Master from Tree Refuge," in Baughman, *Type and Motif-Index,* and Type 303, "The Twins or Blood-Brothers," in Flowers, *West Indian Types and Motifs.* Versions appear in Beckwith, *Jamaican Anansi Stories,* No. 82; Parsons, *Folk-tales of Andros Island,* No. 68; and Harris, *Uncle Remus,* III, 3. This tale has been collected in the Dominican Republic, Antigua, Puerto Rico, Guadaloupe, and Montserrat.

110 Get di Brush, Get di Paint

One day mi and Clem and Brukup a walking, you know, and we see a giant. You nuh seet? So di giant say now, "Anyone can do anyting what mi caan' do, I'll let 'im pass." So through[1] mi see dat now and di oder two man always a run down say dem smarter dan me, so mi stoop down now. So di giant say, "Cool?" Brukup tell him fi jump over a mountain. The Giant did it, and Brukup couldn't pass. So Clem show him a tree and tell him mus' cut it down. Giant say, "Stay so, watch me cut it." Up a yonder deh him jus' go so and him cut di tree. Me say, "Wait, bwoy, dis a man a dangerous!"

So mi jus' say, "Aiiii (I ease di body)![2] Get di brush, get di paint, and jus' paint it."[3]

See him . . . yah. . . . He caan' paint up to now.

Collected in Kingston on October 6, 1978.

See Motif K211, "Devil Cheated by Imposing an Impossible Task," and Motif G303.16.19.3, "One Is Freed if He Can Set a Task the Devil Cannot Perform," in Baughman, *Type and Motif-Index*.

1. Because.
2. Broke wind.
3. He orders the giant to paint it.

111 Green Grass Grows pon Me Grave

Once upon a time three boys were sent to the woods to catch bird by their mother. In the long run the smaller boy had catch more than his two brother. They became envious of his bird and decide to kill and bury their smaller brother.

They did so and bury him under a marble stone.

When they went home their mother asked them for her smallest son. They told her he had left for home before them. Many days passed and he did not return.

One day the mother was working in her yard when a bird came on a tree over her head and began singing: "Fe me brether, Will, fe me brether, Green, don't yu know when you gu home me mother will ask yu for me? Never mind, since I died green grass grows pon me grave."

Then the woman said, "What you say?" And the bird repeat.

In any event, she caught the bird and began comforting and rubbing the bird while it sings. While rubbing, her hand caught something in the bird head, and she drew it out. And lo and behold, the bird turn into her son!

Told by my long dead granny, Aunt Jane.

Given to me in writing by a Kingston resident on October 11, 1978.

See Motif B131.1, "Bird Reveals Murder," in Baughman, *Type and Motif-Index*.

112 Granny Cow

Once upon a time there lived two little boys with their grandmother. But they weren't getting enough food. So they planned to kill their grandmother and sell her. The elder one said go for the kitchen bitch.[1] So the little one went for the kitchen bitch. The elder one went to his grandma and said, "Grandma, may I bathe you?"

Grandma said, "Thank you." The little one hand the kitchen bitch to his brother, and he killed Grandma. Then they cut off her hands, head, and feet, and hid them away. Cut up the remains of her body and put it in a cart. And they the eldest boy said to the little one, "Don't say 'Granny, Granny,' say 'Beef, beef.'"

Then they push the cart out of the yard. The eldest one said, "Beef, beef," and the little one said, "Granny, Granny." A lady then come and said, "How one is saying 'Granny, Granny,' and one is saying 'Beef, beef'?" The little one said, "Because it was an old cow, so we called him granny cow."

Given to me in writing by a Kingston resident on October 11, 1978.

This tale bears some similarity to Beckwith's "Anansi Kills His Grandmother" (*Jamaican Anansi Stories*, No. 135).

1. Knife.

113 Ronnie the Bear

So, Ronnie say him go a foreign now, and 'im see a lady now, dat the lady say, "I know di right place I can carry you, man. They will *readily* accept you dere." So di lady carry him, tek a check now, weh di woman carry 'im, nuh di zoo dem carry Ronnie, and go put Ronnie inna a cage. So Ronnie deh a di zoo—evenin' come for Ronnie go home, Ronnie caan' see him a go home now. So him tek a check; Ronnie jussa realize say dem lock 'im up a di zoo now and gon', man. So Ronnie start mek *noise* now. So dem say all right, dem phone fi di lady. Di lady come back fi Ronnie. So di lady and Ronnie a walk now, and di lady say, "Awright, I goin' carry you somewhere where you can work." And the lady carry Ronnie, tek a subway and go in a different part of di city, come up on a circus. Ronnie come a di circus now, and di circus manager spot Ronnie. Him say [with an American accent], "Say, mate, come 'ere. I've got a job for you."

Hear Ronnie: "You got a job for me. Dat's real cool, man, I readily accept it."

Him say, "But *one* ting, you got to keep a secret."

Ronnie say, "Yeah, man, I can keep a secret, man, you know where I am from? I am from Jamaica. When you tell a Jamaican a secret, man, he only tell . . . one, two, three, four, or five persons. That's how we keep secret."

The man say, "O.K., I am going give you this job, but remember this secret: don't tell anyone what you goin' to do, you gather?"[1]

So di man did have a bear in a di circus. So di bear dead, died di day before now. So di man say, "We goin' give you this bear suit to wear. You act as the bear." Ronnie say all right. So dis man now come now and dress up Ronnie now and put on di bear suit, and Ronnie inna 'im cage: [ferociously] "RRRR-rrrrrr!"

And the man say, "Five cents, look at this Jamaican bear, five cents to look at dis big Jamaican bear." Evening come now, circus done. So the manager now say, "Come back tomorrow you will see dis big Jamaican bear fight a big African lion."

Ronnie say, "But wait, dis man yah nah joke, dis man yah a skin up.[2] How 'im fi go put lion inside a dis place wid me! Oh, no!" Ronnie say, "Dis man yah couldn' serious!" So him come back di nex' day, come back go work di nex' day. So when we tek a check Ronnie go inna di cage di nex' day, him see dis man a come wid a *big* lion. So Ronnie say, "Awright, I goin' mek a Equator, a imaginary line in a di cage. Anyhow him stay over fi him part, everyting cool, but from 'im come over my part, di circus mash up." Him say, "Awright." So Ronnie in a 'im cage a "RRRR-rrrr!" in a 'im cage and 'im bear suit, man. And Everybody believe he's a bear. When you tek a check man, Ronnie see di man open di cage *and trow in di lion*!!! So Ronnie jus' a draw one side, and "RRRR-rrrr!" and di lion "RRRR-rrrr!" and "RRRRRRRRRR!" and the lion "RRRRRR!" So Ronnie say, "Better stay over your part." When you tek a check, di lion nuh jump over Ronnie part, and Ronnie jus', "Watch yah, man, go back over your place, man, I don'. . . ."

So hear di lion nuh, "Stop you noise. You a eediot, man? Mek we cut di capers."

So wen you tek a check, Ronnie believe is a real lion; is a nex' man dat check out like a lion.

Collected in Kingston on October 6, 1978.
1. Understand.
2. Crazy.

114 Him Go a Foreign

Well, you want see a man now, him have a son. Him decide to send the son a foreign fi six week fi a little vacation and ting. So him go a foreign and come back. And when him come back, him watering di garden, doing some work. Him say [very properly], "Mummeee, where is Farter?"

Mummy say, "He is in garden."

So he step out a di garden and see him daddy, the old man. Him say [very properly], "Farter, I'm heah-h."

The father look around. It go on a little more. The man deh pon him verandah; him say, "Sis, you nuh hear what di bwoy say? De bwoy go a foreign, come back and a call me *farter*. If I send him back, dis time when him come back wah him a go call me? Filth!"

Collected in Kingston on September 21, 1978.

115 Man from Mocho

One day now, I was standing up in New York, United States, so I had on a suit and lean up on the corner. Have bredder[1] weh stowaway pon a banana boat, come deh now, but a Mocho[2] 'im come from — a one place deh call it Mocho, no light nuh deh da. So 'im come deh now, and 'im see mi now. But you know di public toilet dem, di public lav dem — you know the public lav? Him come deh now and glimpse me and say: "Hey, mister!"

Mi say, "You caan' call me mister. In talking to me you must sey, 'Tom man' and 'Hey, sir!'"

Him say, "Aah." So him say, "Is there a spot in the lav there I can use?"

Mi say, "Yeah, in dere." So 'im go in dere now, and when him done use the lav now, mi see him come back, and him a wet up himself, you nuh know?

"I never know when you done use the lav you can flush the same place where di filth go through and wash you hand and wash you face," him say.

Ha-a-a!

Collected in Kingston on October 6, 1978.
1. There was a brother, a man.
2. A man who comes from Mocho, a very rural place in the parish of Hanover.

116 You Must Have Cried a Lot

A man went to England one day, and he saw a little girl crying. So he said to the little girl, "Little girl, why do you cry?" And the man tell the little girl that she should not cry. And the little girl ask him why. So he said when you grow up big, you will become ugly. So the little girl look up on the man now and say, "Sir, you must have cried a lot when you were small."

Collected in Kingston on October 30, 1978.

117 Hijack

A passenger on a plane decided to use the bathroom when the plane was airborne. As he was returning from the bathroom, he saw a friend whom he hadn't seen for a long time. On seeing the friend, he shouted, "Hi, Jack!" At this all the passengers stood up with hands in the air, thinking that the man said "Hijack."

Given to me in writing in November 1978 by a Kingston teacher.

118 Nutty Buddy

This lady, once she went to the stadium, and everybody calling out for nutty buddy, so she want three-three, but she don't want to say di buddy.[1] Hear her nuh [very properly]: "Sir, give me three of those nutty ting."

Collected in Kingston on October 30, 1978.
1. Slang for penis.

119 A Pipe Rooster, Please

This man, he had a daughter, you know; she was very sophisticated. And he sent her to buy a pipe cock. So she was so boasy,[1] she don't want to say pipe cock. She said, "Can I have a pipe rooster, please?"

Collected in Kingston on October 30, 1978.
1. Conceited; one who shows off.

120 The Way to Pigley Park?

This lady was going to Hagley Park in Kingston. She didn't want to say *Hagley* Park. She saw a man, and she ask the man, "Could you show me the way to Pigley Park?"

Collected in Kingston on October 30, 1978.

121 Mr. Cashew Cat

There was a man nicknamed Cushu Puss. So one day somebody wanted a favor done by him. So they came to him and said, "Good morning, Mr. Cashew Cat."

Collected in Kingston on October 30, 1978.

122 You Are Full Lawyer

This one is about a boy and a man, his son. This fader want his son to be a lawyer, so they were traveling now to find a lawyer that he could train under him. Then when they reach a river (they have to cross this river to go over), so the fader say, "Lord, I mash a fish." But it was lie that he was telling. And the son said, "Yes, fader, taste de fat."

Him say, "Boy, you done go learn, go home a yu yard now, because you are full lawyer."

Collected in Woodside on September 6, 1978.

See Motif X310, "Jokes on Lawyers," in Baughman, *Type and Motif-Index*. A version appears in Beckwith, *Jamaican Anansi Stories*, No. 14.

123 We Are Trying Our Best

There was this woman who was well sick in the hospital, feeling pain all night. The doctor running the ward the following day—she said to the doctor, "Doctor, I can't stand this pain."

The doctor said, "Oh, how do you mean, you can't stand this pain?"

She said, "Doctor, I would prefer to die than feeling this pain."

The doctor said, "What!"

Say, "Doctor, I prefer to die."

The doctor said, "Just be quiet, lady, we are trying our best."

Collected in Kingston on September 21, 1978.

124 Imitating Monkey

A man have a monkey, and everyting 'im do, di monkey do. Every likkle ting him do, di monkey do. The man waan' come play—di man play wid him wife, di monkey waan' play wid him wife too. So the man say, "Ah-h, I goin' fuck you!"

So him jus' go in front the mirror one mawning and jus' start to shave, you know, and jus' tek the back of di knife and just go so underneath 'im neck, "Ya-ay-ah!" [dramatizing man pretending to cut his throat]. Monkey swear say a di front of di knife. So di monkey go in front of di mirror and soap up and started to shave and jus' use the front of the knife and go so, right through: "Ya-a-a-!" and bus' him owna neck.

So di man come home, come see him dead in front of the mirror, say, "What I tell you goin' get *fuck*!"

Collected in Kingston on September 19, 1978, from a child, exact age unknown.

This is Motif J2413.4.3, "Monkey Cuts His Throat, Thinking That He Is Imitating the Cobbler," in Baughman, *Type and Motif-Index*. For other versions see Dorson, *Negro Folktales in Michigan*, pp.

187–88 (reprinted in Dorson, *American Negro Folktales*, pp. 349–50); Botkin, *Lay My Burden Down*, p. 23; and Dance, *Shuckin' and Jivin'*, No. 451. A variant appears in Legman, *Rationale of the Dirty Joke*, p. 195.

125 Gun Grows

One day I was standing in my yard and I see a policeman come and say, "Pres, what do you, sah?"

I say, "I don't have nutting, sah."

So him come a mi yawd and tek up a gun, a long gun, and say, "Wait, ah can carry you to Gun Court for this gun."

Mi say, "Awright."

Him carry me go to Gun Court, and the judge bawl out and say, "Pres, how long you have this gun?"

I say, "Milawd, I have it from it was a little revolver, until it grow a long, long someting."

The judge say, "Awright, mek it stay over dis place[1] until it turn a cannon."

Collected in Kingston on September 21, 1978.

See Motif J2212.7, "Boat Expected to Grow into Ship," in Baughman, *Type and Motif-Index*.

1. Here; i.e., the judge is going to keep it.

126 Piss-pot

When I was in the army as a private and den I get lance corporal, you have a general dem call General Rasta. So 'im come from Jamaica and went to England, and after him went to England now, him go pon a course. So he not really in the army when he was out here in Jamaica. So by that time him come and see me as lance corporal. So one mawning, mi have a fren' dem call Chambers. One mawning we deh on di parade, idling, and him come down and [loud shout], "ATTENTION!" I just salute. Him come down and him say, "Solja, what's your name?"

"My name is Lance Corporal Fuzzy-B, sah."

He say, "Oh, I hear about you, Fuzzy-Deed."

I say, "No, sah, my name is not Fuzzy-Deed; sah, my name is Fuzzy-B."

So him go a England and ketch dis England tawking. So him look again, say, "Lance Corporal Fuzzy Deed, go down to the mess 'all dere and get me a sloice o' coik and a cup o' tay and two newly laid egg."

So mi say, "What you say, sah?"

"Go down to the mess 'all dere and get me a cup o' tay, a sloice of coik, and two newly laid egg."

So I say, "What you say, sah?" Hear a soldier beside me standing up:

"Cho." Right now he go down a kitchen and get a slice of cake and a cup of tea and two fresh egg. By this time me a lean up pon di verandah, him go to my fren' dem name Charles Chambers. Him say [loud shout]: "SOLDIER!!!"

"Yes sah."

[Very properly]: "What is your name?"

"My name is Chambers, sah."

He say, "Oh-h, Piss-pots!"

"No, sir, my name is not Piss-pots, sah, my name is Chambers, sir."

"Oh, you don't have to tell me. I know your name is Piss-pots."

Him say, "God Almighty, sah, is better you call me *Chambers* more dan call me Piss-pot, sah."

Collected in Kingston on September 21, 1978.

127A One, Two, Three, and a Span

I was standing at Cross Roads one day, and when I tek a stock I see a man, a run come with a long, long machete so—*sharp*—man a run come, come. Mi say, "Wait!" Mi go so, start run now, and him run behind me. Mi run in a place and him still deh behind me. So mi run go into a place which have water in deh and me go so, and me member say me caan' swim, and when 'im go so, mi look round, mi see him go so and touch me and say, "One, two, three, and a span; your time now, friend."[1]

Collected in Kingston on September 21, 1978.
This tale is popular among Black Americans as well.
1. This is a line from a children's tag game.

127B One, Two, Three, and a Span

One time a postman go to di madhouse now to deliver some letters. Him see a madman, di madman say, "Wait, you nuh haf no letter fi me?" And him say no, and the madman jus' say, "Yes, man, you have letter fi me, all di while you bring my letter and mi nuh get." And the madman tek a cutlass and start run him down. Di madman a run him down! And the madman say [dramatizing him tapping the postman on the neck]: "One, two, three, and a span." And the madman go down di bottom and find di letters and a say, "Lawd, one yah a mi grandson, and mi moder send dah one yah, and mi bredder send dah one yah; everybody send letter fi mi." And none of dem a no di madman.

Collected in Kingston on October 6, 1978.

128 Mix-up

One day ah see a man a come up di road and him have a bundle a wood pon him head and a cutlass underneath him arm. A mosquito started to bother his nose. Him look pon him nose. I hear him say, "Ah going clip you, you nuh, and him do so—BOW!—and tek off him nose. In his haste he try and see if he can hitch on back[1] and go do so [reaching to pick it up] and him have fi cut off one a him toe. In his haste he put in the toe for the nose and the nose for the toe. And when he's walking he stepped into a puddle of water and drowned.

Collected in Kingston on September 21, 1978.
1. Put the nose back on.

129 The Escape

Two madmen out at Bellevue, you know, plan a thing one night, and say, "Bwoy, we can't tek this no more."

So one a dem get a big flashlight: "When you reach 'gainst the fence now, whenever I turn on the light, you focus, and being focus, climb up and go over first, man." The next man say to him [gesturing towards the light]: "You madder dan me. You want me climb up and you turn it off and mek me drop."

Collected in Kingston on September 21, 1978.

130 New Bottom

Once upon a time, two man graduate from Bellevue. So them a go to the doctor for examine. So the doctor say to one, "If I give you five hundred dollar, what you woulda do wid it?" So the man say, "I would tek it and build a home and settle down so that I woulda go home, you know, man."

So him set the second blind man and say, Suppose I give you a five thousand dollar; wha you woulda do wid it?" Say, "I would a buy a new bottom because the bottom I have have a hole."

Collected in Kingston from a sixteen-year-old boy, in September 1978.

131 One Pound, One Shoe

Well, you have a madman was at Bellevue deh, you have a madman was at Bellevue a sell a pair of shoes, a "kriss"[1] pair of shoes, and you have dis bred-

der deh now come on now and see di madman a sell di pair a shoes, but thru
'im see is a madman 'im tink him can outwit di madman. So di madman say,
"Two poun'. Two poun'. Two a dem, two poun'." So di bredder a *talk* to di
madman, a try talk 'im out. So di bredder say, "One poun', is only one poun'
mi have, man, gi me di pair a shoes and ting nuh, man, one poun'." So di
madman say, "Awright, ah goin' throw over one foot and you pass di poun'
and I throw over di nex' foot."

So 'im do so ram now, and throw over one foot now, and di bredder
now, 'im a push through di poun', you know. Di madman jus', "Den pay me."
My man say, "One poun', one poun', one poun'." Is outwit him tink him outwit di madman. Di madman jus' gi him one foot a shoe fi di one poun' and
just' say, "One poun', one shoe."

Collected in Kingston on October 6, 1978.

This tale is similar to Motif J1522.1, "Half Price for Half a Shave," in Baughman, *Type and Motif-Index.*

1. Smart, fashionable.

132A Hu-Hu-Huor Fader

There was this man and he sending little boy to school. So he said to
the boy [stammering badly], "We-l-l-l, c-c-can you s-a-y-y O-u-r Fa-a-a-ther
pray-y-er?"

The little boy say, "Yes, Daddy."

Him say, "W-e-l-l-l, s-s-sa-a-say i-i-it."

The little boy, "Our Father which art in heaven. . . . Our Father which
art in heaven."

The man say, "Since y-o-u d-d-don-t k-k-kn-o-w it so g-g-ood sa-say say
af-ta me."

The little boy say, "Say after you, Daddy?"

Him say, "Y-e-s-s, s-s-sa-y af-ter me: Hu-hu-hu-huor F-a-der."

The little boy say, "Hu-hu-hu-huor F-a-der."

The man say, "You must-n't say hu-hu-hu-huor fa-der, you mu-st s-s-sa-y,
hu-hu-hu-hu-h-huor fa-der."

He had to take away the little boy because he couldn't say it.

Collected in Kingston on September 21, 1978.

132B Hu-Hu-Huor Fader

This man he was teaching his son to say his prayers, but the man, you
know, he had a stutter, you know, he stammered. So he was telling his son

to say, "Our Father," you know. But he kept telling the son that "Whatever I say you are to say it." So he said, "Say after me, A-a-a-a-aour f-f-f-father."

So the son said, "A-a-a-a-aour f-f-f-father." So he kept hitting the boy and telling him, you know, "Say after me, A-a-a-aour f-f-a-*ather,*" and the boy say the same thing, and they were there. . . .

Collected in Kingston on October 30, 1978.

133 Mi Never 'Peak nor 'Poke

This lady had three daughters, and they couldn't speak very well. So she wanted husbands for them. So she was leaving one day, and she told them that they are not to talk. So the big sister said to one of the sisters, "Beg you piece a twead."[1] The nex' one say, "You know you musen speak." The nex' one say, "Tank God mi never 'peak not 'poke."

Collected in Kingston on October 30, 1978.
See Motif J2511, "The Silence Wager," and Motif K1984.1, "The Lisping Sisters," in Baughman, *Type and Motif-Index.* A version appears in Smiley, "Folk-lore from Virginia," p. 360 (reprinted in Levine, *Black Culture,* p. 148).
1. May I have a piece of thread?

134 Mi Nuh See di 'Poon

This mother sent this little boy for a spoon. So the boy went, and he came back and said, "Mama, mi nuh see di 'poon."

So his mother said, "Put on di *s.*"

He said, "Mama, mi nuh see di poon-*s.*"

The mother say, "Put on the *s* on the front."

Him say, Mama, mi nuh see di s-poon-s."

Collected in Kingston on October 30, 1978.

135A The Blind Man and the Deaf Man

One time mi go down King Street, and mi see three man deh come up di road. But when you tek check now, one a di man inna a shorts widout pocket, didn' have no pocket; one a di man deaf now; and one blind. So hear di man, the deaf man now: "Man, you hear dat shilling deh drop while a go?"

Hear the nex' man now widout pants pocket now: "Out a my pocket it drop, man."

Hear the blind man: "Is me first see it, give it to me, give it to me quick!"

Collected in Kingston on September 21, 1978.

This is Motif Z18, "Tales Filled With Contradictions," in Flowers, *West Indian Types and Motifs*. Versions have been collected in St. Lucia and St. Thomas.

135B The Blind Man and the Deaf Man

Once upon a time a blind man and a deaf man was walking an' di deaf man hear a money drop and di blin' man say, "Yeah, ah see it too!" And di blind man say to di deaf man, say, "Give mi my own nuh, man." Di deaf man say, "Gi you what? You want ah trow it over in di river?"

So di blind man say,"Den trow it over deh nuh, man, mi wi go fi it, you know."

Him pick up a big stone and trow it over in a di river, man.

The blind man say, "Wah, you gon'?"

Him say, "Yes, man."

Him say, "You find it?"

Him say, "Yes, man, ah-a come wid it."

Him say, "Cho, I haffi come help you search fi it man."

Chuck off and go over deh so. When 'im go over deh now, di two a dem over deh a look, blind man a look you nuh, and di blind man claim say him find it, and di deaf man say "True?" Him say, "Yes, man." And di two a dem jus' come up and him say, "Weh it deh?" Him say, "See it yah." Him say, "See it yah." Him jus' look pon it and say, "Lawd God, a shilling, man, a shilling!"

And di two a dem jus' walk way.

Collected in Kingston on October 6, 1978.

136 Wake Up and Sing

This girl, she was very, very, very ugly, I mean *ugly*, you know, real *ugly*, but she could sing *wonderfully*, and, you know, when she was on the stage, she attract this young man. And [he] decided to, you know, talk to her and so on until they got married.

But when they were married now, the first night there, you know, when he looked on her and saw how *ugly* she was and it was really her singing that attracted him. Him, you know, sort of turn round and say, "Wake up, and *sing, sing*!!"

Collected in Kingston on October 30, 1978.
This tale is popular among Afro-Americans as well.

137 Di Man a Hold Mi

Well, you want see one time dem have two fren', dem directly a grave-robber.[1] Well, all the time a man dead and deh bury him wid jewels and ting. Dem really go dig it up and tek way the jewelry and ting. By dis time dis man dead now and dem bury him wid him gold teeth and him ring and him watch and him chaparita[2] and ting, and the two men wait when di funeral a go on. And as dem gone and night come down now, dem go in. But one a dem is a man who never walk from di day him born, him in a wheelchair, him a di man weh him do the watching, and di oder one do the digging. So dem call him Cripple—di one in a di wheelchair.

So dem go and start to dig and dig till him reach di coffin now and open the coffin and tek out the jewelry and tek off di watch and ting and hear him look pon Cripple: "Cripple, look pon all him suit. Him come naked—so him come, so him shall go back." So him tek off di suit now and ring. So meanwhile him bending down to close back the coffin, him jacket tail, him coat-tail. . . . And screw on down back pon di coffin. So when him ready fi come out a di hole fi pull it back now, him go so, and when you check it out, di coattail hold in a di coffin. So him look pon Cripple and say, "Oh, Crip, you nuh know wha happen?"

Him say no.

"You want see di man a hold mi deh yah."

And Crip just get up out a him wheelchair and do so [dramatizing Crip-ply yelling and running]: "Eeeeeeeppppp!"

Collected in Kingston on September 21, 1978.
See Motif V113.1, "Cripples at Shrine Frightened and Run Away Without Crutches,"and Motif N384.2, "Death in the Graveyard: Person's Clothing Is Caught," in Baughman, Type and Motif-Index. Variants appear in Dance, *Shuckin' and Jivin'*, Nos. 25 and 37; and Fauset, "Tales and Riddles," p. 548. Several other variants of this tale have been collected in Ireland, England, and the United States.
   1. Carlos Nelson informed me that grave robbers in Jamaica sometimes decapitate the corpses and sell the heads to the Obeah men, who need skulls for their practice (interview, Richmond, Virginia, December 14, 1982).
   2. Bracelet.

138 The Moon? The Sun?

There was these two men were drinking one night, all night, well drunk. So they came out the bar, and the moon was shining. One look up and say, "Hey, friend, dat's the moon." The other man say, "Ah, you're drunk, that's the sun." Him say, "No, man, dat's the moon." The other say, "No, man, dat's the sun."

A half-drunk man coming up over the other side of the street, so call to him to verify the fact. Say to him, "Eh, friend, tell dis idiot dat dat's di moon."

"Eh, friend, tell him dat's di sun."

The other half-idiot one say, "Bwoy, from mawning is di first I a pass yah."

Collected in Kingston on September 21, 1978.
This is Motif J2271.1., "The Local Moon," in Baughman, *Type and Motif-Index.*

139 Every Parish Have Dem Own Moon

Once this man and his wife were — they were from the country. So they were coming to Kingston. So after they got to Kingston the night, and he looked up, you know, he saw this moon. He say, "But, Lawd Gawd, me neber know say every parish haf di same moon." He said, "Look here, the same moon lef and come yah."

The wife say, "Shut you mout', John, every parish have dem *own* moon."

Collected in Kingston on October 30, 1978.
See Motif J2271.1, "The Local Moon," in Baughman, *Type and Motif-Index.*

140 Ole Bar Tick

After one time now, some country people out pon trip. So dese people didn't acquainted to lights, you know, electric lights. So one a dem look up on di electric bulb and say, "Coo yah, coo yah![1] Ole bar tick." (Him looking at the light and say is moon and stick.)

Collected in Kingston on September 15, 1978.
1. Look here.

141 Me Never Even Know Him Sick

One time these people they were living, you know, in the country parts where *Gleaner* don't go, so this man send his little grandson to school. So Teacher asked him, "Who died for our sins?" So the little boy didn't know the answer and Teacher flog him. He went home now, you know, and told his grandfather that a teacher flog him because he didn't know who died for our sins. So this man *vex* now, you know, and go to Teacher and start to quarrel, ask Teacher why she beat the boy. So Teacher say, "Well, I asked him who died for our sins, and him couldn't tell me, him couldn't tell me; so that's why I beat him." So the little old man said, "Well, who, *who* died for our sins?" So she said, "Then you never know Jesus Christ died for our sins?" Him say, "Whe you say, man! Me never know him sick, much less him dead. Because me nuh tek *Gleaner*, remember you know, man."

Collected in Kingston on November 8, 1878.

This is Motif J1738.4, "Numbskulls Surprised to Hear That God's Son Has Died," and Type 1833E, "God Died for You," in Baughman, *Type and Motif-Index*. Versions appear in Smiley, "Folk-Lore from Virginia," p. 371, and Dance, *Shuckin' and Jivin'*, No. 173. A variant is "Sister Patsy's Error" in Brewer, *The Word on the Brazos*, p. 22. Baughman cites several white American references.

142 Di Same Puss, Sah

Once upon a time you have two tief, one from the country and one from the town. Well, the country one claim him can tief more dan di town one. Di town one show 'im say, "Me! No, man. All jinnal come from town." So him say, "Awright, prove yourself." So the town man say, "Awright, me fus' a go tief den."

So 'im go inna one Chineyman place, and di Chineyman and him wife and children was sleeping. So 'im mek a bad move. Chineyman say, "Who is dat, who is dat dere?" Him say, "MEOW-W, MEOW-W." Him say, "Oh, dat God damn puss all di while are waking me up." So him tief all weh him could a get an' escape in a one field.

So when him go back now, him tell di country man say, "Awright, see are all my goods weh mi tief yah. *Your* time now." So the country one go in di Chineyman place. So 'im mek di same bad move weh di town tief di mek. So di Chineyman say, "Who is dat?" Hear 'im now: "Di same puss, sah." So di Chineyman just shoot 'im and kill 'im.

Collected in Kingston on October 6, 1978.

A version appears in Dance, *Shuckin' and Jivin'*, No. 152.

143 If Me Dead, Me Dead

A little boy father did not know his prayers, but every night he would beat this little boy and say, "You must know your prayers, man, say it. Say it else I goin' beat you till you dead."

So one night in particular now, the man came and said, "Prayer time." The little boy clasp him hand and say, "Tonight again, O Lord, if me dead, me dead, and if me live, me live."

The father said, "Ah tink you nuh know you prayers."

Collected in Kingston on October 30, 1978.

144 Anyting You Ask God For

One time a parson deh pon a plane a fly wid a whole heap a people in a di plane, passenger. And the parson say, "Anyting you ask God for, God will give you." And him start pray to God, and di plane crash and everybody come out and him say, "Follow me because anyting you ask God for, God will give it to you."

And everybody get lively, man. Same time a bear come into di forest now. Him tek up 'im Bible and, "Oh God, deliver dis bear from me." And the bear still a-come, and him say, "Oh God, please deliver dis bear from me." And di bear still a-come, and 'im jus' dash weh di Bible and say, "Watch me!" And 'im backside [is all you can see now—indicating the man is running].

Collected in Kingston on October 6, 1978.

For variants see Sterling, *Laughing*, pp. 122–23; E. C. L. Adams, *Nigger to Nigger* (New York: Scribners, 1928), pp. 223–24 (reprinted in Botkin, *Treasury of American Folklore*, p. 447); Dobie, *Tone the Bell Easy*, pp. 36–37; Abrahams, *Deep Down*, pp. 204–5; and Dance, *Shuckin' and Jivin'*, Nos. 126–27.

145 My Grace Me a Say

This one is about a lion and a hunter. Now this hunter was hunting in the forest, and he had his gun and, you know, shoot all bout looking things, so he saw this lion coming. And when he pulled his gun, there was no more bullets in the gun, and so he said the only thing to do was to run. And so he started to run. So the lion started to run him down, man, and him run and him run and him couldn't get away. When him see him couldn't get away, him drop down on his knees and started to pray. So while he was praying, he opened his eyes, and when he looked he saw the lion down on his knees too. So him turned to the lion and say, "You praying too?"

The lion say, "Me nuh know wha you a do, you know, but ah my grace me a say."

Collected in Kingston on November 8, 1978.

A version appears in Dance, *Shuckin' and Jivin'* No. 128. A variant appears in Brewer, *Worser Days*, p. 48.

146 It's the Plumber

My aunty told me about a parrot that she had, and one day her bathroom sink began to leak. So she send for the plumber. By that time really she gone to supermarket, and the plumber comes and [elaborate preparations for entry]: "Err-r-rr-r, knock, knock, knock." By this time the parrot (and she only train the parrot talk, "Who is it?" Right? "Who is it?") So the plumber come and knock on the door and the parrot [deep voice]: "Who is it?"

"It's the plumber." Knock, knock, knock, knock.

"Who is it?"

"It's the plumber."

"Who is it?"

[Becoming increasingly frustrated] "It's THE PLUMBER!"

"Who is it?"

"I said, It's THE PLUMBER!"

Who is it?"

"I said, IT IS THE PLUMBER!"

"Who is it?"

By this time him just faint and drop. So by the time now my aunty come from supermarket and start open some compartments, take out her grocery and ting, and come up the steps. She come up and buck up on this man. She never leave anyone at the home. She come now, she say [excitedly], "Who is this?"

The parrot just come out [calmly], "It's the *plumber.*"

And she jus' *drop*! And the thing is that she only train the parrot to say, "Who is it?" And now he learned that part from the plumber.

Collected in Kingston on September 21, 1978.

A version appears in Dance, *Shuckin' and Jivin'* No. 431.

147 Oooooo

This is about the owl. You know the owl saying, "Oooooo, Oooooo." This person was coming one night (he had a letter), so the owl say, "Oooooo!"

Hear him: "A mi Naany Cuckoo, sah."
"Ooooooo."
"Me get one letter, sah."
"Ooooooo."
"Me mumma couldn' read i'."
"Ooooooo."
"Me puppa couldn' read it."
"Ooooooooo."
"Him send me back fi go ask di postmissis, sah."
"Aoooooooooo."
"Me gon', sah."

Collected in Kingston on October 30, 1978.

148 Awhoo Dat!

In the evening when I was a little boy, my mother sent me to the shop to buy some kerosene oil—you know, kerosene oil—we use it to put in the lamp, get a nice flame to cook on. So she sent me for this kerosene oil. She just had an old lamp with an old broken shade, and a wick that wasn't very long, but it touched the oil. And she said, "Run to the shop and buy me some oil, and now see that you come back quickly. *Don't* stop on the road," says she. "Don't stop on the road and play with your little friends. I'm going to spit outside, and see that you get back here before the spit dries. You *hear* me!" "Yes, Maam; yes, Maam." And I looked my most benign, I looked quite cool, calm, religious, angelic. You know how angels look? So that's how I looked, and I said, "Yes, Maam," again. And then I hurried off as *fast* as my two legs could carry me to the corner. And as soon as I got *around* the corner where my mother couldn't see me any more, I slowed up, because right on the little hill around the corner was a guava tree, and no self-respecting, decent boy from Chapelton would ever pass a guava tree with ripe guavas on it. So I had to go and sample the guavas. I bit some of them, you know, and threw them away, but those that were good, I ate—about two or three dozen, and just when mi tummy was hurting me a little bit, I remembered about the kerosene oil. So I started off and I arrived at the next curve, and there I met a friend of mine called Johnnie. And he asked me, "Where are you going? Why are you hurrying like that?"

I said, "Well, my mother sent me to buy some kerosene oil."

He said, "Oh, man, stop and play a little game. Play a little game, man, it's game time now."

So I took off my top out of my pocket on a sort of cord, and I tied it around and I dropped it on the ground, and the gig[1] made quite a pleasant sound. Then he dropped his own, and then the two of us went racing with gigs to see which of the gigs would play longest. And so we went on like that until night began to come down, you know, and I realized it was getting late.

I said, "Look, I have to run to the shop, man, and get that kerosene oil." So away I went again—back to the shop. I asked for a quart of kerosene oil (in those days a quart was about three American cents). So I got my quart of kerosene oil, filled up the bottle, and I started home. No sooner than I got around the curve, no sooner than I got around a curve and was pushing on— what do you think happened? Right around the curve, right around the curve, I heard a voice say, "AWHOOO!" I stopped. I looked to the left. I looked to the right. I saw nobody. I saw nothing. So I began to go a little further, but, you know, I was a little bit *nervous,* and the perspiration was coming down. I heard a voice again, "AWHOO DAT?" [pause] So I looked. I didn't see nobody. The road was deserted. Dark was coming down. Stars began to appear over mi head. So I looked up in the oncoming dark, and I saw two eyes. I saw two eyes way up on a tree. But nobody. And I heard the "AWHOO DAT!" I didn't stop to see anymore. But I fainted, I collapsed, and when I came to, people were there around me, rubbing me up with a thing called asafetida and rum, bay rum, and all sorts of things, and they were saying they didn't know what was wrong, but they came and saw me in the street, flat out on my back. So they tried to get me to talk. Naturally I was very proud that so many people surrounded me, you know. At no time was I the center of attention like that. And I was rather proud of this and I enjoyed it considerably. They asked me who I was. I told them, well, my name was Newsy.[2]

They said, "Newsy what?"

I said, "Newsy Wapps."

They said, "You are Missa Milly's boy?"

I said, "Yes, Missa Milly's boy, one of them."

They say, "What you doing out here?"

I said, "I went to the shop to buy kerosene oil."

They say, "Where's the kerosene oil?"

I said, "I don't know, I had it with me all the time." And I looked at the bush, and there it was nearby. Somebody's flashlight pointed it out—kerosene oil. And I said, "Well, I heard a voice said, 'AWHOO,' then 'AWHOOOOO,' then 'AWHOOOO DAT?'" At the same time while I was saying it to them, I heard it again. And the voice said, "AWHOOOOO DAT?" And all the people who were around me, EVERYBO-O-ODY, they ran away as fast as they could in all directions, and I *ran* for home to Mommie. And when I told Mommie all that happened, she didn't bother to flog me. She just hug me up, rub me down, gave me a good dinner and put me to bed.

Jack Mandora, I don't wan' none.

Collected in Santa Cruz on November 4, 1978.

1. A homemade spinning top constructed of wood, which uses a nail as a prong. String is wound around the nail and then the gig is flung on the ground, where it spins.

2. The storyteller, Eddie Burke, has written a series of tales about his childhood, covering the years 1909–29; including *The Ups and Downs of the Jamaican Boy Newsy Wapps* and *Stories Told by Uncle Newton* (privately published in Kingston, Jamaica, in 1949 and 1950).

149 Duck Calls Names

Once upon a time I 'eard a duck in mi back yard saying, "A Vimora-ma-Cambil! A Vimora-ma-Cambil!"

I run to my uncle called Marse Eric, and when I come out I saw the duck, "A-ra-ra — rara!"

So Uncle Eric say to me, "Why are you saying that the duck is calling your name?"

And I said, "I thought it was because he is saying, "Ar-i-c-k-k, Ar-i-c-k-k!"[1] A-la-la-la.

Collected in Kingston on September 15, 1978.

1. The sounds made by ducks sound like the names of the storyteller, Vernon Campbell, and his Uncle Eric.

150 Jamaican Apples

One time a ship come inna di port, Port Royal, you nuh, a ship wid some white man. And so dem see a woman deh wid some bundle a pepper. So one of dem say to di lady, say, "Eh, lady, is how much for dese Jamaican apples?" The lady say, "Is not apple, is pepper." Hear him, "Oh, cut out di bullshit, man, how much for these Jamaican apples?" Say, "I give you fi' cents." So him buy one and give him fren' one. So him fren' bite di pepper now, and di pepper hot now, bun him. So him start bawl, eye water. So him fren' say, "Hey, Jakes, what you bawling fa?"

Him say, "Just remember the day my moder died."[1]

So him fren', "Cho." Him fren' go so and bite it now, and di pepper bun him go so now and bun him face, and Jakes say, "Jakes, what you bawling for?" You nuh?

"Sorry di day I met a bull fucker like you!"

Collected in Kingston on October 6, 1978.
1. He says this so the friend will be fooled into eating his apple.

151 It's Raining

One time a schoolboy was coming from school, you know. So a very tall fellow, you know, he was very tall [reaching up high], and he was like that. So he said — this little, short little [holding hand down low] schoolboy, you know, came up to him and says, "Hi man, what doin' up there?"

The big tall man just spit on him and said, "It's raining."

Collected in Kingston on September 21, 1978.

152 Steal

One day a country girl went to town. So she had her handbag. And a man just come up and stole it from her and ran away. So a policeman was nearby. So this girl, she was so tush[1] that she just say, "Steal, steal, steal!"

So the policeman look around, and the man come back to the girl and say, "You don't hear I say you mustn't call me 'Steal' next time."

Collected in Kingston on October 30, 1978.
1. Affected, hoity-toity.

153 The Lord Is My Shepherd

You want see one day now one bwoy him real hungry now. So him run and run. Him see a banana tree, but you haffi go over a fence and hide from the rangers. Him sit down and say:

The Lord is my shepherd,
I find what I want.

[The ranger says[1]]

If you touch one of these,
I'll make you lie down in green pasture.

Collected in Kingston on September 21, 1978.
1. A second person delivers the lines of the ranger.

154 Kuffum, Kuffum

One day three of us were at a spot smoking some mariguana, and meanwhile we were *drawing* all this mariguana, there was three cops standing behind the fence. And one of the brodder, after he took three *hawd* draw of the chalice, he started to go "Kuffum, kuffum!"[1] There comes the policeman, say, "'Kuffum, kuffum!' You all ain't gonna kuffum no more."

Collected in Kingston on September 11, 1978.
1. Coughing.

155 Him Out fi Bed You

You have a bad man now, dat cutter[1] in a Kingston deh, you know. So him have a wife now. So him say, "Dawling, go and buy a draw of marijuana deh fi me." And she go down, but as she go deh now, you haf a bad bredder see her now and drape her and cut her a box.[2] Now she go so back and run go to her bad man and say, "You waan' see Tom Stokes cut me a box down deh so." And the man say, "Cho, mi know say a three bad man inna di world yah: me, myself, and I." And she carry him go to the bad man now.[3]

And the bad man come and say, "You cry? Cho, I wouldn' cry, man."
So him [she] look pon him man and say, "This is my man."
And him drape[4] 'im wife and go so—BOW—him box her again.
"Wait! Wha' you do? Box her again!"
So him say, "Who are you?"
Hear him nuh: "A three bad man inna dis world yah, man: I, me, and meself, man."
So di bredder say, "A-oh-h!" So di bredder jus' hole him wife again and go so—BOW-W! And cut her anoder box again, you nuh know.
So: "You box her and mi never a look."[5]
Di bredder go so again and drape her again and go so—BOOP!—box her.
Him say, "Wait, weh you do—box her again?"
So di bredder go so again and hol' her and go so again—BOOP!—box her again.
Hear him nuh: "Come on, mi wife, him out fi bed you."

Collected in Kingston on October 6, 1978.
1. One who sells marijuana.
2. Beat her.
3. Girl leads her boyfriend to the man who hit her.
4. The other man grabs her.
5. The boyfriend claims he didn't see what happened.

156 The Cow Should Blow His Horn

Once upon a time a cow and a donkey was passing on a one-way street, but it 'appen dat di donkey were coming from one direction and the cow is coming from another direction. And it 'appen dat a accident meet up between the cow and dis donkey, but all di people dem been saying di *donkey* wrong, di *donkey* wrong, and rah-ray, everybody just a say di donkey wrong.

But a little women was passing on di street now, and just come up to everybody and just say, "You cannot blame the donkey, the donkey does not have a horn; di cow have a horn, so di cow should blow his horn."

Collected in Kingston on September 18, 1978.

157 You Goin' Dead wid You Foot Skin Up

Once upon a time a parson have a parrot, so Parson couldn't bring nuttin' in a di yard weh di parrot no fuck. So once upon a time, man, parson bring a black bird in a di yawd, so di parrot fucked onto it, man. So next day Parson bring a goat inna di yawd, and di parrot fucked and kill it. So the [parson] say, "You fucker, you, you goin' dead wid you foot skin up inna di air!"

So di parson go out, man, him see a johncrow fly up in a di air, and him [the parrot] tun over 'im two foot so, 'im a go so [dramatizing parrot lying on ground, opening his legs]. Parson come back and say, "You fucker, you, I tell you say you goin' dead wid you foot up inna di air." Hear him nuh, "Sh-h-h, sh-s-h, it's that black fucker I'm waiting on."

Collected in Kingston on September 19, 1978, from a twelve-year-old informant.
A version of this tale appears in Dance, *Shuckin' and Jivin'*, No. 446.

158 3-F

You waan' see now, a man haf a wife, but dis wife de start go a church now, but every time dis man yah waan' sex his wife a tell him say, Fader[1] say she mustn' have any sex. So him just' get vex now and him buy a long cutlass so, and a sharpen it and have a big bokkle a wine and start drink it. So him jus' mark "3-F" pon di board now. So di wife come in and see it, and him say, "You know what this "3-F" for?" Hear her nuh, "Oh, Father, Faithful Father."

Him say, "'Father, Faithful Father!' You know wah dis '3-F' here is for? Fuck, Fight, or Flight!"

Collected in Kingston on October 6, 1978.
1. The parson.

159 Marie Has a Crack

I am married, and I have children, so being a boy and a girl they are about two years apart. The boy is five when the girl was three. So they got mixed up in the bathroom, so the boy seems to have a *good* look at the girl. So when they came out, the boy said to his mummy, "Mummy, where did you get me from?"

She said, "I bought you, son."

He says, "How much did you pay for me?"

She says, "Five pounds, son."

He says, "Then where did you get Marie from?"

She said, "I bought her too, son."

"And how much did you pay for Marie?"

She says, "Five pounds, son."

He says, "No, Mummy, deh tief you because Marie has a crack."

Collected in Kingston on September 21, 1978.

160 Me Want What You Give Me Last Time

You know, I going give you a joke. There was one time here in Jamaica, a sailorman come off a boat, right, come from Japan, right. So still yet him can speak English still, so him go downtown now, and you know some professional down dere and ting and him really want—him go ride it off, you know—a young lady.

Him look at the woman and say, "Hey, you over there, remember the last time I saw you, you give me crab?"

"Then what you want me give you, lobster?"

"Me want what you give me the last time."

Collected in Kingston on September 21, 1978.
A variant appears in Legman, *Rationale*, p. 415.

161 Water on Wood

Two English women came out to Jamaica and went to visit Castleton Gardens.[1] Now they had heard the legend about the sexual prowess of Black men. At Castleton Gardens there was a huge Black man naked, standing on a rock. They decided to seduce the man—both of them—and so they did.

In his fright, the man jumped into the river after the raping. The moral of this story is supposed to be: Water on wood,[2] nuh good!

Given to me in writing by a resident of Kingston on October 5, 1978.
1. Old plantation, now beautiful gardens, in the parish of St. Mary.
2. *Wood* here means penis.

162 What Is Rass?

Once upon a time a little youth come from foreign, so him go out on di street. Him hear a man cuss: "Rass-s!" When him hear dis man cuss, "Rass," him go back and ask him moder, "What is rass?" She say, "Rass is a man axe." So him go back again and him hear a man cuss: "Fuck!" Him go and ask him moder what is fuck. She say, "Fuck is when people tawking." And him go again, and him hear a man cuss: "Bumbo!" Man cuss, "Bumbo," you know. Go and ask him moder say, "What is bumbo?" She say, "Is a man walking stick."

So one mawning now Parson come in fi haf a mawning service, and the parson have fi go to work and ting like dat. And the parson [wanted to] talk to him moder upstairs before him go to work. So di parson come in and him look pon di parson and say, "Hang up you bumbo, put you rass there, sah, Mummy and Daddy upstairs fucking."

Collected in Kingston on October 6, 1978.

163 That's against the Law

One day I was driving in my car, and I get out of my car and start to go to the toilet against the house. There came a policeman and said, "You know that's against the law?"

"No, man, that's against my 'ouse."

Collected in Kingston on September 11, 1978, from a thirteen-year-old informant.

164A When I Lif', You Grab

Once upon a time a Dread deh pon a ship wid a whole lot a sailor and two policeman, so it happen dat a long long time the Dread did want shit, so di Dread jus' go roun' a di back a one, one ole ship deh as a lifeboat and ting, and shit upon a pan and use oder paint pan and cover it down. And see a policeman a walk down di road [whistling]: "phh!" a whistle come down di road. So it happen dat the Dread say to the policeman, say, "Offisa, run come yah, run come yah, man."

And the offisa a run come, and den him say, "You wan' see somepun: mi ketch all a bird underneath da pan yah, but mi fraid fi tek 'im out. Mi one caan' tek 'im out, man. You see weh time mi lif' up di pan, you *grab-b!*" Dat mean say you mus' grab 'im, you nuh see it? So di Dread jus' put 'im han' pon di pan and just say, "One, two three, when I lif', you grab."

And as him lif', him just go so: "Whee-ee!" and grab. And when him grab 'im start grab all shit, a squeeze through all him muscles.

Collected in Kingston on September 19, 1978.

164B When I Lift, You Grab

There was one time you have this yellow man come off a dis boat and come pon di land. Walking—belly start tek him now, well want find a lavatory now fi ease himself now and caan' find no lavatory. But him have on dis bowl hat now. Him start ease himself pon di side. See a constable a come up now. A try, him a try fi cover it. Him say, "Hey, Constable, come here, come here. I got a dove under this cap. When I lift, you grab!"

Collected in Kingston on September 21, 1978.

165 Tack Soup

Well, dis one is about a Chinyman, name Mr. Low, right. So by this time ah go down Barry Street[1] into a restaurant to have a lunch, and after sitting in the restaurant and order a milk shake and steak, and sitting down there waiting for mi order, I see a man come in and order a bowl of soup. And after him order the bowl of soup now, him sit down dere and start drink di soup. So

I stand up and really watch him, and him licking him tongue, a lick him tongue. So I say, "Wait, wah sweet him so?"[2]

So at that point him get up and say, "Mr. Chin."

Him say, "I nuh name no Chin, man, nuh name Chin. I name Low, I nuh name Chin. I name Low."

Him say, "All right, Mr. Low, how dis soup taste so? Wah kind of soup dis?"

Mr. Low say, "Tack soup, man, tack soup, tack soup."

So him say, "Lawd!"

Him say, "I don' use di la-ad. I use di butter."

So him say, "Mi mader!"

Hear him nuh: "Is not you mader, is de puppy."

So him say, "Mi dead now."

So him say, "No, it no dead. Is me kill i'; is me kill i'; if you kill di moder you don't get no mo puppy. I kill di puppy."[3]

Collected in Kingston in November 1978.

1. A Kingston street noted for its Chinese establishments.
2. What does he find so delectable?
3. It is commonly believed in Jamaica that the Chinese eat dogs.

166A Fader Forsythe

Dem have a man dem call 'im Fader Forsythe.[1] ([Addressed to a member of the audience:] You know him, Super? Fader Forsythe. You hear bout him though?) Fader Forsythe a pass one day now, and him a pass one day. So him go see in a little shop where have some likkle puddin' pan and wha bear[2] puddin' and fry dumpling and dem ting deh so. So Fader Forsythe look in and say, "Hey, Fatman, how much fi one tin of that pudding?" Fatman say, "Cho, you caan' eat off that, man." Fader Forsythe say, "How you mean mi caan' eat off dat?" Fatman say, "You caan' eat off dat." Fader Forsythe say, "Awright, mek we see. Ah bet mi eat off everyting in a di shop." Fatman say, "Cho, you a foolishness, man."

So Fader Forsythe go so now and start eat. When him done him eat off di whole a di shelf, and go so and say a look fi Fatman. Fatman drop down a back deh so. Dem haf fi tek him up and gi him ice water.

Collected in Kingston on October 6, 1978.

1. According to this informant, Father Forsythe is a real person. His rival is Battling Johnny. They always have eating contests.
2. Nothing else but.

166B Fader Forsythe

Well, this is a story about a man, two man, by the name of Fader Forsythe and Battling Johnny. Well, in mango season, the period between June
and July, they had a mango-eating contest.[1] Well, only two people really enter
the contest, for two great eater in Jamaica here is Fader Forsythe and Battling
Johnny. Well, Fader Forsythe go up to the eating contest. Battling Johnny was
late. So by the time him coming up now, reaching at a place they call Long
Lane on the Old Stony Hill Road, when him look him see a cartload *full* of
mango seed and skin, coming down. And him look him see anoder dray cart,
which mean a buggy drawn by a mule.

And him really ask the driver whe' him coming from. So the driver say,
"I coming from up the hill—mango-eating contest."

So him say, "Who out dere?"

Him say, "Well, right now you don' know sey Fader Forsythe up deh
jus' a warm up till you come?"

So him say, bwoy, him nah go. Him jus' turn back and jus' mek way,
you nuh. If a warm up the man a warm up and gone a dray cart and a nex'
old cart and still a wait fi him, dat mean no boder go up deh because him
caan' spar.

Collected in Kingston in November 1978.

A comparable tale in which a similarly intimidated contestant accepts defeat before the contest
begins is the popular "Swimming Contest"; versions appear in Dance, *Shuckin' and Jivin',* No. 382,
and numerous other American and African sources.

1. Carlos Nelson informed me that eating contests of many varieties are very popular in Jamaica
(interview, Richmond, Virginia, December 14, 1982).

166C Fader Forsythe

You have anoder one. You haf a bredder dem call 'im Battling John, and
him and Fader Forsythe every year . . . for Fader Forsythe caan' eat better dan
him. Both of dem in mango season—(you know mango?) So Fader Forsythe
stay so now and when him look him see two cart a come down: one is seed
and one is mango skin.[1] So Battling John stay so and him look pon di man
and say, "Eh, whooo do dat?" Him look pon 'im and say is Fader Forsythe,
just get up and a brush 'im teet and ready fi him.

Collected in Kingston on October 6, 1978.

1. One cart has seeds that were left from eating mangoes, and one has the skins.

166D Fader Forsythe

And dem have a patty contes' now up a Tastee deh, wid Fader Forsythe and some more man. So Fader Forsythe si' down so and him say, "Bwoy, dem say di man who eat the most fastest patty. . . ." So Fader Forsythe sit down now and some man a eat. So one man eat off a dozen. When him eat off a dozen. Fader Forsythe eat off two dozen. So when dem start picture[1] now and dem ting now, dem put 'im picture so in a frame, and say 'im oder man dem lose. Him say 'im never know say a so him a eat fas', him tink a di man wah eat di morest. 'Im eat off di whole a Tastee's.

Collected in Kingston on October 6, 1978.
1. According to a member of the audience, the picture appeared in the daily paper.

166E Fader Forsythe

Well, you have this patty place name Tastee's, and they have a eating contest the other day. So a lot of people go dere to show how they can eat, but you have to eat a certain amount—the person who eat the most patties in a di shortest period of time was di winner. So Fader Forsythe now, he is not a fast eater, but he eat plenty. So when everything finish, the contest finish and everything, a man eat three dozen patties within mussi hour and a half. So Father Forsythe, when di contest win and everyting now, Fader Forsythe still a eat, and when you tek a check, Fader Forsythe gon' twelve dozen and still a ask fi more. So when you tek a check now dem haffi say Fader Forsythe is di loser but still di winner, because him take a bigger time but him eat more, double up and triple up what everybody else eat.

Collected in Kingston in November, 1978.

166F Fader Forsythe

Well, this one is Fader Forsythe alone. Well, a Chineyman have a grocery store, and Fader Forsythe come inside dere and say, "Mr. Chin, how much you have to lose? [I'll bet I can] eat off your whole shop." Mr. Chin say, "Get out of my shop! You caan' eat out my shop." So him say, "I bet one hundred pounds." Him say "O.K., if you eat off my shop I give you one hundred pounds."

So Fader Forsythe start eat now and start eat; so when the Chineyman really see Fader Forsythe eat off the whole showglass of cake, bread, cheese,

pastry, and all dose tings, him have to pay Fader Forsythe to stop eat. Because
him know say him goin' lose double, cause Fader Forsythe when him start eat
now is like him nah go stop. Sometime people all wonder which part all the
food deh go. Because him just long and lanky and slim.

Collected in Kingston in November, 1978.

167 The Wheel Just Stop

I goin' give you a joke bout my fader. You want see one time my fader
[was driving] in a Montego Bay, when a train [was coming along]: "Chooka-
chooka-chooka-chooka." Well, you waan' see, when we reach *right* at a railroad crossing—brake!—when you check it out now, him run out a brake! So
you nuh know what him do. Him just push out him foot through di window and just cotch up—and a "Shi-shi-shi." You know wha' happen? The wheel
just stop.

Collected in Kingston on September 21, 1978.

168 Him Stop the Plane

Well, you wan' see what happen now. One time I have a uncle, you nuh
seet? And I was going go pon farm worker to Florida, right? And when I
check it out, the plane a fly, you know, and when I check it out the plane
puncture up in the air, you nuh seet? And him just push out him foot and
stop the plane.

Collected in Kingston on September 21, 1978.

169 Ease Me Up

One day, you know, mi deh a one beach inna Florida, you know. So,
you know, dem big fish dem, butter fish dem. Mi see one a dat, you know,
so mi say, "Cho." So mi look pon a lady and seh, "Ah can swim and ketch dat
fish." Lady look pon me and say, "You caan' ketch di fish." I say, "Awright."
Mi do so and chuck off[1] and hole di fish now, so mi swim and dive and
hole di fish now and do so. And hear di fish now: "Oh, ease mi up nuh, ease
mi up nuh."[2] Mi say, "Ah goin' give you three chance." And mi jus' swim off
again and hole and ketch him again di second time. And him jus' look pon

me and say, "Cho, I have two more chance." Chuck off again and hole him again, and as mi chuck off again a hole di las' time, hear him nuh: "Master, mi never know say you are the king of the sea. Ease me up nuh!"

Collected in Kingston on October 6, 1978.
See Motif X1150, "Lies about Fishing," in Baughman, *Type and Motif-Index.*
1. Take off.
2. Let me go now.

170 Row, Row, Row Your Boat

One night now mi inna mi house a sleep, you know, so mi wake up. Mi haf two stick a matches, a matches box, and one cigarette. So mi go so now [dramatizing] and put di cigarette inna mi mout' and go so—"Shhh" [sound of match fizzling out]. And di match is out, so mi trow it in a likkle pail under di bed now. Mi go so again an' light di oder one and light mi cigarette and trow it and trow di matches box in a pail. Get some sleep now. Mi hear a likkel voice say say:

> Row, row, row your boat
> Gently down di stream,
> Merry, merry, merry, merry
> Life is. . . .

Mi say, "What dat?" So mi go so now and tun on mi light and look and mi nuh see nuttin'. Mi say, "Wait, wha' kind a business dis?" So mi go so now and gone back inna mi bed and sleep again. Dat same night, *again.* So mi say, "Wait!" Mi look an mi nuh see nuttin' out a door, mi nuh see nuttin', but mi think a angel a sing, and mi go so and look. Mi no see no angel. So mi go back now and start sleep again. Di said night, mi tun on mi light and go so and draw di pail and look—is two roaches mi see inna di matches box and a row di matches stick and say:

> Row, row, row your boat
> Gently down di stream. . . .

Collected in Kingston on October 5, 1978.

171 Lef the Water Heng Up

You waan' see, I live in a di country. You waan' see, my old man say he woulda sell some cow and [told me to] give the cow some water. So you waan' see, I gi' a pan of water, and when you tek a stock, I gi' the cow, but the cow don't drink the water. So I just mark up by a tree and heng it up and say, well, the final day I feel, well, the cow may drink the water, if him don' drink the water dis day.

So when I go to find out nex' mawning, wha' you tink really happen? Mosquito eat off the pan and lef' the water heng up. Mosquito eat off the pan and lef' the water heng up. I couldn't believe it. Right deh so.

Collected in Kingston on September 21, 1978.
Versions appear in Beckwith, *Jamaican Anansi Stories*, No. 16, and Burke, *Water*, pp. 25–28.

VIII

Riddles

Introduction

A look at ancient Oriental and Sanskrit writings, at Old Testament accounts, at Greek and Latin literature, at Old English sources, at any contemporary American children's magazine, or at a recent issue of the *Gleaner* reveals something of the enduring and widespread interest in the riddle, not only as a separate genre, but also as a key element in other narratives, such as the *Märchen* that revolve around the hero's finding the solution to a riddle.

Riddles, as Jan Harold Brunvand so effectively puts it, "are traditional questions with unexpected answers — verbal puzzles that circulate, mostly by word of mouth, to demonstrate the cleverness of the questioner and challenge the wit of his audience."[1] One of the key reasons for the popularity of riddles is obviously the love of a battle of wits, particularly in Jamaica, where verbal contests of every variety are so popular. Closely related to this fascination is the appeal of riddling as a form of entertainment. William Hugh Jansen's claim that "in America, riddling is more nearly a performance than a contest" finds support in Jamaican riddling as well, where one might observe that (as Jansen suggests is the case in America), "[the] riddlers do not *ask* riddles or *set* riddles; they *tell* riddles."[2] In Jamaica as in other cultures, another explanation for the popularity of the riddle is the lure of the obscene. Riddles most often begin by presenting a description that is intended to mislead, frequently by clear and inescapable sexual implications. Indeed, it has been suggested that there is thinly veiled sexual symbolism in all riddles.[3]

Riddles take varied forms, but generally they require identifying an object that is compared with something else. Often the riddle is in rhyme and begins with a set phrase, such as "Riddle me this riddle" or "Riddle me, riddle me right," and ends with "What is it?" or some comparable question. In Jamaica the set phrase that I observed at the beginning of most riddles was "Riddle, riddle, guess me this riddle, and perhaps not"; the standard ending was either "What is it?" or "Guess me this riddle."

My experiences suggests that riddling remains a popular pastime for both young and old, rural and urban Jamaicans. Though many of their riddles have a distinctively Jamaican flavor in terms of the metaphors and language, one is immediately struck by the number of them that are traditional, both in form and in subject matter, as is frequently noted in the annotations.

---

1. Jan Harold Brunvand, *The Study of American Folklore: An Introduction* (New York: Norton, 1968), p. 48.

2. William Hugh Jansen, "Riddles: 'Do-It-Yourself Oracles,'" in *American Folklore,* ed. Tristram Coffin III (1968; rpt. Washington, D.C.: Voice of America Forum Lectures, 1974), p. 235.

3. See Brunvand, p. 58.

172 Riddle, Riddle

Riddle, riddle, guess me this riddle, and perhaps not.
Rope run and horse stan' up?

I will guess it now, and say it is pumpkin.

Recorded in Mandeville on September 16, 1978.
A version appears in Beckwith, *Jamaican Anansi Stories,* No. 147.

173 Chin, Cherry Bear

Chin, cherry bear, cedar,
What was that?

That is a plum. That was a plum tree.

Recorded in Mandeville on September 16, 1978.

174 Chin Cherry, Uphill

Chin cherry, uphill,
Chin cherry, downhill,
Not a man can climb chin cherry.

And I will guess it is smoke. Smoke go up and smoke come down and
no man can climb smoke.

Recorded in Mandeville on September 16, 1978.
Versions appear in Beckwith, *Jamaican Anansi Stories*, No. 185; Taylor, *English Riddles*, Nos. 1616a–1617b; Parsons, *Folk-Lore of the Sea Islands*, p. 152, No. 5; and Parsons, *Folk-Lore of the Antilles*, Pt. 3, Nos. 435 and 441.

175 What Is Green Like Grass?

What is green like grass?
But it is not grass.
What juk like macca?[1]
It isn't macca.
What is white like milk?
But it isn't milk.

Soursop.[2]

Recorded in Kingston on September 18, 1978.
Versions appear in Taylor, *English Riddles* No. 1368a; and Parsons, *Folk-Lore of the Antilles*, Part 3, No. 365.
1. A thorn.
2. Soursop is a fairly large kidney-shaped fruit, covered outside with a thin, green, prickly skin. Inside is a white pulp (sour tasting) with seeds. It is very popular for making fruit drink or ice cream, mixed with milk and flavored, or eaten plain. A popular belief is tea brewed with the leaves is good for hypertension.

176 The Shirt pon Mi Back

The shirt pon mi back,
Mi 'air underneat'
Mi Seed underneat' di ear
And mi stick underneat' di seed.
What is dat?

Corn.

Collected in Kingston on September 18, 1978.
Note the sexual suggestiveness: the allusions to pubic hair, the testicles, and the penis.

177 There Is a Cup

There is a cup and within that cup there is a sup,
Within the sup there is a bite.
What am I?

Coconut.

Given to me in writing by a Kingston teacher in November 1978.
See Taylor, *English Riddles*, No. 1241b. A variant appears in Beckwith, *Jamaican Anansi Stories*, No. 83.

178 I Went up Jingle Jangle 'Ill

I went up Jingle Jangle 'ill,
And I 'ear di devil's backbone shake.
What is dat?

Dry gungo.[1]

Recorded in Kingston on September 18, 1978.
    1. Gungo is a variety of small green peas in a pod, used for making soup or dried and used for making rice and peas.

179 My Fader Has Many Wives

My fader has many wives
And all of dem frock tear.
Only one of dem frock does not tear.
What is dat?

A banana tree wid one leaf that does not tear in the center of it.[1]

Recorded in Kingston on September 18, 1978.
    Versions of this riddle appear in Beckwith, *Jamaican Anasi Stories*, No. 113, and Taylor, *English Riddles* Nos. 593a, b, c, and d. It has also been collected in the Bahamas.
    1. Another Jamaican informant said the answer to this riddle is sometimes a virgin.

180 My Father Has Three Children

My father has three children
And di three of dem 'ead black.
What is dat?

Ackee.

Recorded in Kingston on September 18, 1978.
Versions appear in Beckwith, *Jamaican Anansi Stories,* No. 46, and Taylor, *English Riddles,* Nos. 923a and b.

181 What a Chicken Have?

What a chicken have dat a fowl don't have?
You know what a chicken have dat a fowl don't have?

Noodles.

Recorded in Kingston on September 21, 1978.

182 Cornmeal and Flour

Cornmeal and flour come in the same parcel and never mix.
What is that?

Egg.

Given to me in writing in November 1978 by a Kingston teacher.

183 Why Aeroplane?

Why aeroplane and babies are resemble?

Because aeroplane travel from city to city, and babies suck from titty to titty.

Recorded in Kingston on October 30, 1978.

184 Why Lightpost?

Why lightpost and policeman resemble?

The policeman has numbers, and the lightpost has numbers.

Recorded in Kingston on October 30, 1978.

185 Hell a Top

Hell a top, Hell a bottom,
Hallelujah[1] in a middle.

Puddin'.

Recorded in Kingston on September 18, 1978.
See Beckwith, *Jamaican Anansi Stories,* No. 67.
1. Fire; the sexual suggestiveness is very clear here.

186 One Mawning

One mawning mi grandmoder was walking down di street and a lot of Black people stand up to greet her.
What was dat?

Flies.

Recorded in Kingston on September 18, 1978.

187 Mi Father Has Many Money

Mi father has many money and cannot count it off.
What is dat?

Stars.

Recorded in Kingston on September 18, 1978.
Versions appear in Taylor, *English Riddles,* Nos. 1024 and 1028; and Parsons, *Folk-Lore of the Antilles,* part 3, Nos. 370 and 371.

188 Fader Have Twelve

Fader have twelve in all.
The second to the youngest one is the oldest one.
Which is that?

February.

Recorded in Kingston on September 18, 1978.
Versions appear in Parsons, *Folk-Lore of the Antilles,* part 3, No. 433; and Taylor, *English Riddles* No. 984; Taylor has a long discussion of riddles personifying the months and seasons (pp. 370–73).

189 Why Did Paul?

Why did Paul throw the clock outside the window?

Because he wanted to see time fly.

Recorded in Kingston on October 30, 1978.
A version appears in Sutton-Smith, "The Folk Games of the Children," p. 212. This is popular in the United States as a "little moron" joke, one that focuses on the stupidity of a numbskull called simply the little moron.

190 Whitey Whitey Send Whitey Whitey

Whitey whitey send whitey whitey go drive out the whitey whitey out of the whitey whitey.
What is that?

White man send him white dawter go drive out di white fowl out a di white cabbage.

Recorded in Kingston on October 30, 1978.
Versions appear in Beckwith, *Jamaican Anansi Stories,* No. 189; Dorson, *Negro Tales from Pine Bluff,* p. 280; Parsons, "Folk-Lore from Aiken" (No. 66); Parsons, *Folk-Lore of the Antilles,* Pt. 3, Nos. 363, 371, and 437; and Taylor, *English Riddles* Nos. 844a–856. Versions have also been collected in Nova Scotia, Bermuda, and the Bahamas.

191 What Is It?

What is it you find in front of woman,
In the middle of fowl,
And at the back of cow?

The letter *w.*

Recorded in Kingston on October 30, 1978.

192 What Goes In?

What goes in very stiff and come out soft and wet?

Chewing gum.

Recorded in Kingston on November 8, 1978.
A version appears in Knapp and Knapp, *One Potato,* p. 106.

193 I Went up Jingle Jangle 'Ill

I went up Jingle Jangle 'ill and me white kerchief drop
And I couldn't stop to pick it up.
What is dat?

Spit.

Recorded in Kingston on September 18, 1978.
A variant appears in Beckwith, *Jamaican Anansi Stories,* No. 127.

194 London Bridge

London Bridge is falling down
And Jamaica cotch it up.
What is dat?

Brassiere and titty.

Recorded in Kingston on September 18, 1978.

195 Ole England

Ole England dead and gon',
No one to find him.
What is dat?

Bottle.

Recorded in Kingston on September 18, 1978.
A version of this riddle is in Beckwith, *Jamaican Anansi Stories* (No. 148).

196 Red een, Red out

Red een, red out (dis is a riddle, you know),
Red een, red out,
Four corners square,
What is dat?

Brick.

Recorded in Kingston on September 18, 1978.
A version is in Taylor, *English Riddles,* No. 1535.

197 Which Bus?

Which bus was the first to cross the Atlantic Ocean?

Colum*bus.*

Given to me in writing by a Kingston teacher in November 1978.

198 Riddle Me Dis

Riddle me dis, riddle me dat.
My mother have three children and all have one eye.
What is that?

Needle.

Given to me in writing by a Kingston teacher in November 1978.

199 My Father Have a Horse

My father have a horse, and every ride him ride, him ride in a him tail bone.

What is that?

Smoking pipe.

Given to me in writing by a Kingston teacher in November 1978.

Versions are in Beckwith, *Jamaican Anansi Stories*, No. 5; and Taylor, *English Riddles*, Nos. 427a and b. This riddle has also been collected in the Bahamas.

200 Around the Corner

Around the corner there is a tree,
And under the tree there is a school.
And in that school there is a bell.
What is the teacher's name?

Isabell.

Given to me in writing by a Kingston teacher in November 1978.

201 Diggle Daggle

Diggle daggle was the saddle,
Wengy bow was the horse,
What was the man's name?

Watt.

Given to me in writing by a Kingston teacher in November 1978.

202 Why Does a Tailor?

Why does a tailor and a plantain are alike?

The tailor cut to fit and the plantain fit to cut.

Given to me in writing by a Kingston teacher in November 1978.

A version appears in Beckwith, *Jamaican Anansi Stories*, No. 267.

203 Why Do Birds?

Why do birds sleep and hang down their heads?

Because they don't have any pillow.

Given to me in writing by a Kingston teacher in November 1978.

204 What Goes into the Fridge Hot?

What goes into the fridge hot and comes out hot, same way?

Pepper.

Given to me in writing by a Kingston teacher in November 1978.

205 Send Boy Go Call Doctor

Send boy go call doctor, doctor come before boy.

Coconut.

Given to me in writing by a Kingston teacher in November 1978.
Versions appear in Beckwith, *Jamaican Anansi Stories,* No. 135; Taylor, *English Riddles,* Nos. 951a, b, c, d, e, f, and g; and Parsons, *Folk-Lore of the Antilles,* Pt. 3, Nos. 365, 369, 422, and 428. This riddle has also been collected in the Bahamas.

206 Riddle, Riddle

Riddle, riddle, guess me this riddle, and perhaps not.
My father have horse, no man ever ride it
Until the back is sore.
Guess me this riddle.

No man can guess it. I guess it: is a housetop. You don't climb on the roof of you house until you want to repair it.

Collected in Mandeville on September 16, 1978.
Versions are in Beckwith, *Jamaican Anansi Stories,* No. 2; and Taylor, *English Riddles,* No. 435.

207 Going up a Hill

Going up a hill, you face turn up,
Coming down, you face turn up.
What's the meaning of that?

Climbing a tree. You climbing the tree, you face turn up, and you coming down, you face turn up.

Collected in Mandeville on September 16, 1978.

Versions appear in Taylor, *English Riddles,* Nos. 724a, b, c, and d; and Parsons, *Folk-Lore of the Antilles,* Pt. 3, Nos. 372 and 375. A variant is in Beckwith, *Jamaican Anansi Stories,* No. 89. The riddle has also been collected in the Bahamas.

208 It's in Jamaica

And for you[1] now:
It's in Jamaica I am
In America I stand.
What's the meaning of that?

You carry America dust on your shoe and come to Jamaica: in Jamaica I am, American I stand.

Recorded in Mandeville on September 16, 1978.

A version appears in Beckwith, *Jamaican Anansi Stories,* No. 87.

1. The teller addressed me directly at this point.

IX

Rhymes

Introduction

A great many rhymes (and most of those included in this chapter) reveal the irreverence of children, who make parodies of anything considered sacred by adults—the Bible, religious songs, patriotic songs, political events, nursery rhymes,[1] school, church, etc., etc. A great number of these children's rhymes are shocking and ribald verses treating sex, the excretory processes, language (especially obscene language), racial abuses, and other such forbidden subjects.

The pleasure of these rhymes to children pretty clearly stems from the opportunity they afford to briefly escape from or attack societal restrictions. Recitations of these materials win them a certain amount of prestige among their peers—even when, as is sometimes the case, the children are not fully aware of what they are saying; they have witnessed the reactions of others, and knowing the rhyme is a shocker is enough to recommend it.

Another function of children's rhymes, aside from their role as a tool of rebellion and as a means of entertainment, as Mary and Herbert Knapp point out, is their contribution to the child's "grasp of the complexity and richness of language." Such verses, they continue, help the performers to develop "an ear for metaphor, innuendo, puns, tone, and—yes—aesthetic form."[2] That this

155

is quite clearly a significant aspect of the popularity of rhyming among Black Jamaicans is evident to anyone who is aware of the special love of language — its rhythms, melodies, rhymes, and poetry — among Blacks throughout the Diaspora, for whom rhyming in various forms has always been a part of many aspects of life: from traditional rhymes, songs, sermons, speeches, etc., to jive talk, street talk, the dozens, the toast, the Jamaican tracing match, and the Trinidadian picong.[3] Indeed, writers such as Rap Brown, Ralph Ellison, and Louise Bennett have attested to the influence of their exposure to similar verbal practices among Black folk upon their development as writers.[4]

While my emphasis thus far has been largely on obscene children's rhymes, it is important to observe that not all children's rhymes are obscene (certainly not apparently so). Verses such as charms, mnemonic rhymes, and play rhymes are also popular with children, and a few such pieces follow. It is also important to note that not all rhymes are *children's* rhymes. Toasts, political rhymes, work rhymes, military chants, epitaphs, yearbook inscriptions, and the like have all been popular among adults and widely collected. A few of the rhymes in this chapter, especially the political commentaries, very likely have had a currency among adults as well as children. Most of the material here, however, was collected from children or from adults who recalled them as verses from their childhood.

Rhymes frequently accompany games. They may be used to select principals in the game, or they may be an integral part of the game (such as tag, jump rope, clapping, and the like). Such rhymes that I collected in connection with the playing of games are included in Chapter 11. A few other verses that may sometimes appear as rhymes, but that were sung for me, appear in Chapter 10. Those rhymes whose subject is the Rastafarian appear in Chapter 6.

---

1. It is significant to note that "nursery rhymes" presumably originated as satirical mockeries of political figures and situations. This thesis is developed by Katherine Elwes Thomas in *The Real Personages of Mother Goose* (New York: Lothrop, Lee & Shepard, 1930).

2. Knapp and Knapp, *One Potato,* pp. 186–87.

3. The dozens is a verbal dueling popular among Black Americans, particularly males, in which antagonists direct insults at each other, usually in rhyme and frequently aimed at the other's mama. The tracing match and the picong are Jamaican and Trinidadian varieties of the dozens, respectively.

4. H. Rap Brown, *Die Nigger, Die* (New York: Dial, 1969); Ralph Ellison, *Shadow and Act* (New York: Random House, 1964); and Daryl Dance, interview with Louise Bennett, Gordon Town, September 15, 1978.

209 Cain and Abel

Cain and Abel
Sat upon a table.

Cain said to Abel,
"Show me your navel."
Cain took the knife,
And him juk him pon him navel.

Collected in Kingston on October 30, 1978.

210 The Lord Is My Shepherd

The Lord is my shepherd, peng-ge-len-ge-leng,
I shall not mini-mini want,
He maketh me to lie down in potato walk.

[variation in writing]: He maketh me to lie down in a pack of ganga.

Collected in Kingston on October 30, 1978.

211 Hail Mary

Hail Mary, full of grace,
Donkey lick mi round mi waist,
Puss a lick, dog a lick,
All a wi a Catholic.

Given to me in writing by a Kingston teacher in November 1978.
A version appears in Knapp and Knapp, *One Potato,* p. 171.

212 Our Father Who Art in Heaven

Our Father who art in heaven,
Ah buy a shirt fi two an' eleven,
Ah wear it once, ah wear it twice,
Ah give it back to Jesus Christ.

Given to me in writing by a Kingston teacher in November 1978.

213 Forty Days and Forty Nights

Forty days and forty nights,
Paul donkey ketch a fight,

John came in and pick a fight,
And swear to God.

Collected in Kingston on October 30, 1978.

214 String Pop, Baggy Drop

Ting-a-ling-a-ling
School bell a ring.
Teacher baggy tie with a big broad string.
String pop,
Baggy drop,
Send for the mop
To pick it up.

Collected in Kingston on October 30, 1978.

215 For Health and Strength

For health and strength,
And dollars and cents,
We praise thy name,
For Shearer's own cent.[1]

Given to me in writing by a Kingston teacher in November 1978.
1. It was while Shearer was prime minister that Jamaica changed from pounds and pence to dollars and cents.

216 Every Night

Every night
Dance a light
In a Shearer house.

Collected in Kingston on October 30, 1978.

217 Queen Victoria

> Orange in the market,
> One for a penny,
> Queen Victoria
> Reign for many.

Collected in Kingston on October 30, 1978.

218 If You White, You Quite All Right

My grandmother told me that the lady that she grow up with, her mother told her that this is what the whitey brother told the slaves:

> If you white you quite all right,
> If you brown you hang around,
> But if you black you stay back.

Collected in Kingston on October 30, 1978.

It does not appear that this popular American verse has much currency in Jamaica. I heard a more popular Jamaican variant of the verse in the United States from a Jamaican who grew up in Savanna-La-Mar:

> If you're black, you're fancy,
> If you're brown, you're dancy,
> If you're white, you're red ants.

219 I Am a Man from Back a Wall

> I am a man from Back a Wall,[1]
> I eat potatoes big and small,
> But when I turn my back against the wall,
> I eat goat skin and all.

Collected in Kingston on October 30, 1978.

1. A major ghetto of Western Kingston.

220 I Am a Gal from Back a Wall

> I am a gal from Back a Wall,
> I nyam potato big and small,

But when mi back is agains' di wall,
I nyam di very skin and all,
Ayyiyi!

Collected in Kingston on October 30, 1978.

221 Bulla Is a Noun

Bulla is a noun,
Big and round,
Soft and tender.
When we take a bite
We bound to surrender.

Collected in Kingston on October 30, 1978.

222 Line a Banana

Line a banana,
Jump in a corner,
Eat out Miss Vera,
Ripe banana.

Collected in Kingston on October 30, 1978.

223 Mi Name Johnny Flower

Mi name Johnny Flower,
Mi eat one pound of flour,
But if you give mi a *tousand* dummplin',
Ah nyam it off in a half a hour.

Collected in Kingston on October 30, 1978.

224 Hot, Hot Patty

Hot, hot patty,
Two fi quattie,[1]

Jus' come out
A Miss Nancy batti.

Collected in Kingston on October 30, 1978.
1. Three farthings.

225 Popeye the Sailor Man

Popeye the sailor man
Lives in a garbage can,
He eats all the worms
And spits out the germs,
Popeye the sailor man.
'E lift up my auntie and take off her pantie,[1]
I'm Popeye the sailor man.

Given to me in writing by a Kingston teacher in November 1978.
Versions appear in Knapp and Knapp, *One Potato,* pp. 164, 184, and 188.
1. Carlos Nelson suggested that this verse was motivated by the many sailors who visited Jamaica during the fifties and their relationships with the Jamaican women of the night.

226 Haile Selassie

Lawd a massy
Donkey have fassi,[1]
Who fi wash i'
But Haile Selassie?

Collected in Kingston on October 30, 1978.
1. Sores.

227 I Married to a Millionaire

Believe me, I nuh care,
All I know, I married to a millionaire.
If him die,
I nah cry,
All I do
Just pop another guy.

Collected in Kingston on October 30, 1978.

Versions appear in Botkin, *Treasury of American Folklore,* p. 797; and Sutton-Smith, "Folk Games of the Children," p. 214.

228 The Way You Spell Japan

A woman and a man siddown pon a pan,
Dat is the way you spell Japan.

Collected in Kingston on October 30, 1978.

229 The Way You Spell Mathematics

Matta in the eyes,
Ticks in the batti,
That is the way you spell mathematics.

Collected in Kingston on October 30, 1978.

230A Once upon a Time

Once upon a time Piggy was a swine
Jump over car line and bruk him behin',
Mr. Valentine[1] was just in time
To take white lime and rub him behin'.

Collected in Kingston on October 30, 1978.
1. A possible allusion to a famous cricketer in Jamaica during the fifties and sixties.

230B Once upon a Time

Once upon a time
Monkey was a swine,
Jump over car line,
Broke him behin'.
Dere come Miss Nancy
Rolling down the line
Wid plain white lime
To rub him behin'.

Look at dat!
A-aw-w-w-w-w!

Collected in Kingston on September 15, 1978.

230C Once upon a Time

Once upon a time
When Piggy was a swine,
Piggy went up the hill
To break some bar vine.
Piggy fall down and break his behin'.
Doctor Valentine was just in time
With a pint of turpentine
To well up back Piggy's behin'.

Collected in Kingston on September 10, 1978.

230D Once upon a Time

Once upon a time
Big Bwoy was a swine
And broke 'im behin',
Jump over the train line,
And run fi a lime
And rub 'im two behin'.

Collected in Kingston on September 18, 1978, from an eleven-year-old boy.

231 Engine, Engine, Number Nine

Engine, Engine Number Nine,
Running pon Chicago line,
Please tell me the correct time.
The correct time is nine.

Collected in Kingston on October 30, 1978.
Versions appear in Brewster, *Children's Games,* p. 168; Botkin, *Treasury of American Folklore,* p. 768; and Abrahams, *Counting-Out,* No. 161, in which thirty-two other sources are listed.

232 Three Little Monkeys

Three little monkeys jumping on the bed,
One fell off and bumped his head.
Call the doctor and the doctor said,
"That's what you get for jumping on the bed."

This popular children's rhyme was recorded from my five-year-old daughter in Kingston on September 21, 1978. She had lived in Kingston for about four months and was attending school in Mona Heights, where she learned the verse from her schoolmates.

233 Rain a Fall

Rain a fall,
Breeze a blow,
Chicken batti out the door.

Collected in Kingston on October 30, 1978.

234A Mosquito One

Mosquito one,
Mosquito two,
Mosquito jump in a hot callaloo.
Light the lamp,
Mosquito come,
Pitch him batti out the lamp.

Collected in Kingston on October 30, 1978.

234B Mosquito One

Mosquito one,
Mosquito two,
Mosquito jump in a hot callaloo.
Baby caan' walk,
Baby caan' talk,
Baby caan' eat wid knife and fork.

Collected in Kingston on October 30, 1978.

234C Mosquito One

Mosquito one,
Mosquito two,
Mosquito jump in hot callaloo.
Bake the bread,
Bring me the pork,
But save me the change.

Collected in Kingston on October 30, 1978.

235 No Beer

In 'eaven we have no beer,
That's why we are drink it 'ere.
When we are gone from 'ere,
Our friends will be drinking all di beer.

This toast was collected in Kingston on September 18, 1978, from a child, exact age unknown.

236 Chinee, Chinee

Chinee, Chinee, never die;
Flat nose and Chinky eye!

Collected in Kingston on August 25, 1978, from an informant from Trinidad.
Similar children's insults against the Chinese may be found in Knapp and Knapp, *One Potato,* pp. 198–200.

237 Down by the Creek

Down by the creek where nobody goes,
I saw Sandra without any clothes,
There came Otis and a swinging chain,
Pull down his zip and out it came:
Two shaky balls an' a 'ell of a cock
Give Sandra a 'ell of a shock.

Collected in Kingston on September 11, 1978, from a thirteen-year-old informant.

X

Songs

Introduction

Certainly no aspect of Jamaican folklore is as familiar to the American and international audience as the music, which has been popularized both by a large number of prominent and well-known Jamaican singers (from Harry Belafonte to Bob Marley) whose recordings have been internationally acclaimed and by the many local groups who entertain tourists at the numerous popular resorts throughout Jamaica. Furthermore several collections of traditional folk songs have served to make this form of Jamaican folklore easily accessible. A great deal of important work in the collection and preservation of folk music continues with the ongoing organized efforts to make field recordings of traditional and contemporary folk songs throughout the country, particularly by such notable music scholars as Marjorie Whylie and Olive Lewin. Their important work in collecting and interpreting Jamaican folk music, in tracing influences, and in arranging that music for schools promises to contribute to the preservation and perpetuation of this significant area of Jamaican life and culture.

    Because of the wealth of material available, I made little effort to collect the well-known traditional folk songs. Such songs as appear here are presented because they are variants to the popular versions or because they have not been as commonly anthologized. Most of the materials in this chapter are more current, topical pieces.

Included among these selections are calypsos, work songs, children's songs, and numerous parodies of religious and patriotic songs. Several of the contemporary pieces, especially those collected from children, satirize every conceivable social, economic, and political situation in contemporary Jamaican life.

A great many of the children's parodies ridicule school and teacher. It is perhaps to be expected that Jamaican schools might incur such lampooning, since in Jamaica the school system is more pressure ridden throughout than it is in America. There, from elementary school on, students are compelled to struggle with the behemoth of periodic exams that must be passed in order to advance within the system. Furthermore, in most schools the teaching techniques are traditional and *strict* — there is a great deal of drilling and recitation and no lack of harsh discipline, including the use of the rod.

It is perhaps also to be expected that a great many of the current, topical songs are political. Such pieces are, of course, usually short-lived, since they are no longer relevant once the situation that motivated them changes. The political verses that I collected stemmed from the 1972 contest between former Prime Minister Hugh Shearer and his successor, Michael Manley. Some of those same songs were recast during the election in 1976, when Manley was challenged by Edward Seaga, who defeated him in 1980. Such songs as the political ones in this chapter reflect the fact that Jamaicans, like their counterparts in many third-world countries, take their elections seriously, and thus political contests take on a passion rarely experienced in the United States. In the last election, for example, the violence was so great that many Jamaicans fled the country in fear for their lives. I had one friend who had, months in advance, purchased airline tickets so that he and his family were booked on flights leaving Jamaica the morning after the election, in the event that the candidate he supported lost. Indeed, during the 1980 campaign, as *Newsweek* reported, the death toll from violence was averaging a dozen a day[1] (in a country of two million people), and Edward Seaga reportedly charged "that on election day alone gunmen fired 'no less than 2,000 rounds' at his entourage."[2]

Several of the songs that I collected from children are clearly associated with games, and they are included in Chapter 11.

1. *Newsweek,* November 3, 1980, p. 56.
2. Ibid., November 10, 1980, p. 72.

238 Auntie Monica

I have an auntie, an auntie Monica,
And when she go shopping,

She all say do or that.
And so the axe were swinging,
The axe were swinging so,
And so the axe were swinging,
The axe were swinging so.

And I have an auntie, an auntie Monica,
And when she go shopping,
They all say do or that.
And so the church were singing,
The church were singing so,
And so the church were singing,
The church were singing so.

And I have an auntie, an auntie Monica,
And when she go shopping,
They all say do or that.
And so the broom were sweeping,
The broom were sweeping so,
And so the broom were sweeping,
The broom were sweeping so.

And I have an auntie, an auntie Monica,
And when she go shopping,
They all say do or that.
And so the axe were swinging,
The axe were swinging so,
And so the axe were swinging,
The axe were swinging so.
And so the church were singing,
The church were singing so,
And so the church were singing,
The church were singing so.
And so the broom were sweeping,
The broom were sweeping so,
And so the broom were sweeping,
The broom were sweeping so.

Finish.

Recorded in Kingston in September 1978 from a fifteen-year-old informant.

239 Will You Marry Me?

I am a soldier, young and gay,
Just come 'ome from sea today.
Will you marry, marry, marry, marry,
Will you marry me?

And if you're a soldier, young and gay,
Just came home from sea today,
I won't marry, marry, marry, marry,
I won't marry you.

And if I give you a rocking chair,
To rock from the gun that you get 'ere,
Will you marry, marry, marry, marry,
Will you marry me?

And if you give me your rocking chair,
To rock from the gun that I get 'ere,
I won't marry, marry, marry, marry,
I won't marry you.

And if I give you a bouncing ball,
To bounce from the kitchen straight thro' the 'all?
Will you marry, marry, marry, marry,
Will you marry me?

And if you give me a bouncing ball,
To bounce from the kitchen straight thro' the 'all,
I won't marry, marry, marry, marry,
I won't marry you.

And if I give you the key of my chest,
With all the money that I possess,
Will you marry, marry, marry, marry,
Will you marry me?

And if you give me the key of your chest,
With all the money that you possess,
I will marry, marry, marry, marry,
I will marry you.

Ha, ha, you are funny,
You don't want me but you want my money.

I won't marry, marry, marry, marry,
I won't marry you.

Recorded in Kingston in September 1978 from a ten-year-old girl.
Similar lines appear in a game song noted in Brewster, *Children's Games*, p. 155.

240 Mango Time

Me nuh drink coffee, tea, mango time,
Care how nice it may be, mango time,
[At the height of] the mango crop,
When the fruit dem a ripe and drop,
Wash you pot, tun dem down,
Mango time.

Mek we walk mango walk, mango time,
For is only we talk, mango time.
Mek we jump pon wi big jackass,
Ride him round [and not 'top a path][1]
Ride him fast, one more [time],
Mango time.

This song was sung for me in Kingston in September 1978 by a group of five youngsters ranging in age from eight to ten. Some sections of the tape were unclear, and the words in brackets were provided by another informant after the recording session.
　1. Don't stop on the way.

241 Run, Mongoose

Run, Mongoose, run, Mongoose,
Run, Mongoose, run, Mongoose.
Mongoose tek up a piece of stick,
Well me tek up a whole a brick.
Mongoose sey, "Mi nah tek las' lick."
Run, Mongoose.

But we met up a Gallaghan wire,
Seek a job of an operator,
Operator say, "Gu back in deh."
Run, Mongoose.
Run, Mongoose, run, Mongoose.

Mongoose went up a Teacher Ben,
Seek a room fi rent,
Mongoose began to teach his thing.
Run, Mongoose.
Run, Mongoose, run, Mongoose,
Run, Mongoose, run, Mongoose.

Mongoose tek up a whole a brick,
Ben took up a piece of stick.
Mongoose sey, "Mi nah tek las' lick."
Him say, "Run, Mongoose."
Run, Mongoose, run, Mongoose.

Mongoose went up a police station,
Seek a job of an operation,
Mongoose say, "Mi nah tek las' lick."
Run, Mongoose.

Recorded in Woodside on September 6, 1978.

According to Ms. Olive Lewin, noted Jamaican folk-song scholar, this is not a standard version of the popular folk song, which originated from the suggestion that the Prophet Bedward had an affair with one of the girls among his followers. It was originally a bawdy song with the suggestiveness carefully concealed, according to Ms. Lewin.

242 Sweetie Charlie

Mi gat mi business a mi yard,
Mattie carry i' go out a 'treet,[1]
Mi gat mi business a mi yard,
Mattie carry i' go out a 'treet.
Mi chat mi business a mi yard,
Mattie carry i' go out a 'treet,
But Sweetie Charlie deh go bruk Mattie back
Wid 'im coocoomacca.[2]
Sweetie Charlie,
Ask dem gal bout Sweetie Charlie.
Sweetie Charlie deh go bruk Mattie back
Wid di coocoomacca.

Collected in Gordon Town on September 15, 1978.

1. Gossips.

2. With his coocoomacca stick, a prickly branch from the coocoomacca tree, which is noted for its hardness.

243 Hold 'Em, Joe

Well, ["Hold 'Em, Joe"] from my research, comes from Manchester, the neighboring parish. And the story goes that a girl, a young attractive girl, with lots of bulges here and there, met one or two village boys one morning [as] she was *returning* home, and she met them going to take the train. Now in those days there was a terminus for the train at a little town called Kendal. . . .[1] And when she met these boys, they were going to take the train at five o'clock in the morning. So she met them at about four. Now, no decent girl was supposed in those days to be on the roads at four *a.m.* coming from anywhere. At four a.m., if she was going to take the train, you know, that would be understood, but not coming *from*. So the boys met her, greeted her, and very innocently went about their business and took the train, went to Kingston. They came back in the evening, and they came to the village, where she came from . . . and they called upon this leader to sing a song. And to the consternation of the girl, she heard the fellow begin like this:

> One Monday morning . . .

And he told the crowd to sing, "Hold them, Joe." His name was Joe. "Hold them, Joe," means "Give us the song, Joe. Hold on to the rhythm, Joe. Give it to us, Joe." So everybody sang, "Hold them, Joe." So he starts:

> One Monday morning.
> Hold them, Joe.
> Mi duh go to Kingston.
> Hold them, Joe.
> Mi bump up Kesiah.
> Hold them, Joe.
> Uh, where she uh come from?
> Hold them, Joe.
> She say she coming from the doctor.
> Hold them, Joe.
> [John] is a doctor.
> Hold them Joe.
> [Art] is a doctor.
> Hold them, Joe.
> Everybody done doctor.
> Hold them, Joe.

And so everybody goes in the chorus after that. But you see, the girl just broke down. She had to pull away. She had to escape because she knew it was about her; but in these folk songs, as you know, it is a parable. Each folk song is a parable. Each folk song is supposed to be a legend. It's not supposed to be true. If it were a written story, you would say all the names given here are fictitious. Well, of course, people know it's not fictitious, but so you call this man—she's coming from the doctor. She's coming from her boyfriend. And her boyfriend is her doctor. After all, who is a doctor? A doctor is a man who attends to you. A doctor is a man who makes you happy . . . a doctor, you know, a doctor normally, he gives you hope. He says, "Oh, that's all right. After you take these tablets and drink this medicine, you'll be quite all right, you know. You don't need to come back and see me. If anything, in two weeks, if you're not quite better, you can come." But you know, he's so pleasant and nice and so on that that does it. So after all, there is not much difference between a boyfriend and a doctor. They serve the same purpose.

This song was recorded in Santa Cruz on November 4, 1978.
The singer spoke about the origin and meaning of the song. His comments are presented verbatim.
A version appears in Courlander, *Treasury of Afro-American Folklore,* pp. 107–8.
1. Kendal is the site of the famous train crash in the fifties, in which over one hundred people were killed.

244 Colon Man a Come

One, two, three, four, Colon man a come,
One, two, three, four, Colon man a come,
One, two, three, four, Colon man a come,
Wid 'im brass chain a lick 'im belly,
Bang, bang, bang!

Ask 'im what's de time an' 'im look
Up pon de sun.
Ask 'im what's de time an' 'im look
Up pon de sun.
Ask 'im what's de time an' 'im look
Up pon de sun.
Wid 'im brass chain a lick 'im belly
Bang, bang, bang.[1]

Zoot suit an' brass chain 'Merican a come,
Big boot an' gold watch 'Merican a come,
Wid' 'im brass chain a lick 'im belly,
Bang, bang, bang!

So fass 'im leave de ilan,
So quick 'im come back.
So fass 'im leave di ilan,
So quick 'im come back.

So fass 'im leave de ilan,
So quick 'im come back
Wid 'im brass chain a lick 'im belly,
Bang, bang, bang!

Given to me in writing by a Kingston teacher.
1. This popular folk song makes fun of the Jamaicans who went to help build the Panama Canal (Colon men), and who showed off their wealth (watches) when they came back to Jamaica. Some-times, however, they did not actually have a watch on the end of their chains, as is the case in this version. See Olive Lewin, *Brown Gal in de Ring* (London: Oxford University Press, 1974), p. 1.

245 Mek ah Tell You When the Worl' Is Made

Come 'ere you little bit of sambo girl,
Mek ah tell you when the worl' is made.
World made six, God bless the seven,
Seven was the contract . . . eleven.
Adam was the first one, Eve was the second.
Cain was a wicked man. . . .

Recorded in Woodside on September 6, 1978. This version is obviously incomplete.

246 If You Want to Hear Duppy Laugh

If you want to hear duppy laugh,
Gu down a riverside Sunday mawning.
If you want to hear duppy laugh,
Gu down a riverside Sunday mawning.
Man duppy laugh, "Ha-ha-a-a!"
'Oman duppy laugh, "Ki-ki-ki-king-king!"
Man duppy laugh, "Ha-ha-a-a-a!"
'Oman duppy laugh, "Ki-ki-ki-king-king!" Ah tell you,
You should not beat him fi hear duppy laugh
On dat bright Sunday mawning.
Man duppy laugh, "Ha-ha-a-a-a!" Ye-ah-h-h!
And 'oman duppy laugh, "Ki-ki-ki-king-king!"

Recorded in Kingston on September 11, 1978.
A version appears in *Jamaican song,* No. 82, where Jekyll identifies it as a digging song.

247 A Duppy

Last week Sunday mawning,
Ah fall down a Rio Bueno River,
Fi gu hole[1] a shower
In a di cool, cool water.
Ah 'eard a scream
Coming from up di stream.
Ah climb a tree
And see what that could be,
But to my surprise
It was a duppy from up di stream.

Recorded in Kingston on September 11, 1978.
1. Get.

248 Missa Ramgoat

Ah, Missa Ramgoat, oh-h,
Barba[1] deh-a,
I beg you lend me you razor,
Baba deh,
A fi go cut off mi long bade,[2]
Barba deh,
A Missa Fittin' goat, oh-h,
Baba deh.
Ah beg you lend me you razor,
Baba deh,
A fi go cut off mi long bade,
Barba deh-a.
Awright.

This popular Jamaican work song was collected in Kingston from a fourteen-year-old informant.
1. Barber.
2. Beard.

249 'Oman Is a People

Leader: 'Oman is a people.
Others: Grumble too much. [All lines in this song alternate between the leader
and his audience.]

'Oman is a people.
Grumble too much.
'Oman is a people.
Grumble too much.
'Oman is a people.
Grumble too much.
'Oman is a people.
Grumble too much.
Dem a walk, dem a grumble.
Grumble too much.
Dem a nyam, dem a grumble.
Grumble too much.
Dem a eat, dem a grumble.
Grumble too much.
Dem a sing, dem a grumble.
Grumble too much.
Dem plant corn and grumble.
Grumblę too much.
Dem reap corn, dem grumble.
Grumble too much.
'Oman is a people.
Grumble too much.
'Oman is a people.
Grumble too much.
'Oman is a people.
Grumble too much.
'Oman is a people.
Grumble too much.
'Oman is a people.
Grumble too much.
Kingston woman, dem a grumble.
Grumble too much.
American woman, dem a grumble.
Grumble too much.
Dominican woman dem a grumble.
Grumble too much.
Dentist woman dem a grumble.[1]
Grumble too much.
'Oman is a people.
Grumble too much.

This work song was recorded in Santa Cruz on November 4, 1978. The informant noted that he had changed some words, since the words that the men would use out in the fields would not always "be suitable for the drawing room."

A version appears in Burke, *Water*, pp. 16–24.

1. During this session the singer had in his audience people from Santo Domingo, Kingston, and the United States, including the wife of a dentist. His citations illustrated his observation that the leader of this song always makes up his verses as he goes along.

250 The Cake Couldn't Bake

Once upon a time a lady bake her cake. A man come in there and eat it. So the lady go call a police, and the police say, "Why did you eat up the lady cake?"

> The cake couldn' bake
> And it give me bellyache.

And the police say: "I goin' to put you in the jail."

Man: If you put me in the jail,
I will cock up mi tail,
And piss in the pail,
And must get bail.

Recorded in Kingston on September 10, 1978, from a six-year-old informant.

251 While Shepherds Washed Their Socks

> While shepherds washed their socks by night,
> And set them out to dry,
> Some dirty rogues were passing by,
> And said those socks are mine.
> I do believe, I must believe
> That chinch is bigger than flea,
> For on the wall they play football,
> Without a referee.
> [And when I go to bed at night,
> They come and bite me up.]

Recorded in Kingston on October 27, 1978. The song is sung very solemnly to the tune of "While Shepherds Watched Their Flocks by Night."

The two lines in brackets are a varient ending given to me in a written version by a Kingston teacher in November 1978.

252 My Soul Shall Fly

And when I die,
And when I die,
I hope that my,
I hope that my,
My soul shall fly,
My soul shall fly up
Rader than I.

Recorded in Kingston on October 30, 1978. A leader sings the first lines, and the group repeats his lines.

253 Mr. Kennedy Is Now Dead

Mr. Kennedy is now dead,
Oswald shot him in the head.
Coco Cola went to town,
Pepsi Cola lick him down.
Desnoes and Geddes[1] pick him up,
Carry to Fanta[2] to fix him up.
Tra-la-la-la-la-la,
Tra-la-la-la-la-la.

Recorded in Kingston on October 27, 1978.
A version appears in Knapp and Knapp, *One Potato*, p. 165. The Knapps discuss parodies of commercials on pp. 162–66.
1. Desnoes and Geddes is the name of the big soft-drink bottling company in Jamaica that makes Pepsi products.
2. Another drink made by Desnoes and Geddes

254 Shearer in the Garden Hiding

Shearer[1] in the garden hiding, hiding, hiding.
Shearer in the garden hiding.
Hiding from Joshua.[2]
Shearer, where art thou?
Shearer, where art thou?

Shearer, where art thou?
Shearer hiding from Joshua.

Recorded in Kingston on October 27, 1978. This song is sung to the tune of "Adam in the Garden Hiding." The tune is still sung at political rallies and was changed during the last elections to "Seaga in the Garden, etc."

1. A former prime minister of Jamaica.
2. Joshua is the nickname of Michael Manley, the former prime minister, who lost to Edward Seaga.

255 Ride Him, Shearer

Manley a Shearer donkey. Whooa!
Manley a Shearer donkey. Whooa!
Everywhere you go you hear them say,
Manley a Shearer donkey. Whooa!

Ride him, Shearer, ride him. Oooh!
Ride him, Shearer, ride him. Oooh!
Everywhere you go,
You hear them say,
Manley a Shearer donkey. Oooh!

Recorded in Kingston on October 27, 1978. I have a written version given to me by a Kingston teacher in November 1978, with the notation that those who wanted Manley to win sang, "Ride him, Manley, ride him." The song is sung to the tune of "Dip Them, Bedward, Dip Them." It too was sung during later political elections with appropriate changes in names.

"Ride Him, Shearer" bears an interesting similarity to the popular folktale of the hero riding the fool. (See Tale 19, above.)

256 Manley, Row the Boat Ashore

Manley, row the boat ashore, hallelujah.
Manley, row the boat ashore, hallelujah.
Manley, row the boat ashore, hallelujah.
Manley, row the boat ashore, hallelujah.

Shearer's boat is a sinking boat, hallelujah.
Shearer's boat is a sinking boat, hallelujah.
Shearer's boat is a sinking boat, hallelujah.
Shearer's boat is a sinking boat, hallelujah.

Given to me in writing by a Kingston teacher in November 1978. The song is sung to the tune of "Michael, Row the Boat Ashore." This too continues to be sung during campaigns with appropriate changes in names.

257 Keep Us from Counter Flour

Eternal Father, bless our land,
Guide us with thy mighty hand.
Keep us free from Counter Flour,
Lest we perish within the hour.
To our leaders, great defenders,
Jumped through the window and broke their fingers.
Justice truth be ours for ever,
Potato land we love.
Potato, potato, potato land we love.

Given to me in writing by a Kingston teacher in November 1978. Sung in the tune of the Jamaican national anthem, this song developed after the flour disaster in St. Thomas, when the flour had been infected with insect killer and about twenty people died.

258 Blessed Assurance

Blessed assurance, dumpling is mine,
Ackee and salt fish with coconut oil.
When Mama cook it, it's sweeter than wine,
When Mama cook it with coconut oil.
[God bless dumpling and coconut oil.]
[Me lick me finger plop, plop, plop.]
[When Papa taste it, he lick his finger.]

Recorded in Kingston on October 27, 1978. This selection is sung very solemnly in the tune of "Blessed Assurance." Several variant ending lines were given to me in written versions by a Kingston teacher in November 1978. They appear above in brackets.

259A We Three Kings

We three kings of curry and rice,
Bearing gifts we travel afar,
One on a bicycle, two on a tricycle,
Three on a donkey cart.
Oh-h-h rice and peas, it taste so nice,

Let us make a sacrifice.
One on a bicycle, two on a tricycle,
Three on a donkey cart.

Recorded in Kingston on October 27, 1978.
Variants appear in Knapp and Knapp, *One Potato*, p. 167.

259B We Three Kings

We three kings of Cassius Clay,
Bearing gifts of curry and rice.
One on a bicycle, two on a tricycle,
Three on a donkey cart.
Oh rice and dumplin' taste so nice,
One on a bicycle, two on a tricycle,
Three on a donkey cart.

We three kings of curry and rice,
Bearing gifts we traverse afar,
One on a bicycle, two on a tricycle,
Three on a donkey cart.

Oh, ackee and salt fish, bulla and pear,
Let us make a sacrifice.
One on a bicycle, two on a tricycle,
Three on a donkey cart.

We three kings of Orient are
Trying to smoke a rubber cigar.
It was loaded, it exploded
And scattered us all afar.

Given to me in writing by a Kingston teacher in November 1978.

260 Missa Potta

Mawnin', Missa Potta, good mawnin' to yuh, sah!
Ah cum to lodge a complain to yuh now, sah.
Ah plant a piece a red peas a Red Sally lan'!
Mary Jane ah pigin cum eat e out, sah!
Cum out a mi yard! Mi neva call yah!

Cum out a mi yawd! Mi neva call yah!
Fah de 'ouse rent money no dun pay fah.

Given to me in writing by a Kingston teacher in November 1978.

261 There Is a Bulla Shop

There is a bulla shop
Five miles away,
Where the children stop five times a day.
Lawd, Lawd, the bulla sweet!
Lawd, Lawd, it edge me teet,
Right a the bulla shop five miles away.

Given to me in writing by a Kingston teacher in November 1978. This song is sung to the tune of "There Is a Happy Land."

262 Trust and Don't Pay

Trust and don't pay,
For there is no other way
To be happy at Tuck Shop,
But to trust and don't pay.

Given to me in writing by a Kingston teacher in November 1978. The song is sung to the tune of "Trust and Obey."

263 Mi No Get No White Rum

From mi come yah mi no get no white rum,
From mi come yah mi no see no [unclear],
From mi come yah mi no get no white rum.
Mi a go sit down di boat
And gu way,
Mi a go sit down di boat
And gu way,
One a dese fine, fine day.

Recorded in Kingston on October 30, 1978.

264 All Hail the Power

All hail the power of rice and peas,
Let dumplin' prostrate fall,
Bring forth the royal ackee and fish,
And crown them, crown them, crown them,
Crown them with coconut oil.

Given to me in writing by a Kingston teacher in November 1978. This song is sung to the tune of "All Hail the Power of Jesus' Name."

265 There's a Boarding School

There's a boarding school
Close by the way,
Where the children eat rotten eggs
Three times a day.
How the children yelled
When they heard their dinner bell!
Smell how the eggs them smell
Nine miles away.

Come to the boarding school
Close by the way,
And eat some of the rotten eggs
Three times a day.
How the children yelled
When they heard their dinner bell!
Smell how the eggs them smell
Nine miles away.

Given to me in writing by a Kingston teacher in November 1978, this song is sung to the tune of "There's a Happy Land."

266 One More Day

One more day of school,
One more day of sorrow,
One more day of this old dump,
And we'll be home tomorrow.

Given to me in writing by a Kingston teacher in November 1978.

267 Mine Eyes Have Seen the Glory

Mine eyes have seen the glory of the burning of the school.
We have tortured every teacher, we have broken every rule.
We are going to hang the principle tomorrow afternoon.
We start at half past two.

Glory, glory, hallelujah,
Teacher hit me with the ruler.
Glory, glory hallelujah,
For the school we burned it down.

[Teacher hit me with a ruler,
I met her at the door with a colt 44,
And she ain't going to teach no more,
Glory, glory, hallelujah,
She ain't going to teach no more.

The ruler turned red,
And the teacher dropped dead,
And there won't be any school anymore.
Glory, glory, hallelujah,
There won't be any school anymore.]

Recorded in Kingston on October 17, 1978. The lines in brackets were provided in a written version given to me by a Kingston teacher in November 1978. This song is sung to the tune of "Battle Hymn of the Republic."

A version appears in Knapp and Knapp, *One Potato,* pp. 173–74.

268 Happy Birthday to You

Happy birthday to you,
You come from a zoo,
You look like a monkey,
And smell like one too.

Happy birthday to you,
I went to the zoo,
I saw a gorilla
And it looked just like you.

Given to me in writing by a Kingston teacher in November 1978.
A version appears in Knapp and Knapp, *One Potato,* p. 223.

269 Sister Joy

Sister Joy, bun'[1] out mi rice,
Ketch her in a bed,
She bawl, "Jesus Christ!
Hole mi tight,
Squeeze mi right.
Gi mi di same ting
You gi mi las' night.
Shut di door,
Gi mi more,
And if you want,
You can a take it pon di floor."

Recorded in Kingston on September 15, 1978.
1. Burn.

270A Sister Potter

Sister Potter,
Go like she fat,
She waan fi gi mi
Pon di wing bus stop.[1]
And when mi ketch 'er in a granstan' box,
When mi started to discharge,
Say she run lef' her blue drawers,
And she tear down di back yard.
And when dey came to di landlord,
Say, "You, Sister Potter,
Why you acting like dat?
You, Sister Potter,
Why you acting like dat?
You a gwan like a acro-b-a-t."
But see di frock
Wid di spit[2] a it a lick.[3] Ow!
Di frock wid di spit a it a lick.
See di frock,
Wid di spit a it a lick.
Man, we say dat tie and dye frock a lick,
But not nuh sweet.

Recorded in Kingston on September 15, 1978.

1. Side of the bus stop.
2. Split.
3. Stylish.

270B Sister Potter

Tek a looks at di gal a wear slingshot,
Sister Potter.
She batti black.
Di gal waan fi gi mi pon di wing bus stop,
And when mi ketch her round a grandstan' box,
And when mi started to discharge,
Di gal say she run lef her blue drawers.
And she tear down di back yard,
And den deh coming to di landlord,
And then they charge mi fi fr-a-u-d.

Recorded in Kingston on September 15, 1978.

XI

Children's Games

Introduction

Folk games are alive and well in Jamaica. Indeed, it has been established by folklorists that folk games survive throughout industrialized countries among children of *all* backgrounds and classes; however, there is no question that the style of life in Jamaica contributes even more to the persistence, even the flourishing, of traditional children's games. Folklorists have discovered that, despite the fact that some children in countries such as the United States spend most of their time engaging in supervised and organized activities (school, camp, Y activities, organized sports, supervised club activities), and despite the fact that they spend a great deal of their remaining time watching television, attending movies, listening to records, and engaging in other similarly passive entertainment, whenever they find time to themselves away from adults, they frequently participate in group folk activities—whether it be during recess at school, on the bus en route to school, in the car on the way to the movies, or in their backyards. Opportunities for participation in group games are more frequent in Jamaica, however, because most Jamaican children do not have constant access to televisions, radios, movies, and other such entertainment as does the average American child. Further, the year-round temperate weather conditions in Jamaica, coupled with the organization of Jamaican neighborhoods in urban areas around a central yard, are more conducive to continual group congregation and interaction than is the case in the United States. The fact that a large number of the children live in tiny little huts that are frequently very cramped and also hot during the day encourages the children to spend many of their waking hours outside in the company of others. After school the opportunity for the kinds of organized activities so common to American children is available only to the well-to-do Jamaican child. All of these conditions contribute to the popularity of games among Jamaican children — and in this regard, they perhaps enjoy an advantage over their American counterparts.

Children's games are significant factors in teaching children to govern themselves, for in such games they set up rules and learn, as Mary and Herbert Knapp note, "how to make sophisticated juridical distinctions that strike a fine balance between the self-interest of individuals and the good of the group." Other important benefits that accrue to participants in folk games are also discussed by the Knapps: "They let off steam, releasing tensions created by the repressive atmosphere of the school. They mock the larger culture, distancing themselves from the intrusive demands of advertising. They play with the emotion of fear, thus becoming less fearful."[1]

Many of the games that are popular with children in Jamaica have versions that have been prevalent in diverse places and times. They include jumping rope to set rhymes. Of the more than six hundred jump-rope rhymes that have been collected by folklorists,[2] I collected some of the more popular ones, such as "Cinderella, Cinderella" (No. 290) and "Down by the Ocean" (No. 289), from Jamaican children.

They include clapping games — that intimate play between two friends challenging and helping each other as they go through well-rehearsed routines, which usually require reciting memorized verses but also sometimes challenge the particpants to furnish original ideas. Several of the traditional clapping games remain popular with Jamaican children, including what the Knapps label "the *grand dame* of the claps,"[3] "Mary Mack" (No. 280).

They include skill games that require the manipulation of objects with dexterity, the most popular of which in Jamaica is clearly "Manuel Road" (Nos. 271A, B, and C).

They include the singing ring games in which children take turns being "It," the principal(s) who performs some act within or without the circle.

They include the dancing ring games in which the center individual or couple dances within the ring or around the ring, or winds through the ring, performing the dance steps indicated or suggested by the group song, but often also having an opportunity to improvise. Sometimes in these dancing ring games the whole group dances around together in a circle. The players may sometimes form two lines, and the dancing takes place as couples move through the lines. An example of a popular form of these dance games that I collected in Jamaica is "It's a Very Fine Motion" (No. 277).

If, indeed, as some scholars have suggested, children's games help to develop more independent, imaginative, social, and healthy children, Jamaican children by and large enjoy a distinct advantage.

1. Knapp and Knapp, *One Potato,* p. 2.
2. Ibid., p. 127.
3. Ibid., p. 136.

271A Manuel Road

Go down on Manuel Road, gal and boy,
Fi go bruk rock stone.
Go down on Manuel Road, gal and boy,
Fi go bruk rock stone.
Bruk them one by one, gal and boy,
Bruk them two by two, gal and boy,
Play wi' dem, play, gal and boy,
Knock your finger, no cry, gal and boy.

Recorded in Kingston on October 21, 1978.
A version appears in Jekyll, *Jamaica Song,* No. 98. In this game each person sits in a circle with stones piled in front of him. The stones are passed around as the song directs, faster and faster, according to the rhythm of the song; for if one misses the beat, he may get his knuckles hit with the stone. At the end of the game, stones are usually piled up in front of the one who misses his turn, and he is out of the game.

271B Manuel Road

Go down a Manuel Road, gal and boy,
Fi go bruk rock stone, gal and boy.
Go down a Manuel Road, gal and boy,
Fi go bruk rock stone, gal and boy.
Bruk dem one by one, gal and boy.
Bruk dem two by two, gal and boy.
Bruk dem three by three, gal and boy.
Bruk dem four by four, gal and boy.
Teacher have no time, gal and boy.

Go down a Manuel Road, gal and boy
Fi go bruk rock stone, gal and boy.

Bruk dem one by one, gal and boy.
Bruk dem two by two, gal and boy.
Bruk dem three by three, gal and boy.
Bruk dem four by four, gal and boy.
Keep them by yourself, gal and boy.
Mek dem [unclear], gal and boy.

Recorded in Kingston on October 30, 1978.

271C Manuel Road

Come we go Manuel Road, gal and boy,
Fi go break rock stone.
Break them one by one, gal and boy.
Break them two by two, gal and boy.
[Break them three by three, gal and boy.]
Break them four by four, gal and boy.

Given to me in writing by a Kingston resident on October 11, 1978.

272 Shine-Eye Gal

The shine-eye gal is a trouble to a man,
The shine-eye gal is a trouble to a man,
The shine-eye gal is a trouble to a man,
And she want and she want and she want everyting.
Her heel favor river and she want high heel,
Her heel favor river and she want high heel,
And she want and she want and she want everyting.

Shine-eye gal is a trouble to a man,
Shine-eye gal is a trouble to a man,
Shine-eye gal is a trouble to a man,
And she want and she want and she want everyting.
Waist favor wire and she want broad belt,
Waist favor wire and she want broad belt,
Waist favor wire and she want broad belt,
And she want and she want and she want everyting.

Shine-eye gal is a trouble to a man,
Shine-eye gal is a trouble to a man,
Shine-eye gal is a trouble to a man,
And she want and she want and she want everyting.
The lip favor liver and she want lipstick,
The lip favor liver and she want lipstick,
The lip favor liver and she want lipstick,
And she want and she want and she want everyting.

[Shine-eye gal is a trouble to a man,
Shine-eye gal is a trouble to a man,
Shine-eye gal is a trouble to a man,
Her eye favor toad and she want eyeglass,
Her eye favor toad and she want eyeglass,
Her eye favor toad and she want eyeglass,
And she want and she want and she want everyting.

Shine-eye gal is a trouble to a man,
Shine-eye gal is a trouble to a man,
Shine-eye gal is a trouble to a man,
And she want and she want and she want everyting.
Her neck favor bottle and she want necklace,
Her neck favor bottle and she want necklace,
Her neck favor bottle and she want necklace,
And she want and she want and she want everyting.

Shine-eye gal is a trouble to a man,
Shine-eye gal is a trouble to a man,
Shine-eye gal is a trouble to a man,
And she want and she want and she want everyting.
Her finger favor thread and she want gold ring,
Her finger favor thread and she want gold ring,
Her finger favor thread and she want gold ring,
And she want and she want and she want everyting.]

That's why never spen' you money pon a shine eye gal,
Never spen' you money pon a shine eye gal,
Never spen' you money pon a shine eye gal,
For she want and she want and she want everyting.

Collected in Kingston on October 27, 1978.
In this popular ring game the "Shine-Eye Gal" stands in the ring with her hands on her hips, and the others shake their fingers at her.
The verses in brackets were given to me in writing in November 1978.

273 Right through, Right through the Rocky Road

Right through, right through the rocky road,
Sing Charlie, Molly, Charlie.
Right through, right through the rocky road,
Sing Charlie, Molly, Charlie.
Dem barefoot gal mi nuh chat to dem,
Sing Charlie, Molly, Charlie.
Dem barefoot gal mi nuh chat to dem,
Sing Charlie, Molly, Charlie.

Right through, right through the rocky road,
Sing Charlie, Molly, Charlie.
Right through, right through the rocky road,
Sing Charlie, Molly, Charlie.
Dem dry-head gal mi no chat to dem,
Sing Charlie, Molly, Charlie.
Dem dry-head gal mi no chat to dem,
Sing Charlie, Molly, Charlie.

Right through, right through the rocky road,
Sing Charlie, Molly, Charlie.
Right through, right through the rocky road,
Sing Charlie, Molly, Charlie.
Dem talking gal mi nuh chat to dem,
Sing Charlie, Molly, Charlie.
Dem talking gal mi no chat to dem,
Sing Charlie, Molly, Charlie.

Right through, right through the rocky road,
Sing Charlie, Molly, Charlie.
Right through, right through the rocky road,
Sing Charlie, Molly, Charlie.
Dem big-foot gal mi no chat to dem,
Sing Charlie, Molly, Charlie.
Dem big-foot gal mi no chat to dem,
Sing Charlie, Molly, Charlie.

Recorded in Kingston on October 27, 1978.

This is a dancing game in which a set of partners goes through the line of the other players when they sing, "Right through, etc.," doing whatever improvisations they desire.

274 Poor Mass Charlie

Old Mass Charlie,
Him have a bulldog
In a him backyard.
A weh him get dat?
Chain haffi chain him,
Wire haffi wire him,
Rope haffi rope him.

Poor Mass Charlie,
Him have a bulldog
In a him backyard.
A weh him get dat?
Chain haffi chain him,
Wire haffi wire him,
Wood haffi beat him,
Rope haffi rope him.

This ring game was recorded in Kingston on October 27, 1978.

265 Stagolee

Stagolee:	I am Stagolee.
Others:	Stagolee stole the cookie from the cookie jar.
Stagolee:	Who me?
Others:	Yes, you.
Stagolee:	Couldn't be.
Others:	Then who?
Stagolee:	Number four stole the cookie from the cookie jar.
Number Four:	Who me?
Others:	Yes, you.
Number Four:	Couldn't be.
Others:	Then who?
Stagolee:	Number six stole the cookie from the cookie jar, etc.

Recorded in Kingston on October 21, 1978.
A version of this game appears in Knapp and Knapp, *One Potato,* p. 132; another is in box 1, Folklore Research Project, Institute of Jamaica. Except for the name, this seems to have no connection to the popular Black American toast, "Stagolee."
Each person in this ring game has a number, and he must respond if his number is called by Stago-

lee, or he is put out of the game. If Stagolee calls the number of someone who is out of the game, Stagolee is also put out. Stagolee stands inside the circle as long as he is in the game.

276 Zuzuwah

Now this game is played in a ring, and this man is going to town, and he is telling this woman:

> Mi gawn a town, Mary.
> Ai, Zuzuwah. (Everybody in the circle sings)
> Mi gawn a town, Mary.
> Ai, Zuzuwah.
> Mi bring one boot fi you.
> Ai, Zuzuwah.
> Mi bring one frock fi you.
> Ai, Zuzuwah.
> Mind mi goat fi me.
> Ai, Zuzuwah.
> Mind mi pig fi mi.
> Ai, Zuzuwah.
> But nuh mek no man come yah.
> No, Zuzuwah.
> But nuh mek no man come yah.
> No, Zuzuwah.

Then he lifts his voice now:

> Mi gawn a town.
> Oh-h-h, Zuzumah.

This other one sings, Zuzu*mah,* you see:

> Mi gawn a town.
> Oh-h-h, Zuzumah.

He turns to the woman and says:

> Mind da bwoy, Zuzu,
> Zuzumah.
> Mind da bwoy, Zuzu,
> Zuzumah.
> Mind da bwoy, Zuzu,
> Zuzumah.
> MI GAWN A TOWN!!!

He lifts his voice to say it loud that Zuzumah can hear that he gone to town. No sooner than you see Zuzumah coming through. . . .

Hi, you cook the food?
Ai, Zuzumah. [laughter]

Then she is about to hand him this plate of dinner:

Mi got corn pork.
Oh-h Zuzumah.
Mi got breshe,
Oh-h, Zuzumah.
The roast breshe deh yah?
Ai, Zuzumah.
Roast banana too?
Ai, Zuzumah.
Nuff sinting da yah.[1]

And she is about to give him now, and says:

See fi you own yah,
Zuzumah.
Tenk yu, Miss Marta.

And everybody says:

ZUZU*WAH*!!!

That time Zuzuwah comes back, and, boy, then they have a time. They have stick-fighting thing to do. Oh, boy! Now in that one Zuzuwah generally is the conqueror, you know, but you never know. Sometimes Zuzumah beat him.

This game was described to me by the famouse diseuse Louise Bennett. The text above is exactly as she gave it to me, the lyrics often interspersed with Ms. Bennett's descriptions of the action.
1. Lots of things are here.

277 It's a Very Fine Motion

Mary on the mountain,
Two by two.
Mary on the mountain,
Two by two.
Mary on the mountain,
Two by two.
And then you rise up, sister, rise.
Then you show me your motion,
Two by two.
And then you show me your motion,
Two by two.

And then you show me your motion,
Two by two.
And then you rise up, sister, rise.
It's a very fine motion,
Two by two.
It's a very fine motion,
Two by two.
It's a very fine motion,
Two by two.
And then you rise up, sister, rise.

Collected in Kingston on October 27, 1978.

Versions of this game are found in Brewster, *Children's Games*, pp. 71, 131. In this game two people stoop in the center holding hands. When they are told to "rise up" and "show . . . your motion," they begin dancing, and the people forming the circle must do whatever steps they do.

278 My Boyfriend Is a Sailor

I am a pretty little Dutch girl,
As pretty as can be, be, be,
And all the boys around my way
Are crazy over me, me, me,
My boyfriend is a sailor,
He comes from Palisadoes,[1]
With a big, big nose,
And ten long toes,
And this is what he says to me.
"I l-o-v-e love you,
I'll k-i-s-s kiss you,
I'll kiss, kiss, kiss you in the
D-A-R-K dark, dark, dark."
Bam chi-chi-la-la, bam bam!
Bam chi-chi-la-la, bam bam!
One day he gave me chocolate,
One day he gave me pear,
One day he gave me fifteen cents
And kicked me down the stair.
Bam chi-chi-la-la, bam bam!
Bam chi-chi-la-la, bam bam!
I gave him back his chocolate.
I gave him back his pear,

I gave him back his fifteen cents
And kicked him down the stairs.
Bam chi-chi-la-la, bam bam!
Bam chi-chi-la-la, bam bam!

Recorded in Kingston on October 27, 1978.
This is a clapping game. A version appears in Knapp and Knapp, *One Potato,* p. 123.
1. The name of the piece of land sticking out that almost encloses Kingston Harbour. Port Royal is at the end of Palisadoes, and the airport is halfway along. (See map of Jamaica.)

279 Come Out and Play with Me

My pretty playmate,
Come out to play with me.
Bring out your dolly things.
Climb up my apple tree.
All along my rain-n-bow
Into my cellar door,
For jolly friends we are forevermore.
One, two, three, four.

Oh, no, Miss Brownie,
I cannot play with you.
My dolly has the flu, flu, flu-u-u.
One, two, three, four.

Recorded in Kingston on October 27, 1978. I also received a written version in November 1978 from a Kingston teacher. See Knapp and Knapp, *One Potato,* p. 131.
This clapping game, with lyrics borrowed from a popular song, is pretty clearly alien to Jamaica, where apple trees and cellars are rare.

280 Mary Mack

Miss Mary Mack, Mack, Mack,
All dressed in black, black, black,
With silver buttons, buttons, buttons,
All down her back, back, back.
She asked her mother, mother, mother
For fifty cents, cents, cents,
To see a white elephant, phant, phant
Jump over the fence, fence, fence.

He jumped so high, high, high,
He reached the sky, sky, sky,
And he never came back, back, back
Till the fourth of July, July, July.
She went upstairs, stairs, stairs,
To make her bed, bed, bed,
But by mistake, stake, stake,
She bumped her head, head, head.
She went downstairs, stairs, stairs,
To cook her dinner, dinner, dinner,
But she made a mistake, stake, stake,
She cooked her shoe, shoe, shoe.

Recorded in Kingston on October 27, 1978. The version above is a composite of the recorded version and a written one give to me by a Kingston teacher in November 1978.

For other versions see Courlander, *Treasury of Afro-American Folklore*, pp. 535–36; Abrahams, *Counting-Out*, No. 352; Taylor, *English Riddles*, No. 656; and Abrahams, *Jump-Rope*, p. 120. This popular clapping game was the first one my five-year-old daughter learned when she got to Jamaica.

281 Yes, No, Maybe So

Marlene, Marlene,
Do you love Aston?
Yes, no, maybe so.
Yes, no, maybe so.

This popular clapping game was recorded in Jamaica on October 27, 1978. The verse is also used in jumping rope.

Versions appear in Knapp and Knapp, *One Potato*, p. 254; and Botkin, *Treasury of American Folklore*, p. 792.

282 Tell Me the Name of the B-o-y

All merry, all merry, puddin' and pie,
Tell me the name of the B-o-y.
Kkkkkkkk.

This clapping game was recorded in Kingston on October 27, 1978.

283 Ride Him, Jackie

Ride him, Jackie, but nuh bruk him back,
Ride him, Jackie, but nuh bruk him back.
Ah say, ride him, Jackie, but nuh bruk him back.
Ah say, ride him, Jackie, but nuh bruk him back.
Ah tell you, ride him, Jackie, but nuh bruk him back.

This clapping game was recorded in Kingston on October 27, 1978.

284 Donna, Donna

Donna, Donna, a biscuit.
Ooo, Sis sis, wow, wow, a biscuit.
I met a boy, a biscuit.
He sold sweets, a biscuit.
Like my cherry tree, a biscuit.
Ice cream soda with the cherry on top,
Hey, boy, you looking at me!
You think you can buy my belly skin?
No fi, no fi, no cha, cha, cha.
I have a pain in mi belly, go ho-ha, ho-ha,
So bam, bam, bam, stick it up.
So bam, bam, bam, stand at ease.
So bam, bam, bam, stick it up.
So bam, bam, bam, stand at ease.

This clapping game was recorded in Kingston on October 27, 1978. A written version was given to me by a Kingston teacher in November 1978. The text above is a compilation of the two versions.

285 I Went Downtown One Day

I went downtown one day,
And I met Miss Brown one day,
With a bunch of cane one day,
And ah beg her piece one day.
And she gave me piece one day.
Papsy, papsy, go pingo shell,
Bus a go bite me tenda toe.

I salute you kimbo,
Kimbo to kimbo, kimbo,
Rub 'im belly, rub 'im,
Kick 'im, Nellie, kick 'im,
Box 'im, Nellie, box 'im,
Thump 'im, Nellie, thump 'im.

This clapping game was given to me in writing by a Kingston teacher in November 1978.

286A Room for Rent

Room for rent,
Supplies you need,
When I run out,
You run in.

Collected in Kingston on October 21, 1978.

A version appears in Botkin, *Treasury of American Folklore,* p. 793. I also received a written version of this verse from a Kingston teacher in November 1978. The jumper must run out and another jumper must run in at the point indicated in this jump-rope rhyme.

286B Room for Rent

Room for rent,
Apply within.
When I run out,
Then you run in.

Recorded in Kingston on October 27, 1978.

287 Stars Shining

Red, white, and blue,
Stars shining over you.

Collected in Kingston on October 21, 1978.

In this jumping game the jumper must stoop at the second line, and the rope is turned over his head. If he causes the rope to stop, he is out.

See Abrahams, *Counting-Out,* Nos. 468, 469, 471, and 472; and Abrahams, *Jump-Rope,* pp. 167–68.

288 When You Set the Table

When you set the table,
You must-t remember
Salt, mustard, pickle, pepper,
Pepperpepperpepperpepperpepper. . . .

Recorded in Kingston on October 27, 1978.
When they get to *pepper*, the rope turners turn the rope as fast as they can, repeating *pepper* and increasing the speed until the jumper misses.
Versions appear in Knapp and Knapp, *One Potato*, p. 112; Brewster, *Children's Games*, p. 172; and Botkin, *Treasury of American Folklore*, p. 792.

289 Down by the Ocean

Down by the ocean, down by the sea,
Johnny broke a bottle and blame it on me.
I told Ma, Ma told Pa,
And Johnny got a beating with a ha ha ha.
Johnny skipped on one foot, one foot, one foot,
Johnny skipped on two feet, two feet, two feet,
Johnny skipped on three feet, three feet, three feet,
Johnny skipped on four feet, four feet, four feet.

This jump-rope rhyme was given to me in writing by a Kingston teacher in November 1978.
A version appears in Knapp and Knapp, *One Potato*, p. 113.

290 Cinderella, Cinderella

Cinderella, Cinderella, dressed in yellow,
Went downtown to meet her fellow,
How many kisses did she get?
I, 2, 3, 4, 5, 6, etc.

What kind of dress is she going to marry in?
White silk, satin, crocus bag, etc.

What kind of drink is she going to have?
Rum, wine, sugar and water, etc.

How many children are they going to have?
1, 2, 3, 4, 5, 6, etc.

These verses to the ever-popular jump-rope rhyme "Cinderella" were given to me in writing by a Kingston teacher.

With each verse, the numbers continue, or the words are repeated until the jumper misses.

Versions appear in Brewster, *Children's Games*, p. 171; Botkin, *Treasury of American Folklore*, pp. 800–801; and David C. Laubach, *Introduction to Folklore* (Rochelle Park, N.J.: Hayden Book Company, 1980), p. 97.

291 Christopher Columbus

Christopher Columbus sailed across the ocean
The wind blows higher and higher.
Then over.

This jump-rope rhyme was given to me in writing by a Kingston teacher in November 1978. The rope is swung from side to side until the words *then over,* at which point it is turned normally.

292 1, 2, 3, Jamaica

1, 2, 3, Jamaica,
4, 5, 6, Independence,
7, 8, 9, Celebration,
10, sixth of August,[1]
1, 2, Manley,
3, 4, Beverley,
5, 6, Have a baby,
Natasha, Natasha, Natasha,[2]

This jump-rope rhyme was given to me in writing by a Kingston teacher in November 1978.
1. Jamaica got its independence on the sixth of August.
2. Then-Prime Minister Michael Manley and his wife, Beverley, had a baby girl called Natasha.

293 Auntie Lou

1, 2, 3, Auntie Lou lo,
4, 5, 6, Auntie Lou lo,
7, 8, 9, Auntie Lou lo,
10, Auntie Lou lo.

This jump-rope rhyme was given to me in writing by a Kingston teacher in November 1978.

The rope is skipped normally during the recitation of the numbers. Then the jumper crouches and the rope is turned high above his head.

"Auntie Lou" may possibly be a reference to Louise Bennett.

294 Children, Children

Mumma: Children, children.
Children: Yes, Mumma.
Mumma: Where have you been to?
Children: Grandpuppa.
Mumma: What did he give you?
Children: Bread and tea.
Mumma: Where is my share?
Children: Up in the air.
Mumma: How can I reach it?
Children: Climb on a broken chair.
Mumma: Suppose I fall?
Children: I do not care.
Mumma: Who taught you that manners?
Children: The dawg.
Mumma: Who is the dawg?
Children: Youuuuuuuu!

This dialogue between one child representing the mother and the rest being the children was recorded in Kingston on October 30, 1978.

295 Little Miss Lulu

Suitor: Little Miss Lulu, I love you.
Miss Lulu: Love me? [She stops sweeping the floor and points to herself.]
Suitor: Little Miss Lulu, I love you.
Miss Lulu: Love me? [She stops sweeping again and points to herself.]
Suitor: Little Miss Lulu, see mi pickney dem deh.[1] [He points.]
Miss Lulu: See fi mi deh.[2]
Suitor: Little Miss Lulu, see mi house and land.
Miss Lulu: See fi mi deh.
Suitor: Little Miss Lulu, I love you.
Miss Lulu: Love me?
Suitor: Little Miss Lulu, I love you.
Miss Lulu: Love me?
Suitor: Little Miss Lulu, see mi 'usband yah.

Miss Lulu: See mi fi mi deh.
Suitor: Little Miss Lulu, see mi 'usband yah.
Miss Lulu: See fi mi deh.
Suitor: Little Miss Lulu, see mi pickney dem dah.
Miss Lulu: See fi mi deh.
Suitor: Little Miss Lulu, see mi money yah.
Miss Lulu: ME LOVE YOU!!!! [Embraces him enthusiastically.]

This dialogue between the child representing Miss Lulu and another representing the suitor was collected in Kingston on September 10, 1978. The performers were two sisters, eight and ten years old.

1. See my children there.
2. See mine there.

296 Mawning, Buddy

Mawning, buddy.
Me nuh buddy fi you.
Which ten?
Ten a flash.
Which flash?
Flash a bodda me.
Is a di man a go play?
Play fi di young gal.
Rosie identical funny like a fi mi gal.
Poppa doo.
Oh come.
No but, no bat.
Oh come.
No but, no bat.

Recorded in Kingston on October 30, 1978.

This is another game in which a leader speaks and the group responds, but evidently the others did not respond properly, since after a few lines my informant insisted, "Mek me alone say it!" and proceeded to recite both roles.

The sexual allusions here lead to two levels of interpretation—one obscene. *Buddy* may be interpreted as friend or as penis.

297 You Do the Cha-Cha-Cha

Si Puss Club, Si Puss Club.
Eenie-meenie dixie-wallie,
You are the tambourine,

Ack-a-lacka, baby, I love you-u,
Yes I do.
I saw you with a boyfren' las-s-s night-t-t,
How do you know?
Ah peek through the key hole—NO-S-EY!
Wash your dishes, lad-d-y-y.
Beg you piece a candy-y-y. GR-E-E-DY!
You see the house upon the hill,
Where me and my b-a-b-y live.
What's her name?
Mary-y Jane.
What's her number?
Koo-ba-koomba.
What she eat?
Pig feet.
What she drink?
Black milk.
So come on, baby,
Let's go to bed.
Na-na-na-a-a-a, a biscuit.
Why sissi-wa-wa-a, a biscuit.
Like my cherry tree, a biscuit.
She's so-o sweet, a biscuit.
Knock, knock.
Ice cream.
Ice cream.
Soda pop.
Soda pop.
A ginger ale.
Ginger ale.
Do your thing.[1]
You got a a, b, c, d, e, f, g,
You got a q, r, s, t, u, v, w, x, and y.
You do the back, you do the front. [They jump.]
You do the cha-cha-cha. [They shake their hips.]
You do the back, you do the front.
You do the cha-cha-cha.
You do the back, you do the front.
You do the cha-cha-cha.
And *freeze*! [Lively dancing stops suddenly.]

Recorded in Kingston on September 10, 1978.

This game is played in a circle, with one child speaking and the others responding. At the end they dance as directed. The five children who played this game for me were eight, nine, and ten years old.

For several eenie-meenie verses, see Abrahams, *Counting-Out*, pp. 45–68.

1. With this line, the children began to dance, and an onlooker exclaimed, "Rock on!" causing a great deal of laughter.

298 When Johnny Was One

When Johnny was one, he learned to suck his thumb,
Thumb Tilda, thumb Tilda, half past one, cross over.
When Johnny was two, he learned to clean his shoes,
Shoes Tilda, shoes Tilda, half past two, cross over.
When Johnny was three, he learned to climb a tree,
Tree Tilda, tree Tilda, half past three, cross over.
When Johnny was four, he learned to shut the door,
Door Tilda, door Tilda, half past four, cross over.
When Johnny was five, he learned to dig and dive,
Dig and dive Tilda, dig and dive Tilda, half past five, cross over.
When Johnny was six, he learned to pick up sticks.
Sticks Tilda, sticks Tilda, half past six, cross over.
When Johnny was seven, he was on his way to heaven.
Heaven Tilda, heaven Tilda, half past seven, cross over.
When Johnny was eight, he learned to shut the gate.
Gate Tilda, gate Tilda, half past eight, cross over.
When Johnny was nine, he learned to feed the swine.
Swine Tilda, swine Tilda, half past nine, cross over.
When Johnny was ten, he learned to feed the hens.
Hens Tilda, hens Tilda, half past ten, cross over.

This game was given to me in writing by a Kingston teacher in November 1978.

Glossary

Ackee   a fruit (brought to Jamaica from Africa) with a red and cream outer covering. The inside is made up of a cream-colored pulp with black seeds. The fruit is eaten when it breaks open. The ackee is supposedly poisonous if it is eaten before it opens naturally. Ackee is the Jamaican national fruit; and salt fish and ackee is the national dish.

Ah   I.

Anancy   the most popular folk figure throughout the West Indies. This cunning spider man is generally involved in a contest with other, stronger animals. See the Introduction to Chapter 2 for an extended discussion of Anancy.

Babylon   modern society that oppresses, including particularly the police and other governmental forces and agencies.

Back o' Wall   a Rasta-dominated section of the Dungle (q.v.), located off Fourshore Road in Western Kingston. In July 1966 (three months after Emperor Haile Selassie's visit to Jamaica) Back o' Wall was razed to construct new government housing.

Backra   *see* Buckra.

Baggy   panties.

Bammy   cakes made from cassava.

Batti   buttocks.

Bellevue   mental institution on Windward Road in Eastern Kingston.

Blood clat   obscene expression alluding to cloth used during menstruation.

Bradder   brother, boy.

Breadfruit   popular and common fruit in Jamaica, which when baked has the texture of bread.

Bredder   brother, boy.

Bredren   brothers, friends, fellow Rastafarians.

Brer   brother.

Buckra, Backra   white man, master, boss; derives from an Efik word meaning the ruling class.

Buck up   meet, bump into.

Bulla   small, flat, round, sweet cake.

Bungo   ignorant person, country bumpkin.

Bwoy   boy.

Caan'   cannot.

Callaloo   a popular Jamaican vegetable, usually prepared as a soup called pepperpot.

Calypso   traditional West Indian ballad originating in Trinidad and popular in Jamaica as well, which frequently satirizes an individual or an event. Calypsos are often sexually suggestive and obscene.

Chalice   pipe used to smoke ganga during Rastafarian rituals.

Chat   talk too much.

Cho   an exclamation with no precise meaning. It is used as a response, and it may serve as an expression of scorn, disgust, dissension, displeasure, or unreceptiveness.

Colon   Panama; The Jamaicans who went to Panama to work on the Panama Canal were called Colon men.

Coolie   Indian.

Craffing   tricking, being dishonest.

Cum   come.

Daughta   girl, woman, girlfriend, wife.

Deh   there.

Deh da   there.

Dinky   wake.

Don', doan   don't.

Dread   a Rastafarian, especially one who wears dreadlocks. As an adjective *dread* suggests Rastafarian (as in dreadlocks or dread talk) or it may be interpreted as terrible or bad, often in the positive sense suggested by the Black American *ba-ad*.

Dreadlocks   an ancient hair style popularized by the Rastafarians, in which the uncombed hair partitions itself into locks or braids. Rastafarians cite Leviticus 21:5 as the directive for this hair style: "They shall not make baldness upon their head, neither shall they shave off the corner of their beard."

Duckanoo   dough made up of corn meal, salt fish, raisins, and scallions.

Dungle   a slum area in Western Kingston. Jamaican novelist Orlando Patterson told me in an interview at Harvard on December 10, 1979, that the name *Dungle* is a play on the words *dung hill* and *jungle*.

Duppy   ghost, spirit, soul of the dead in human form. For a fuller discussion of this popular African-derived figure, see the Introduction to Chapter 3.

Fenky-fenky   fastidious, meticulous, effeminate.

Festival   national Jamaican celebration including competitive events in all the arts. The competitions take place in spectacular shows at the National Stadium in Kingston. Festival culminates the Independence Celebration during the first week in August.

Foo-foo   a dish of West African origins made from ground cassava.

Football   soccer, the second most popular Jamaican sport after cricket.

Foreign   abroad, a foreign nation. The expression *go a foreign* means to go abroad or to travel to another country.

Ganga   marijuana. Ganga is used in some Rastafarian religious rites, where it is identified as the sacred herb of the Bible. To justify its use, Rastafarians cite Genesis 1:29, Psalms 18:8, Revelations 22:2, Exodus 10:12, and Proverbs 15:17.

Gi'   give.

Gleaner   popular Jamaican daily paper, published in Kingston.

Goady, gourdy   a calabash with a hole in it, used for carrying water.

Goin'   going.

Gon'   gone.

Gourdy   *see* goady.

Gun Court   Rehabilitation Center on Camp Road in Kingston.

Gungo   variety of small green peas in a pod, used for making soup, or dried and cooked with rice.

Higgler   a peddler of produce or other goods. In the marketplaces of Jamaica, higglers vigorously and competitively thrust their goods at shoppers, who must often bargain for them.

Him   may be either male or female, him or her.

Hooker stick   a stick with a prong on the top, used to pick fruits.

I and I   Rastafarian substitute for several pronouns, including *my, I,* and *we.*

Jack Mandora   from the traditional Jamaican closing to folktales: "Jack Mandora, me nuh chose none," which is the tale-teller's way of disclaiming responsibility for the tale he has just related. For a fuller discussion see the Introduction to this book.

Jah   Jehovah, God, Haile Selassie.

JAMAL   a program launched by the Jamaican government in 1973 to stamp out illiteracy throughout the country. The program is organized by the Jamaican Movement for the Advancement of Literacy (JAMAL), which has offices throughout the island.

Jipijapa   straw used in making hats.

Jinnal   con man, one who plays smart.

Journey cake, Johnny cake   a fried dumpling.

Juk   jab, stab, strike.

Likkle   little.

Mariguana   marijuana.

Maroons   slaves released by the Spaniards in 1655, who lived in mountain retreats and offered refuge to other fleeing slaves until the English negotiated a peace treaty with them in 1738.

Mek   let, allow.

Mento   traditional Jamaican music and dance with a strong Spanish and African influence.

Missa   mister

Mussi   must be, must have been.

Nah, nuh   not, am not, is not, are not.

Nuh   now, know, don't, or not.

Nyam   to eat; an Africanism.

Obeah   witchcraft; derives from the Ghanaian *obayi*. The practice of Obeah still exists in Jamaica, despite the fact that it is illegal.

Obeah man   sorcerer who uses a variety of magical powers and herbs to work witchcraft upon others.

Patty   a semicircular pastry filled with highly seasoned ground meat, the most popular of the fast goods in Jamaica, where patty shops are as common as hamburger chains in the United States.

Pickney   child, variant of *pickaninny*.

Pocomania   revivalist religious practice in Jamaica, characterized by frenzied dancing and speaking in tongues by those possessed by the ancestral spirits.

Rahtid, raatid   exclamation, an expression of shock or anger.

Rass   a profanity with no exact translation. It is often used in phrases where *ass* or *damn* might be equivalents, but it is used in many variations—it may be a noun, a verb, an adjective, or an expletive.

Rasta   short for Rastafarian.

Ras Tafari   Haile Selassie. Before his coronation in 1930, Selassie's title was Ras. His personal name was Tafari. Members of the Rastafarian movement prefer to be called Ras Tafari.

Rastafarian   member of a religious sect that believes in the divinity of Haile Selassie. For a fuller discussion see Chapter 6.

Rasta man   male Rastafarian.

Reggae   popular contemporary Jamaican music that makes use of the language of the Rastafarians and was popularized by such musicians as Bob Marley and Jimmy Cliff. Much of the outside world was introduced to reggae through the movie *The Harder They Come* in 1972. Reggae lyrics usually comment upon the political and social situation in "Babylon" (q.v.). The hit single "Do the Reggay" was recorded by the Maytels in 1968.

Rock steady   Jamaican music developed in the sixties. A mixture of ska and American soul music, rock steady was a forerunner of reggae. The hit song "Rock Steady" was recorded by Alton Ellis.

Rude   obscene, impertinent, coarse, bad.

Seet, see-it   understand, comprehend.

Ska   a Jamaican musical form that combines mento and American rhythm and blues. Ska is a predecessor of rock steady and reggae.

Spliff   marijuana, "joint."

Tastees   a patty (q.v.) chain in Jamaica.

Tacuma   frequent character in the Anancy tales. Sometimes Tacuma is Anancy's companion, sometimes his son, sometimes his spouse, sometimes his neighbor.

Tief, thief   thief. As a verb, *tief* or *thief* means to steal.

T'ree   three.

Waan'   want.

Wha'   what.

Whe   where.

Wood   slang for *penis.*

Yah   there, here.

Yard   urban communities in the West Indies having an open area that serves often as a gathering place for both recreational and work purposes for the inhabitants of the many tiny huts clustered around it. Kingston city yards date back to a 1770 law requiring that any time there were four slave huts on the same plot of land, they must be enclosed by a seven-foot-high wall and they could have only one entry.

You nuh seet?   You see? Understand?

Biographies of Major Contributors

As was noted in the Introduction, my methods of collecting often made it impossible to gather biographical data. Thus some of the following biographies are incomplete and others are disproportionate in terms of the kinds and amounts of information presented. Those people who were interviewed individually are the main ones represented here. Almost none of the many students who gave me material at St. Joseph's College or the residents of Jamaican yards or the scores of others who were interviewed in groups are listed here.

Ballie, Henry   A teenage gardener in Woodside, Henry Ballie was a somewhat reticent but prolific storyteller.

Bennett, Louise   Born in Kingston, Jamaica, on September 7, 1919, Louise Bennett, better known as Miss Lou, was educated at St. Simon's College and Excelsior College, after which she studied at the Royal Academy of Dramatic Art in England. Much of her life has been devoted to the study of Jamaican folklore, and she spent many years visiting and observing the Maroons, old-time tea meetings, digging matches, religious ceremonies, Dinkies, country weddings, concerts, and field days throughout her country. Her extensive collections of Anancy stories, folk songs, folk legends, proverbs, riddles, and games, and her use of these folk materials, including the dialect, in her poetry and dramas (she has performed her work on radio, on the stage, and in art festivals in Europe, Canada, the United States, and throughout the Caribbean) have represented perhaps the single most significant contribution to the preservation and appreciation of Jamaican folk culture. Her works include *Verses in [Jamaican] Dialect* (Kingston: The Herald Ltd., 1942); *Jamaican Humour in Dialect* (Kingston: The Jamaica Press Assoc., 1943); *Jamaican Dialect Poems* (Kingston: The Herald Ltd., 1948); *M's Lulu Sez: A Collection of Dialect Poems* (Kingston: Gleaner Co., 1949); *Anancy Stories and Dialect Verse* (Kingston: Pioneer Press, 1950, 1957, and 1973); *Laugh with Louise: A Pot-pourri of Jamaican Folk-Lore, Stories, Songs, and Verses* (Kingston: City Printery, 1961); *Jamaican Labrish* (Kingston: Sangster's, 1966); *Anancy and Miss Lou* (Kingston: Sangster's, 1979); and *Selected Poems* (Kingston: Sangster's, 1982 and 1983). When I visited her at her home in Gordon Town in September 1978, Mrs. Bennett not only shared some of her favorite folk selections with me but she also granted me a lengthy interview in which she talked about and responded to my many questions concerning Jamaican folklore.

Blackwood, Constantine   A resident of Kingston, Mr. Blackwood was forty-five years old in the fall of 1978 during our interviews. He is a professional cabinet-maker, an assistant teacher in the JAMAL program, and a singer.

Brown, Edward   Born and raised in Kingston, Mr. Brown was twenty-two years old in the fall of 1978 during our interviews. He described himself as a drummer, a singer, and a comedian.

Brown, Headley   Mr. Brown was the acknowledged storyteller among a group of young men whom I accidentally stumbled upon in a Kingston yard where my self-appointed guide Cynthia Jones had taken me to interview someone who was not in. When I decided to approach a group sitting around enjoying conversation and spliffs, Cynthia protested: "Lawd, Miss, no, no, I no want them for insult you. Dem bad boys, dem!" Despite Cynthia's protests, Mr. Brown and his compatriots welcomed me into their group and provided much interesting material, though he refused to tell me some of the tales his friends requested.

Brown, Herbert   Born and raised in Kingston, Mr. Brown was thirty-two years old at the time of our interviews in the fall of 1978. An assistant teacher in the JAMAL program, he is a writer, dramatist, actor, and musician. He won a gold medal for acting and two silver medals for directing and writing in the Jamaica National Festival for 1978.

Burke, Eddie   The Reverend Eddie Burke grew up in Chapelton, where at night when he had finished his duties around the house, he and his friends would meet and exchange stories or listen to the tales told by the "*big* people." In addition to his work in the ministry, his extensive travels in Africa, and his work as a teacher, the Reverend Mr. Burke has long been a devotee and a student of Jamaican folklore. He is the author of *The Ups and Downs of the Jamaican Boy Newsy Wapps* (Kingston: privately published, 1950) and several other tales of the adventures of Newsy Wapps, based upon his own childhood experiences, as well as a collection of folktales that he did with Annie Garside, *Water in the Gourd and Other Jamaican Folk Stories* (London: Oxford University Press, 1975). During my interview with the Reverend Mr. Burke in Santa Cruz, where he now lives, he told me tales, sang songs, and shared with me his views, interpretations, and assessment of Jamaican folklore.

Campbell, Vernon (Shine)   A resident of Kingston, nineteen-year-old Shine was the acknowledged raconteur of his yard. When he strolled up to the group assembled around me on a September afternoon in 1978, everyone reacted to his arrival, and immediately deferred to him. With a confident smile, he acknowledged their accolades as his due, reached over for the microphone, and proceeded to recite rhymes, pose riddles, sing songs, and tell tales, all of which were enthusiastically received by his audience. Though Shine participated in several sessions, he would never really tell me anything about himself. All requests for information were met with cute retorts, the performance of another piece, or some other evasive maneuver.

Clarke, Paul   Paul Clarke was one of the most prolific storytellers among the students from whom I recorded at St. Joseph's College in October and November 1978.

Dixon, Paul   Born and raised in Kingston, Mr. Dixon was twenty-three years old at the time of our interviews in September and October of 1978. Mr. Dixon went to Cane River Primary School. He is interested in mechanics and drama.

Duncan, Clive   Born and raised in Kingston, Clive Duncan was nineteen years old when I interviewed him in the fall of 1978. He attended Boys Town School. A dramatic storyteller, he wants to be a comedian.

Gibbs, Michael   Born and raised in Kingston, twenty-one-year-old Mr. Gibbs attended Kingston Junior Secondary School. He is interested in singing.

Gordon, Roger   Born and raised in Kingston, twenty-year-old Roger Gordon is a football fan.

Henry, Theresa Adina   Born in Cassava River, Mrs. Henry was eighty-three years old at the time of our interview in July 1978. Her mother, who was a cocoa chocolate vendor, told her children stories at night while she made her chocolate. Later, when Mrs. Henry was growing up, everyone in Cassava River, Above Rocks, and Stony Hill (the neighboring areas) used to plait jipijapa hats and shell corn. While they engaged in these tasks, they told Anancy stories. The stories that Mrs. Henry so masterfully recounts today were all recalled from those childhood days. Many of the storytelling sessions and other rituals and celebrations that Mrs. Henry fondly recalled from her childhood days no longer continue in Cassava River, she told me, because "the children — everybody turn aristocrat." A delightful lady and a master storyteller, Mrs. Henry was brought by her grandson to my apartment in Kingston, where she regaled me all afternoon with her endless repertoire of tales.

Johnson, Mary   Born in Top Hill in St. Elizabeth in 1888, Mrs. Johnson grew up relishing the tales related to her by her mother and her grandmother, the latter of whom was born in slavery. She later moved to Mandeville and worked at the Mandeville Hotel. When I arrived to interview her at her home in Mandeville, where she lived with her daughter, Mrs. Ivy Marrett (who also contributed a few pieces to this collection), Mrs. Johnson was energetically working in her garden. We could not proceed with our interview until she had prepared one of the most sumptuous Jamaican meals I enjoyed during my stay. After a few sips of her homemade liqueur, we spent the afternoon enjoying her many memorates, riddles, and tales. Mrs. Johnson died soon after my return to the United States.

Jones, Thelmira.   Mrs. Jones, who is a schoolteacher in Woodside, is a superb storyteller whose contributions to this collection were accidental. In September 1978, I went to interview a gentleman who had fallen ill, and she was at his home caring for him. He suggested that she tell me certain stories, and with his prompting, she shared with me a great deal of interesting material.

Palmer, Clinton   Born and raised in Kingston, Mr. Palmer was twenty-eight during the fall of 1978, when he contributed to this collection. He was educated at Boys Town School and was a steelworker.

Parks, Franklin   Born, raised, and educated in Kingston, Mr. Franklin enjoys writing and acting.

Rhoden, Frank   Climbing to Mr. Rhoden's home up a steep hill in Kingston after a heavy rainstorm was an adventure in itself, but one that resulted in some of my best Anancy stories.

Riley, J. P.   Born and raised in Woodside, Mr. Riley has spent most of his life there except for brief periods when he was a migrant worker in the United States. I interviewed him at his home in September 1978.

Rose, Alfred   Twenty-four-year old Mr. Rose attended Campion High School, Kingston Senior School, Kingston College, and Congregational School. He has worked as a contractor.

Talbot, Vivian   Born and raised in Kingston, twenty-four-year-old Mr. Talbot attended Durham College. He is a poet and an actor and won a gold medal for acting in the Jamaica National Festival for 1978 as well as a silver medal for production. He is a superb storyteller and organized several productive sessions for me. He also helped me on several occasions to transcribe materials that I recorded from him and his friends.

Thomas, Junior   Born and raised in Kingston, Junior Thomas was twenty years old when he contributed to this collection in the fall of 1978. An assistant teacher in the JAMAL program, his main interests are poetry and music.

Thompson, Clive   Born and raised in St. Catherine, Clive Thompson was nineteen years old when I interviewed him in the fall of 1978. He attended Bernard Lodge Secondary School and worked as an apprentice to an electronics technician. He enjoys singing.

Works Cited

Published Sources

Abrahams, Roger D. *Counting-Out Rhymes: A Dictionary.* Austin: Univ. of Texas Press, 1980.

———. *Deep Down in the Jungle: Negro Narrative Folklore from the Streets of Philadelphia.* Rev. ed. Chicago: Aldine, 1970.

———. *Jump-Rope Rhymes: A Dictionary.* American Folklore Society, Bibliographical and Special Series, Vol. 20. Austin: Univ. of Texas Press, 1969.

———. *Positively Black.* Englewood Cliffs, N.J.: Prentice-Hall, 1970.

Bacon, A. M., and E. C. Parsons. "Folk-lore from Elizabeth City County, Va." *Journal of American Folklore*, 35 (Jan.–March 1922), 250–327.

Baughman, Ernest W. *Type and Motif-Index of the Folktales of England and North America.* The Hague: Mouton, 1966.

Beckwith, Martha Warren. *Jamaican Anansi Stories.* 1924; rpt. New York: Dover, 1966.

Bennett, Louise. *Anancy and Miss Lou.* Kingston: Sangster's, 1979.

Botkin, B. A., ed. *Lay My Burden Down: A Folk History of Slavery.* Chicago: Univ. of Chicago Press, 1945.

———, ed. *A Treasury of American Folklore.* New York: Crown, 1944.

———, ed. *A Treasury of Southern Folklore.* New York: Crown, 1949.

Brewer, J. Mason. *American Negro Folklore.* Chicago: Quadrangle, 1968.

———. *Dog Ghosts and Other Texas Negro Folk Tales.* Austin: Univ. of Texas Press, 1958.

———. *The Word on the Brazos: Negro Preacher Tales from the Brazos Bottoms of Texas.* Austin: Univ. of Texas Press, 1953.

———. *Worser Days and Better Times: The Folklore of the North Carolina Negro.* Chicago: Quadrangle, 1965.

Brewster, Paul G. *Children's Games and Rhymes.* New York: Arno, 1976.

Burke, Eddie. *Water in the Gourd and Other Jamaican Folk Stories.* London: Oxford Univ. Press, 1975.

Courlander, Harold. *The Drum and the Hoe: Life and Lore of the Haitian People.* Berkeley: Univ. of California Press, 1960.

———. *A Treasury of Afro-American Folklore.* New York: Crown Publishers, 1976.

Dance, Daryl Cumber. *Shuckin' and Jivin': Folklore from Contemporary Black Americans.* Bloomington: Indiana Univ. Press, 1978.

Dobie, J. Frank. *Tone the Bell Easy.* Dallas: Southern Methodist Univ. Press, 1932.

Dorson, Richard M. *American Negro Folktales.* Greenwich: Fawcett, 1967.

———. *Buying the Wind.* Chicago: Univ. of Chicago Press, 1964.

———. *Negro Folktales in Michigan.* Cambridge: Harvard Univ. Press, 1956.

———. *Negro Tales from Pine Bluff, Arkansas, and Calvin, Michigan.* Bloomington: Indiana Univ. Press, 1970.

Fauset, Arthur Huff. "Tales and Riddles Collected in Philadelphia." *Journal of American Folklore*, 41 (Oct.–Dec. 1928), 529–57.

Flowers, Helen L. *A Classification of the Folktales of the West Indies by Types and Motifs.* New York: Arno Press, 1980.

Harris, Joel Chandler. *The Complete Tales of Uncle Remus.* Boston: Houghton Mifflin, 1955.
  I. *Uncle Remus: His Songs and His Sayings.*
  II. *Nights with Uncle Remus.*
  III. *Daddy Jake, the Runaway.*
  IV. *Uncle Remus and His Friends.*
  V. *Told by Uncle Remus.*

Hughes, Langston, and Arna Bontemps, eds. *The Book of Negro Folklore.* New York: Dodd, Mead, 1958.

Hurston, Zora Neale. *Dust Tracks on a Road: An Autobiography.* Philadelphia: Lippincott, 1971.

———. *Mules and Men.* Philadelphia: Lippincott, 1935.

Irvin, K. Leroy. "Negro Tales from Eastern New York," *New York Folklore Quarterly*, 11 (1955), 165–76.

Jekyll, Walter. *Jamaican Song and Story.* 1907; rpt. New York: Dover, 1966.

Johnson, John H. "Folklore from Antigua, British West Indies." *Journal of American Folklore*, 34 (Jan.–March 1921), 40–88.

Knapp, Mary, and Herbert Knapp. *One Potato, Two Potato: The Secret Education of American Children.* New York: Norton, 1976.

Leach, MacEdward. "Jamaican Duppy Lore." *Journal of American Folklore*, 74 (July–Sept. 1961), 207–15.

Legman, G[ershon]. *Rationale of the Dirty Joke: An Analysis of Sexual Humor.* New York: Grove, 1971.

Levine, Lawrence W. *Black Culture and Black Consciousness.* Oxford Univ. Press, 1977.

Parsons, Elsie Clews. "Barbados Folk-lore." *Journal of American Folklore*, 38 (April–June 1925), 269–92.

———. "Folk Lore from Aiken, South Carolina." *Journal of American Folklore*, 34 (Jan.–March 1921), 1–39.

———. *Folk-Lore of the Antilles, French and English.* Memoirs of the American Folklore Society, Vol. 26, Parts 2 and 3. New York: American Folklore Society, 1936.

———. *Folk-Lore of the Sea Islands, South Carolina.* 1923; rpt. Chicago: Afro-American Press, 1969.

———. *Folk-tales of Andros Island, Bahamas.* Memoirs of the American Folklore Society, Vol. 13. New York: American Folklore Society, 1918.

Perdue, Charles L., Jr., Thomas E. Barden, and Robert K. Phillips, eds. *Weevils in the Wheat: Interviews with Virginia Ex-Slaves.* Bloomington: Indiana Univ. Press, 1980; originally published by the Univ. Press of Virginia, 1976.

Perdue, Chuck. "I Swear to God It's the Truth if I Ever Told It." *Keystone Folklore Quarterly*, 14 (Spring 1969), full issue.

Smiley, Portia. "Folk-Lore from Virginia, South Carolina, Georgia, Alabama, and Florida." *Journal of American Folklore*, 32 (July–Sept. 1919), 357–84.

Spalding, Henry D., ed. *Encyclopedia of Black Folklore and Humor.* Middle Village, N.Y.: Jonathan David, 1972.

Sterling, Philip. *Laughing on the Outside: The Intelligent White Reader's Guide to Negro Tales and Humor.* New York: Grosset and Dunlap, 1965.

Sutton-Smith, Brian. "The Folk Games of the Children." In *American Folklore,* ed. Tristram Coffin III, pp. 203–15. 1968; rpt. Washington, D.C.: Voice of America Forum Lectures, 1974.

Taylor, Archer. *English Riddles from Oral Tradition.* Berkeley: Univ. of California Press, 1951.

Thompson, Stith. *Motif-Index of Folk-Literature.* Rev. ed. 6 vols. Bloomington: Indiana Univ. Press, 1955.

Wake, Charles E. "Anancy Stories." *Folklore Journal,* 1 (1883), 280–92.

Zumwalt, Rosemary. "Plain and Fancy: A Content Analysis of Children's Jokes Dealing with Adult Sexuality." In *Readings in American Folklore.* Ed. Jan Harold Brunvand, pp. 345–54. New York: Norton, 1979.

Unpublished Materials

Folklore Research Project. Unpublished materials from a folklore research project in Jamaica, directed by Jeanette Grant during 1967–69. The tapes and transcripts are at the Institute of Jamaica in Kingston.

Index of Motifs and Tale Types

Tale type numbers and motif numbers are from Ernest W. Baughman, *Type and Motif-Index of the Folktales of England and North America,* unless otherwise indicated. Tale type numbers and motif numbers followed by "(Flowers)" are from Helen L. Flowers, *A Classification of the Folktales of the West Indies by Types and Motifs.* The number following each entry indicates the tale number in this collection.

Motifs Cited in the Text

Tale Types Cited in the Text

General Index

Folklore from Contemporary Jamaicans was composed on the Compugraphic digital phototypesetter in eleven point Bembo with one point of spacing between the lines. The book was designed by Ed King at Hillside Studio, typeset by Metricomp, Inc., printed offset by Thomson-Shore, Inc., and bound by John H. Dekker & Sons. The paper on which the book is printed carries acid-free characteristics for an expected life of at least three hundred years.

THE UNIVERSITY OF TENNESSEE PRESS : KNOXVILLE